Writing the Economic Subject in Modern Western Europe

LITERATUR — KULTUR — ÖKONOMIE
LITERATURE — CULTURE — ECONOMY

Herausgegeben von / Edited by
Christine Künzel, Axel Haunschild, Birger P. Priddat,
Thomas Rommel, Franziska Schößler und / and Yvette Sánchez

VOLUME 9

Zu Qualitätssicherung und Peer Review der vorliegenden Publikation

Die Qualität der in dieser Reihe erscheinenden Arbeiten wird vor der Publikation durch einen externen, von der Herausgeberschaft benannten Gutachter im Double Blind Verfahren geprüft. Dabei ist der Autor der Arbeit dem Gutachter während der Prüfung namentlich nicht bekannt; der Gutachter bleibt anonym.

Notes on the quality assurance and peer review of this publication

Prior to publication, the quality of the work published in this series is double blind reviewed by an external referee appointed by the editorship. The referee is not aware of the author's name when performing the review; the referee's name is not disclosed.

Aileen Behrendt / Nicholas Courtman (eds.)

Writing the Economic Subject in Modern Western Europe

Representation, Contestation, Critique

PETER LANG

Bibliographic Information published by the Deutsche Nationalbibliothek
The Deutsche Nationalbibliothek lists this publication in the Deutsche Nationalbibliografie; detailed bibliographic data is available online at http://dnb.d-nb.de.

Library of Congress Cataloging-in-Publication Data
A CIP catalog record for this book has been applied for at the Library of Congress.

The publication of this book was made possible by the generous support of the Potsdam Graduate School and the Tiarks German Fund of the University of Cambridge.

Cover illustration: Factory workers at Armstrongs, c. 1940s
(archive ref DDPD-2-2-6)
by East Riding Archives, dedicated to the public domain.

ISSN 2364-1304
ISBN 978-3-631-83999-7 (Print)
E-ISBN 978-3-631-85753-3 (E-Book)
E-ISBN 978-3-631-85754-0 (EPUB)
E-ISBN 978-3-631-85755-7 (MOBI)
DOI 10.3726/b18541

Peter Lang – Berlin · Bern · Bruxelles · New York · Oxford · Warszawa · Wien

This publication has been peer reviewed.

www.peterlang.com

Acknowledgements

The contributions in this volume grew out of papers that were given at two separate events in 2018. The first such event was a workshop at King's College London organised in cooperation with the Humboldt-Universität zu Berlin entitled 'Cultures of Work'. The second event was the trilateral colloquium between the University of Cambridge, the University of Chicago, and the Friedrich Schlegel Graduate School for Literary Studies of the Free University Berlin, on the topic of 'Economic Subjects in Modern German and Comparative Culture'. The colloquium was held at Jesus College, University of Cambridge, and was financed through the Schröder Fund (German and Dutch, University of Cambridge). The editors would like to thank Professor Erica Carter and Dr Lizzie Stewart for organising the workshop at King's College London and for their early support of this project. We would also like to thank the graduate student organisers of the Cambridge colloquium, Melina Mandelbaum, Margarete Thiessen, and Isabelle Zirden, as well as Ulrike Balser, Professor Andrew Webber, and Professor Sarah Colvin for their support of that event. We are further indebted to the Potsdam Graduate School at the Universität Potsdam and the Tiarks German Fund of the of the University of Cambridge for their generous funding of this publication. A special thanks goes to Michael Rücker for guiding us expertly through the publication process at Peter Lang.

Last but not least, we would like to thank our contributors for all the work they have put into their chapters and their commitment and support throughout this project.

Table of Contents

Aileen Behrendt and Nicholas Courtman

Introduction

Over the last decade, literary and cultural scholars have increasingly turned their attention towards the ways in which authors, artists, and thinkers engage and have engaged with economic subjects in the widest possible sense of the term – that is to say, both with the subject of the economy and its various facets, as well as with the way in which economic processes, institutions, and dynamics form and shape individual subjectivity.[1] This surge in critical interest is undoubtedly linked to the after-effects of the Financial Crisis of 2007–2008 and the ensuing years of austerity politics, which have seen the intensification of existing inequality in the distribution of wealth and resources, both within individual Western nations and on a global scale. Economic concerns have also begun to receive more mainstream attention in both public discourse, aided by the popular success of authors like Paul Mason and David Graeber,[2] and in political discourse and policy settings, as evidenced by the growing number of politicians expressing support for Universal Basic Income. While the outcome of these

1 A great deal of the recent scholarship on this issue has come out of Germany: See Erdbrügger, Torsten et al. (eds.): *Omnia Vincit Labor? Narrative der Arbeit – Arbeitskulturen in medialer Reflexion*. Frank & Timme: Berlin 2013; Stevanovic, Vid et al. (eds.): *Literatur und Arbeit*. Frank & Timme: Berlin 2018; Lillge, Claudia: *Arbeit. Eine Literatur- und Mediengeschichte Großbritanniens*. Wilhelm Fink: Paderborn 2016; Brogi, Susanna et al. (eds.): *Repräsentationen von Arbeit. Transdisziplinäre Analysen und künstlerische Produktionen*. For relevant volumes from other areas, see Attridge, John / Ryland, Helen (eds.): *Modernist Work. Labor, Aesthetics and the Work of Art*. Bloomsbury: London 2019; White, Claire: *Work and Leisure in Late Nineteenth-Century French Literature and Visual Culture. Time, Politics and Class*. Palgrave MacMillan: Basingstoke 2014; Cotes, Nicholas / Lauter, Paul (eds.): *A History of American Working-Class Literature*. Cambridge University Press: Cambridge 2017; Goodridge, John / Keenan, Bridget (eds.): *A History of British Working-Class Literature*. Cambridge University Press: Cambridge 2017; see also the special issue of *Framework. The Journal of Cinema and Media* 53(1), 2012, pp. 43–227.

2 See Mason, Paul: *Postcapitalism. A Guide to Our Future*. London: Allen Lane, 2015; Graber, David: *Bullshit Jobs. A Theory*. Allen Lane: London 2018.

policy debates is uncertain, such initiatives are only likely to gain in significance in the wake of the large-scale furlough and *Kurzarbeit* programmes that have been introduced in numerous countries following the outbreak of the COVID-19 pandemic. The economic recession that is projected for the coming years as a result of the economic shutdown that followed the global outbreak of COVID-19 in 2020 will surely further exacerbate many of the central problems of modern societies. The developments and tensions surrounding work's value not only as a factor in the calculation of economic gain, or in the formation of material to satisfy human needs, but also as a source of meaning, personal and social identity, and as a vector for social integration and exclusion, run through many of the contributions in the current volume.

Even though the surge in critical interest is partly a result of contemporary political and economic developments, the numerous scholarly publications on economic subjects as reflected and refracted through literary and philosophical texts from earlier centuries demonstrate that this interest is by no means restricted to the current moment. One could rather claim that the financial crisis, in (once again) revealing the fundamental instability of the contemporary global capitalist economic system, has reinvigorated interest in the origins of that system, and its historical trajectory towards global dominance.[3]

Prior to this renewal of scholarly interest, matters of the economy and work had, with the exception of several significant publications,[4] spent

---

3 Some examples of recent edited volumes collecting essays from the field that examine material from the early twentieth century and earlier include Waite, Marcus and Claire White (eds.). *The Labour of Literature in Britain and France, 1830–1910. Authorial Work Ethics*. Palgrave MacMillan: Basingstoke 2018; Lemke, Anja / Weinstock, Alexander (eds.): *Kunst und Arbeit. Zum Verhältnis von Ästhetik und Arbeitsanthropologie vom 18. Jahrhundert bis zur Gegenwart*. Wilhelm Fink: Paderborn 2014; Albracht, Miriam / Balint, Iuditha / Frank Weiher (eds.). *Goethe und die Arbeit*. Wilhelm Fink: Paderborn 2018; Vogl, Joseph / Burkhardt Wolf (eds.): *Handbuch Literatur und Ökonomie*. De Gruyter: Boston 2019.

4 E.g. Vogl, Joseph: *Kalkül und Leidenschaft. Poetik des ökonomischen Menschen*. Diaphanes: Zürich 2002; Tinkcom, Matthew: *Working Like a Homosexual. Camp, Capital, Cinema*. Duke University Press: Durham 2002; Lesjak, Carolyn: *Working Fictions. A Genealogy of the Victorian Novel*. Duke University Press: Durham 2006; Blaschke, Bernd: *Der homo oeconomicus und sein Kredit*

several decades on the periphery of literary and cultural studies in the wake of the so-called 'linguistic turn' and poststructuralism's emergence as the dominant critical paradigm within the discipline from the 1980s onwards. The collapse of "really existing" socialism and the integration of the former Eastern bloc into the capitalist system, heralded by Francis Fukuyama as the 'End of History',[5] undoubtedly also contributed to this process, thoroughly detracting from the appeal of the Marxist and Marxian theoretical frameworks that had informed the study of the relationship between labour, economics, and cultural production since the late 1960s, and indeed for much of the twentieth century.

Although Marx never produced a systematic aesthetic theory, his writings contain a number of remarks and reflections on literature and other arts that proved to be extremely influential for later theorists and critics.[6] The origins of the most significant trends in twentieth-century Marxist literary theory and scholarship can be traced to two diverging strands that emerged at the beginning of the 1930s. One of these was the state-ordained doctrine of socialist realism, developed first in the Soviet Union in the early 1930s,[7] before later being prescribed, emulated, and reworked in the various states behind the Iron Curtain in the post-war period. The other strand finds its origin in the works of members of the Frankfurt School, such as Walter Benjamin and Theodor Adorno, and other associated figures, such as Georg Lukács and Ernst Bloch.[8] Despite their differences in approach, both of these strains of Marxist-inspired literary criticism were united by their understanding of literary and cultural criticism as a form of ideology critique, operating within the fundamental

bei Musil, Joyce, Svevo, Unamuno und Céline. Wilem Fink: München 2004; Saller, Reinhard: Schöne Ökonomie. *Die poetische Reflexion der Ökonomie in frühromantischer Literatur*. Königshausen & Neumann: Würzburg 2007.

5 Fukuyama, Francis: *The End of History and the Last Man*. Penguin: London 1992.

6 The disparate statements are collected in volumes such as Marx, Karl / Engels, Friedrich: *Über Kunst und Literatur*. 2 vols. Dietz: Berlin 1967.

7 For an overview of some of the variant forms of socialist realist literature in different European national and linguistic literary traditions, see Tate, Dennis / Scriven, Michael (eds.): *European Socialist Realism*. Berg: Oxford 1988.

8 Some of the key texts documenting the debates between the originators of this strand of Marxist approaches to the study of literature are collected in Adorno, Theodor et al: *Aesthetics and Politics*. Verso: London 2006.

ideological tenets of a more-or-less traditional Marxism.[9] By the late 1980s, at the same time that many of the central tenets of traditional Marxism seemed to have been disproved by the course of history, several scholars had begun to approach the study of the intersections of literature, the arts, and the economy in a manner that was less aligned with traditional rhetoric of class struggle, and instead, drawing upon the methodologies of New Historicism and Foucauldian discourse analysis, examined the relationship between the economic and cultural spheres as one of interpenetration, mutual influence, and reciprocal exchange, in which metaphors, concepts, figures, and narratives crossed over between them.

This 'New Economic Criticism', as it was named in the title of a significant 1999 collection of essays espousing such approaches,[10] was of a less overtly political bent, seeking to identify, describe and analyse the relations between economic developments, economic thought, and the arts, without immediately setting such analysis in the service of an existing political agenda or within an overarching political (master)narrative, as had been the case in much Marxist literary criticism. Since the Financial Crisis, though the numerous works examining the historical semantics of the term 'work'/'labour' and their antitheses (play, idleness, laziness, etc.) in modernity, for example, still draw heavily on the methodological toolkits of the New Economic Criticism,[11] recent scholarship has often been far more overtly political and critical in its tone, both in its analysis of contemporary neoliberalism, and in its analysis of works of art from earlier historical periods. Our volume reflects these analytical trends and the more overtly political tone of recent scholarship, presenting essays that trace Marxist thought and its influence in theories of economic criticism

---

9 For an account and critique of the central elements of traditional Marxism, see Postone, Moishe: *Time, Labor, and Social Domination: A Reinterpretation of Marx's Critical Theory*. Cambridge University Press: Cambridge 1993.

10 See Woodmansee, Martha / Osteen, Mark (eds.): *The New Economic Criticism. Studies at the Intersection of Literature and Economics*. Routledge: London 1999.

11 See for example Schäfer, Martin Jörg: *Die Gewalt der Muße. Wechselverhältnisse von Arbeit, Nicht-Arbeit, Ästhetik*. Diaphanes: Zurich, 2013; Etzold, Jörn / Schäfer, Martin Jörg (eds.): *Nicht-Arbeit: Politiken, Konzepte, Ästhetiken*. Bauhaus-Universitätsverlag: Weimar 2011.

alongside contributions that follow the methodology of Foucauldian discourse analysis.

The essays collected in this volume enter the ongoing scholarly discussion with analyses of the engagement with economic subjects and their formation in key texts from Western European intellectual and literary history, from the nineteenth century to the present. The following chapters explore how different literary narratives and critical theorists have imagined or analysed the economic subject to show how this subject is conditioned by, challenges, resists, or even undermines the economic order in which it is situated. By doing so, the contributors tease out and make visible different dynamics within various forms of capitalist economic orders, and explore, and at times question, their attendant market logics and commodification mechanisms. Despite the differences separating the texts discussed in the individual contributions, the authors share an interest in critical inquiry into the ideologies that underpin those economic orders, and in tracing how economic discourses and structures produce economic subjects through the co-formation of individual subjectivity. This focus on the construction of the economic subject within society not only reveals the significance of work and the subject's relationship to capital in subject formation, but also how such structural positions in relation to capital intersect with other identity categories, such as gender, race, or, with increasing relevance in relation to transnational labour migration regimes, citizenship, play a crucial role in subjecting agents differently. The contributions in this volume throw a critical eye onto the interplay of such categories, exploring the different constricting and enabling factors for agency which follow from them, and the different modes of resistance to hegemonic economic discourses and structures which arise in response to them. Before we expand on the individual contributions, we want to provide a short overview of the relation between the economic order, work, and the economic subject in modern Western societies.

Exploring the Economic Order: Work and Society in Capitalist Modernity

In his 1820 *Grundlinien der Philosophie des Rechts*, G.W.F. Hegel elaborates his political philosophy of modern society. Such a society, he argues, consists of three essential elements – the family, *die bürgerliche Gesellschaft*, and the state. Modern society and the modern state, Hegel argues, differentiate themselves from the ideal state of antiquity primarily through the inclusion of the *bürgerliche Gesellschaft*. While this term has traditionally been translated in English as 'civil society', what Hegel actually discusses in relation to that term is a modern, free-market based economy. One of the central tenets of Hegel's argument is that such a free-market economy, if left to its own devices, would have deleterious consequences for society as a whole.[12] Such negative consequences can only be prevented, in Hegel's argument, by the regulatory intervention of the institutions of the state, which, due to its fundamental orientation towards the collective rather than individual good, functions as the guarantor of *Sittlichkeit*, or ethical life. Hegel does, however, identify one element of ethical life that operates within the *bürgerliche Gesellschaft*, namely:

> [D]ie *Rechtschaffenheit* und die *Standesehre*, sich, [...] durch seine Tätigkeit, Fleiß, und Geschicklichkeit [...] zu erhalten und nur durch diese Vermittlung mit dem Allgemeinen für sich zu sorgen sowie dadurch in seiner Vorstellung und der Vorstellung anderer *anerkannt* zu sein.[13]

For individuals in modern societies, Hegel argues, work is not merely a means to secure the necessities for material sustenance, but instead becomes a central mechanism of social integration through which individuals not only develop a sense of their own identity – themselves being formed (*gebildet*) through the type of formative activities that comprise their labour – but also seek recognition from themselves and from others

---

12 Hegel, G.W.F.: *Grundlinien der Philosophie des Rechts*. Suhrkamp: Frankfurt a.M. 1986. See especially §§ 240-47. For a fundamental reconstruction of Hegel's critique of liberal conceptions of the state, see Smith, Steven B: *Hegel's Critique of Liberalism*. Yale University Press: New Haven 1989.

13 Hegel, *Grundlinien der Philosophie des Rechts*, § 207, italics in original. Hegel, G.W.F / Nisbet, Barry (transl.): *Elements of the Philosophy of Right*. ed. by Allen W. Wood. Cambridge University Press: Cambridge 1991, p. 238: 'The ethical disposition within this system is therefore that of *rectitude* and the *honour of one's estate*, so that each individual [...] supports himself through his own activity, diligence, and skill [...] and only through this mediation with the universal does he simultaneously provide for himself and gain *recognition* in his own eyes and the eyes of others'.

on that basis.[14] Looking back from the present, we can see that what Hegel described was the emergence of a form of society in which we still find ourselves today, in which work functions as the central point of a network of social institutions and the mechanism through which the individual is integrated into those institutions.

The labour historian Jürgen Kocka identifies the early nineteenth century as the point at which Western European nations began the transformation into *Arbeitsgesellschaften.*[15] This transformation was accompanied by a number of fundamental shifts both in the organisation of labour itself – such as the rise to dominance of the capitalist wage form over other labour relations, or the introduction of a spatial delineation between workplace and the home – and also in the fundamental understanding of which types of activities enjoyed the status of work at all. This renegotiation of what counted as work had particularly serious consequences for the societal recognition accorded to traditionally feminine work, with many types of work associated with women gradually losing that status.[16] Moreover, those forms of activity that retained the status of work were subject to increasing specialisation and fragmentation in the course of the industrial organisation of labour and the growing rise of large-scale, machine-based production.[17]

Karl Marx describes and reconstructs this historical process in minute detail in the first volume of *Capital*, terming it the 'real subsumption of labour under capital'.[18] This 'real subsumption' brings with it the proliferation of unsafe, monotonous, exploitative, and physically gruelling forms

---

14 See Herzog, Lisa: *Inventing the Market. Smith, Hegel, and Political Theory.* Oxford University Press: Oxford, 2013, pp. 73–79.

15 See Kocka, Jürgen: "Mehr Last als Lust. Arbeit und Arbeitsgesellschaft in der europäischen Geschichte". In: Kocka, Jürgen: *Arbeiten an der Geschichte. Gesellschaftlicher Wandel im 19. und 20. Jahrhundert.* Vandenhoeck & Ruprecht: Göttingen 2011, pp. 203–224

16 Ibid., pp. 212–15. See also Bock, Gisela / Duden, Barbara: "Arbeit aus Liebe – Liebe als Arbeit. Zur Entstehung der Hausarbeit im Kapitalismus". In: Gruppe Berliner Dozentinnen (ed.): *Frauen und Wissenschaft. Beiträge zur Sommeruniversität für Frauen, Juli 1976.* Courage: Berlin 1977, pp. 118–99.

17 Kocka 2011, p. 216.

18 Marx, Karl: *Das Kapital Band 1. Der Produktionsprozess des Kapitals* Berlin: Dietz 1962, pp. 356–531.

of labour, in which the individual subject was often reduced, in Marx's terms, to little more than a human appendage of a machine. The workers' movements of the nineteenth century emerged partly in response to the proliferation of such horrific working conditions. Yet rather than rejecting work altogether, those movements frequently staked their claims to legitimacy on the basis of work's supposedly innate honour and moral value,[19] drawing upon the celebration of work that had been elaborated in the preceding decades within bourgeois circles, where it had also been used to delegitimise workers, accusing them of laziness while claiming the status of 'real workers' for the bourgeoisie.[20]

Throughout the twentieth century, work-related matters continued to play a central role in the political narratives of capitalist and state socialist nations alike and their negotiation of social processes of inclusion and exclusion.[21] These discourses around work also addressed issues that could not be reduced to material concerns, often taking on violent, racist, or otherwise discriminatory ideological elements.[22] These were exacerbated

19 See Hake, Sabine: *The Proletarian Dream. Socialism, Culture, and Emotion in Germany, 1863–1933*. De Gruyter: Berlin 2017; Campbell, Joan: *Joy in Work, German Work. The National Debate, 1800–1945*. Princeton University Press: Princeton 1989; Thompson, E.P.: *The Making of the English Working-Class*. Gollancz: London 1963.

20 Kocka, 'Mehr Last als Lust', p. 217.

21 For a representative analysis of this in a state socialist context, see Barck, Simone / Mühlberg, Dietrich (eds.): "Arbeiter-Bilder und Klasseninszenierung in der DDR. Zur Geschichte einer ambivalenten Beziehung." In: Hübner, Peter / Kleßman, Christoph / Tenfelde, Klaus: *Arbeiter im Staatssozialismus. Ideologischer Anspruch und soziale Wirklichkeit*. Böhlau: Weimar 2005, pp. 163–89; for this process in capitalist countries, see Hachtmann, Rüdiger / von Saldern, Adelheid: "Das fordistische Jahrhundert. Eine Einleitung". *Zeithistorische Forschungen* 6(2), 2009, pp. 174–85.

22 The antisemitic instrumentalization of the discourse of "deutsche Arbeit" in the German interwar context is perhaps the most striking example of this. See Buggeln, Marc / Wildt, Michael (eds.): *Arbeit im Nationalsozialismus*. De Gruyter: Berlin 2014; Axster, Felix / Lelle, Nikolas (eds.): *Deutsche Arbeit. Kritische Perspektiven auf ein ideologisches Leitbild*. Wallstein: Göttingen 2018. For other examples of the intersections between labour discourses and other forms of social exclusion and marginalisation, see Colin, Nicole / Schößler, Franziska (Eds.): *Das nennen Sie Arbeit? Der Produktivitätsdiskurs und seine Ausschlüsse*. Heidelberg: Synchron 2013.

following the economic crises of the 1970s, which led to transformations in the organisation of employment and broader social structures which then prompted several prominent scholars to question whether the 'End of Work Societies' was imminent.[23] While this prophesised end did not arrive, the ringing of the alarm bells served to register the broader social crisis that was initiated by the dissolution of the Fordist economic model in the final quarter of the twentieth century.[24] In the wake of the Financial Crisis at the beginning of the twenty-first century, the critical discussion of waged work and the value systems of capitalist nations and global systems have turned to addressing the problems of labour organisation and social structures with a new urgency. Topics such as the intensifying precarity among the middle classes, or the new forms of insecurity and pressure that arise as the side-effects of digitisation, be that in the increasing porousness of the spatial and temporal boundaries separating work and everyday life,[25] or in the structure and organisation of the gig economy, are now an integral part of the debate.[26]

Yet many of the central questions at the heart of these debates – How fair is a society that predicates social inclusion upon employment, and how can one guarantee these participatory dynamics within an economic system in which full employment is impossible? What should replace work as the main source of meaning in our everyday lives? – have remained constant alongside these significant changes.[27] Our volume shows the

---

23 See for example Dahrendorf, Ralf: "Im Entschwinden der Arbeitsgesellschaft. Wandlungen in der Konstruktion des menschlichen Lebens". *Merkur* 34(8), 1980, pp. 749–60.

24 On the significance of these changes, see Doering-Manteuffel, Anselm / Rapahel, Lutz: *Nach dem Boom. Perspektiven auf die Zeitgeschichte seit 1970.* Vandenhoeck & Ruprecht: Göttingen 2010.

25 See Rosa, Hartmut: *Beschleunigung. Die Veränderung der Zeitstrukturen in der Moderne.* Suhrkamp: Frankfurt a.M. 2005. 269; Crary, Jonathan: *24/7. Late Capitalism and the Ends of Sleep.* Verso: London 2013.

26 For an analysis that situates these 'new' forms of work within the broader historical context of labour relations under real subsumption under capital, see Huws, Ursula: *Labor in the Digital Economy. The Cybertariat Comes of Age.* Palgrave MacMillan: London 2014.

27 Compare, for example, the contributions in Beck, Ulrich (ed.): *Die Zukunft der Arbeit und der Demokratie.* Suhrkamp: Frankfurt a.M. 2000, with those in Dörre, Klaus et al. (eds.): *Kapitalismustheorie und Arbeit. Neue Ansätze*

different iterations of these questions in different social and historical contexts from the 19th century to the present day to discuss the paradoxes of such a society, and the different modes of participation and resistance available to individual subjects.

Writing the Economic Subject

The emergence of modern societies as *Arbeitsgesellschaften* was accompanied by the elaboration of a new understanding of the nature or essence of human subjectivity. While earlier understandings may have emphasised rationality, religiosity, or sociality as the defining characteristic of human subjectivity, this new model – often referenced under the catchword of the *homo oeconomicus* – conceived of individual subjects as rational free agents whose decisions and actions were driven by the desire to maximise profit and minimise loss.[28] This model, which had its most influential proponent in Adam Smith, seldom stood, as many of Smith's contemporaries and later critics noted, in accordance with the empirical reality of most subjects, whose actions and agency were constrained by numerous conditions outside of their control, and whose decisions were often made in compliance with entirely different sets of priorities. Many critiques of this model of subjectivity in the eighteenth and nineteenth centuries were formulated from a theoretical or political position, with Hegel's aforementioned theory of modern society in the *Grundlinien der Philosophie des Rechts* providing a prime example. Yet literature also played an important role in both the constitution and circulation of this understanding of subjectivity, and in questioning, contesting, and critiquing it. Many authors sought to do this by drawing out the fault lines that separated the *homo oeconomicus* as ideal type (and ideal subject) of classical liberalism from the social reality of their age, or indeed of later ages. The contributions of

---

soziologischer Kritik. Campus: Frankfurt a.M. 2013. See also Jaeggi, Rahel / Kübler, Lukas: "Pathologien der Arbeit. Zur Bedeutung eines gesellschaftlichen Kooperationsverhältnisses", *WSI-Mitteilungen* 7, 2014, pp. 521–27.

28 Felix Maschewski, 'Homo oeconomicus'. In: Vogl, Joseph / Wolf, Burkhardt: *Handbuch Literatur und Ökonomie*. De Gruyter: Berlin 2019, pp. 160–63; see further Vogl, Joseph: *Kalkül und Leidenschaft. Poetik des ökonomischen Menschen*. Diaphanes: Munich 2002.

Elena Stingl, Anat Marcus, and Simon Godart in this volume, which respectively focus on George Bataille, Walter Benjamin, and Walter Benjamin in conjunction with Charles Baudelaire, examine attempts by cultural and social theorists (and, in Godart's case, literary authors) to understand the relationship between the economy and the individual subject in a far different mode from that taken by Smith and other early theorists of modern society who took an affirmative stance towards capitalist market economies. Their essays foreground some of the resistant analytical work that critical theorists have performed in order to understand the unexpected and harmful ways in which economic structures condition and produce individual subjectivity and collective social dynamics.

Many studies emphasise that discourse and narrative analysis can draw attention to dynamics and processes that often remain overlooked in economic thought and scholarship.[29] Literature can, of course, play a significant role in propping up, further elaborating, and lending ideological credence to the models of subjectivity prescribed and presented in classical economic thought. But it can also undermine and subvert them, partly through the confrontation of such ideal types with the less-than-ideal social conditions within which they must be lived out – thereby re-introducing the negative elements that are glossed over in the beautified ideal types of abstracted theory – and partly through the exploration of other prototypical economic subjects, whose existence may cast doubt upon the normative legitimacy of a given social or economic order. One might here think of the figure of the pauper, the slave, the professional failure, the

29 See for example Poovey, Mary: *A History of the Modern Fact. Problems of Knowledge in the Sciences of Wealth and Society*. Chicago University Press: London and Chicago 1998; Poovey, Mary: *Genres of the Credit Economy: Mediating Value in Eighteenth- and Nineteenth-Century Britain*. Chicago University Press: Chicago and London 2008; Wagner, Tamara: *Financial Speculation in Victorian Fiction: Plotting Money and the Novel Genre, 1815–1901*. Ohio State University Press: Columbus, Ohio 2010; Kornbluh, Anna: *Realizing Capital. Financial and Psychic Economies in Victorian Form*. Fordham University Press: New York 2013; Courtemanche, Eleanor: *The 'Invisible Hand' and British Fiction, 1818–1860. Adam Smith, Political Economy, and the Genre of Realism*. Palgrave Macmillan: Basingstoke 2011; or more recently, Saul Morson, Gary / Schapiro, Morton: *Cents and Sensibility: What Economics can Learn from the Humanities*. Princeton University Press: Princeton NJ 2018.

has-been, or the 'economic migrant', a roundly demonised figure of the contemporary moment. Figures such as these offer ample ground for forms of literary exploration and treatment that can critically question the ideological mechanisms which idealise certain figures while demonising others, drawing attention to the underlying economic, political, or social interests that drive such representational processes.

The engagement with individual ideal types or representative figures focuses on clearly delineated examples of the interplay between economic processes and individual subjectivation. Yet the subject of the economy in the twenty-first century, in the sense of the interconnected structures of economic production, exchange, and interdependence which cross national boundaries as part of a global system, is often too complex and entangled to be easily grasped. Literary works can illuminate the connections between the accumulation of wealth in the global North and the impoverishment of the global South, and draw attention to how these dynamics propel other dynamics, such as the economically motivated global migration of peoples. In this volume, Dorothea Trotter's contribution focuses on literary critiques of state responses to such migration flows. Elsewhere in the volume, Nora Weinelt and Aileen Behrendt show how literary texts from earlier historical periods can perform similar critical functions, arguing that literary narratives of failure and ruined lives also outline the dangers and risks that circumvent the realm of individual freedom, even in its ideal form, while simultaneously questioning the significance of a loosely defined "happiness" as motivating force or attainable goal of the economic subject. By putting this subject in a narrative, and thus always within a network of other subjects, literature reflects the complexity of conflicting social positions that can pose a challenge to overly simplistic or reductionist economic theories of human subjectivity or sociality.

In the past four decades, economies and societies in the Global North have been fundamentally wrought by neoliberal capitalism, seeing the erosion of the welfare state and the forms of Fordist state-controlled capitalism that had emerged in the wake of the Second World War.[30] The

30 In his relatively early essay of 1998, "The Essence of Neoliberalism", Pierre Bourdieu described neoliberalism as a "programme for destroying collective

restructuring of the world of work in the course of its neoliberal reorganisation, a process which was partially informed by critiques of Western capitalism that had been articulated as part of the New Left,[31] placed a premium on individual flexibility, creativity, and adaptability, creating new ideal economic subjects in its wake – the 'Ich-AG', or individual subjects as 'self-entrepreneurs', a new form of subjectivation that was analysed by Ulrich Bröckling in 2007.[32] Much contemporary fiction of the late twentieth and early twenty-first century showcases the destructive and destabilizing impact of neoliberalism, confronting capitalist thought and ideology with its negative consequences.[33] A wealth of critical literature written in a variety of disciplines – sociology, literary and cultural studies, philosophy – since the millennium has focused on showing the dark underbelly of the neoliberal rhetoric of creativity, flexibility, and self-determined working in digital capitalism – burnout, exploitation, and the looming threat of precarity.[34]

---

structures which may impede pure market logic." See Bourdieu, Pierre: "The Essence of Neoliberalisms" *Le Monde diplomatique*, Translation Jeremy J. Shapiro. *Le Monde diplomatique*, December 1998. Retrieved March 27, 2020, from https://mondediplo.com/1998/12/08bourdieu. Over the decades, more critics have responded to the increasingly visible negative impact on social structures left in the wake of neoliberal policies and reforms. For a representative early and later response to neoliberal reform, see Hall, Stuart / Massey, Doreen / Rustin, Michael (Eds.): *After Neoliberalism? The Kilburn Manifesto*. Lawrence & Wishart: London 2015; and Braedley, Susan / Luxton, Meg: *Neoliberalism and Everyday Life*. McGill-Queen's University Press: Montreal 2010, respectively.

31 See Boltanski, Luc / Chiapello, Eve / Elliott, Gregory (trans.): *The New Spirit of Capitalism*. Verso: London and New York 2007.

32 Bröckling, Ulrich: *Das unternehmerische Selbst. Soziologie einer Subjektivierungsform*. Suhrkamp: Frankfurt a.M. 2007.

33 Several novels have been read with a focus on how they narrate neoliberal structures. Among them McCarrthy, Tom: *Satin Island. A Novel*. Jonathan Cape: London 2015; late novels by J.G. Ballard, such as *Millennium People*. Harper Perennial: London 2003; or Margaret Atwood's dystopian fiction. In the German-language context, see also Röggla, Katrin: *wir schlafen nicht*. Frankfurt a.M.: Fischer 2004; Götz, Rainald: *Johann Holtrop. Abriss der Gesellschaft*. Suhrkamp: Berlin 2013. For further research, see: Johansen, Emily/ Karl, Alissa G. (eds.): *Neoliberalism and the Novel*. Routledge: London 2017.

34 There is a wealth of secondary literature examining this: Heimberger, Susanne: *Kapitalistischer Geist und literarische Kritik. Arbeitswelten in*

Our volume covers these issues that seem particular to the neoliberal age in the aforementioned contributions from Dorothea Trotter and Nora Weinelt, but different iterations of these existential concerns have informed literature across the last three centuries. The authors in this volume look at the fallacies of neoliberal and capitalist systems and how they produce economic subjects from the 19th century to the present day. They are interested in the literary representation of market and commodity structures that create agents that can affirm but also undermine, challenge and resist their subjection. Studies have shown how identity politics play a crucial role in the allocation of resources and have therefore identified the constituents according to (predominantly) class, race and gender categories.[35] The contributions by Katrin Frisch, Aileen Behrendt, and Dorothea Trotter also reflect on how economic subjects are gendered, classed and racialised, exploring how these categories condition subjects' positions in the economic order. In keeping with the preoccupation with power dynamics in contemporary critical literary and cultural studies, these contributions critically focus on how the idea of 'pure market logic' is constructed and serves to sustain the power of the privileged few who benefit from this system.

---

deutschsprachigen Gegenwartstexten. edition text + kritik: Munich 2010; Ring, Annie: 'System Error. Complicity with Surveillance in Contemporary Workplace Documentaries', *Seminar* 52(4) 2016, pp. 465–89; Biendarra, Anke: *Germans Going Global. Contemporary Literature and Cultural Globalization*. De Gruyter: Berlin 2012, pp. 89–147; Solty, Ingar / Stahl, Enno (Eds.): *Richtige Literatur im Falschen? Schriftsteller – Kapitalismus – Kritik*. Verbrecher: Berlin 2016; Matthies, Annemarie: *Spielbälle. Neuverhandlungen der Arbeitswelt im Medium Literatur*. Herbert von Halem: Köln 2016; Cosgrove, Mary: "The Slothful Protest: *Acedia* in Terézia Mora's Darius-Kopp Trilogy and Iris Hanika's *Das Eigentliche*", *German Life and Letters* 74(1), 2021, pp. 47–66.

35 As has been analysed by Weeks, Kathi: *The Problem with Work. Feminism, Marxism, Antiwork Politics, and Postwork Imaginaries*. Duke University Press: Durham and London 2011, p. 9; and Hennessy, Rosemary: *Profit and Pleasure. Sexual Identities in Late Capitalism*. Routledge: New York 2000.

On the Contributions

The first three essays in this volume discuss theories of economic order influenced by Marxist thought and work out the implication of power struggles for a critical reading of economic discourse. The collection of essays opens with Elena Stingl's chapter "Marxian Undercurrents in Bataille's Analysis of Fascism", in which she proposes a re-evaluation of Bataille's analysis of fascism in his early writings. After showing how Bataille scholarship has conventionally underplayed the significance of Marx's thought for Bataille's writings on fascism in the 1930s, Stingl demonstrates that Bataille's analysis of the charisma of fascist leaders via the concepts of social homogeneity and heterogeneity draws upon Marx's account of the qualitative transformation of the labour process and social relations as part of the real subsumption of labour under capital, and of the subjection of social relations to the principle of exchange.

The volume continues this discussion of exchange and transaction and their centrality for the economic order in the contributions by Anat Messing Marcus and Simon Godart, who reflect on the positions of the economic subject in these constellations. The second contribution in our volume, Anat Messing Marcus's "The Economic Body and the Incompletion of Time. On Walter Benjamin's 'Capitalism as Religion' ", focuses on Walter Benjamin's political-theological analysis of modern capitalist societies. Marcus sets Benjamin's enigmatic fragmentary text of 1921 alongside concepts and methods developed by Benjamin in his later writings, and the work of later cultural theorists such as Eric Santner and Giorgio Agamben, in order to shed new light on Benjamin's reflections on the links between ostensibly pre-modern political-theological forms of sovereignty and rule, and modern capitalist societies. In doing so, Marcus not only makes a valuable contribution to scholarship on Walter Benjamin, but her analysis of the commodity culture of the sexual market and the paradox of the prostitute as an economic subject who sells goods and embodies goods at the same time also identifies space for feminist critique of some aspects of Benjamin's, and of wider Marxian, thought.

While Marcus focuses on Walter Benjamin's theoretical writing, Godart's interest lies largely in his use for the study of literature. In the chapter " 'Un pauvre petit speculateur': Baudelaires *La fausse monnaie*" Godart examines Walter Benjamin's readings of Baudelaire's poetry and the methodological debate that these initial readings sparked between himself and Theodor W. Adorno on the function and nature of Marxian literary criticism. After reconstructing this debate and its significance for different ways of making economic processes and socio-historical developments visible in literary criticism, Godart turns his attention towards Baudelaire's prose-poem *La fausse monnaie*, providing an exemplary reading of the text that puts the methodological insights of Adorno and Benjamin – still relevant for much literary criticism today – into action. Godart's reading explores how the economic subject emerges – as flaneur, as gambler, as worker and importantly as speculator – within a conflicting field of the supply and demand logic.

The volume continues this investigation of the position of the economic subject within capitalist orders by examining subjective experiences and performances of failure, and how these moments of failure can shed light on some of the fallacies of the market. Nora Weinelt's essay "Being a Failure. The Malfunctioning of the Subject in Work Environments around 1900" traces how 'being a failure' became a biographical category and situates failure in language concepts and literary contexts of the 19th century. She works out the difference between the two German expressions "versagen" ("to be a failure") and "scheitern" ("to fail") to show how the concept of 'being a failure' is constructed in the midst of the development of new ideologies of economic and professional performance that saw the growing bureaucratisation of professional life and the proliferation of institutionalised modes of performance assessment. Reading Italo Svevo's *Una vita* and Herman Melville's short story "Bartleby, the Scrivener: A Story of Wall Street", she argues that 'being a failure' is a bourgeois mode of fulfilment and stands in stark contrast to literary notions of tragic failure. Weinelt asks why the idea of "being a failure" seems so deeply connected to a modern, historically young figuration of work. She questions the office cultures and power relations that produce failing subjects, but also critically notes how literary texts about failing so often focus on white-collar workers, yet almost never on the working class. Weinelt follows this development to our neoliberal age and questions the myths of failures-as-(eventual)-success-stories.

In alignment with Marcus's notion of the economic subject as a prostitute and Weinelt's observations on failure, Aileen Behrendt focuses on 'failure' with a discussion of precarious economic positions for women during the interwar years. In "Against the Capitalist Narrative of Success and Failure – the Precarious Lives of Jean Rhys's Interwar Women", Behrendt explores how Jean Rhys's 1930s novels can be read as critiques of capitalism as they challenge many of capitalism's underlying assumptions. Rhys's failing protagonists remain unimpressed by capitalist promises of work as the bringer of happiness, revealing the significant constructivist efforts behind the ideology of capitalism. Moreover, Behrendt's reading shows how Rhys's women, who occupy an array of subject positions on the economic periphery, complicate these positions further on account of their gender, as they can neither be the bourgeois failures that Weinelt analyses, nor the flaneurs that Godart identifies. These positions seem unavailable to the female characters at the heart of Rhys's texts, who can be read as vagabonds but never as tourists, to borrow Zygmunt Bauman's metaphors,[36] within the confines of a discriminatory economic system.

This focus on how gender and class shape economic subjects is taken up again by Katrin Frisch, who examines two more recent texts with an eye to their differing articulations and judgements of violence, as refracted through two very different class positions. Frisch does this through a comparative reading of two violent scenes involving skinheads in Alan Hollinghurst's *The Swimming Pool Library* (1988) and DJ Stalingrad's *Exodus* (2011). Her essay "The Language of Violence – Writing Lower-Class Masculinities in a Capitalist System" tries to untangle and decipher different forms of violence – physical, political, structural – which operate at different levels in her chosen texts, reading all three types against the backdrop of social class. With reference to DJ Stalingrad's text in particular, Frisch enquires into the conditions and repercussions of authors who are usually associated with 'non-literary' classes writing literature – a question which is also relevant in Nora Weinelt's contribution to this volume – while also examining the ways in which gender is treated within such examples of male working-class resistant writing.

36 See Bauman, Zygmunt: *Postmodernity and its Discontents*. Polity Press: Cambridge 1997.

Our volume closes with the contribution of Dorothea Trotter's chapter 'The Right to Work. The Humanitarian Migrant as Economic Subject in Contemporary German Literature' that focuses on the paradoxes of work, citizenship, and social integration in contemporary Germany, exploring the type of ideal subjects which the state constructs, while at the same time preventing members of certain social groups from engaging in the activity necessary to perform that desired identity. Taking a closer look at recent literary engagements with the situation of refugees and other migrants within the context of Germany and Austria, Trotter explores how works by Elfriede Jelinek, Jenny Erpenbeck, and Abbas Khider reflect upon the situation of migrants who are denied the right to work in a society in which not only material security, but a sense of self and identity is so tightly linked with one's own employment. Trotter shows that while doing this, these authors occupy variably critical positions towards the value ascribed to work within European societies, with some drawing upon it positively in their critique of contemporary European nation-states, while others seek to criticise both the states' treatment of migrants and the ideologies of labour which those states fail to realise in that treatment.

While the discussions in this volume encompass different centuries and Western nations, from Great Britain, Italy, Austria, Germany, France to the U.S., this temporal and geographical diversity emphasises the ubiquity of problems with the dominant economic orders and their impact on economic subjects. Spanning from the 19th century to today, the essays have identified recurring struggles and conflicts that arise from uneven power dynamics which continuously tip in favour of the privileged. However, by critically engaging with the narratives of economic subjects, with the paradoxes and quandaries of subjectivation in relation to economic structures and systems, and theories of economic order, the essays show the productive potential of literature and theory, when read alongside or against the grain of economic discourses, in contesting and critiquing aspects of capitalist order.

References

Adorno, Theodor W. et al.: *Aesthetics and Politics*. Verso: London 2006.

Albracht, Miriam et al. (Eds.): *Goethe und die Arbeit*. Wilhelm Fink: Paderborn 2018.

Attridge, John / Ryland, Helen (Eds.): *Modernist Work. Labor, Aesthetics and the Work of Art*. Bloomsbury: London 2019.

Axster, Felix / Lelle, Nikolas (Eds.): Deutsche Arbeit. Kritische Perspektiven auf ein ideologisches Leitbild. Wallstein: Göttingen 2018.

Barck, Simone / Mühlberg, Dietrich: "Arbeiter-Bilder und Klasseninszenierung in der DDR. Zur Geschichte einer ambivalenten Beziehung." In: Hübner, Peter / Kleßman, Christoph / Tenfelde, Klaus (Eds.): *Arbeiter im Staatssozialismus. Ideologischer Anspruch und soziale Wirklichkeit*. Böhlau: Weimar 2005, pp. 163–189.

Bauman, Zygmunt. *Postmodernity and its Discontents*. Polity Press: Cambridge 1997.

Beck, Ulrich (Ed.): *Die Zukunft der Arbeit und der Demokratie*. Suhrkamp: Frankfurt a.M. 2000.

Biendarra, Anke: Germans Going Global. Contemporary Literature and Cultural Globalization. De Gruyter: Berlin 2012.

Blaschke, Bernd: Der homo oeconomicus und sein Kredit bei Musil, Joyce, Svevo, Unamuno und Céline. Fink: Munich 2004.

Bock, Gisela / Duden, Barbara: "Arbeit aus Liebe – Liebe als Arbeit. Zur Entstehung der Hausarbeit im Kapitalismus". In: Gruppe Berliner Dozentinnen (ed.): *Frauen und Wissenschaft. Beiträge zur Sommeruniversität für Frauen, Juli 1976*. Courage: Berlin 1977, pp. 118–99

Boltanksi, Luc / Chiapello, Eve / Elliott, Gregory (trans.): *The New Spirit of Capitalism*. Verso: London 2007.

Bourdieu, Pierre: "The Essence of Neoliberalisms" *Le Monde diplomatique*, Translation Jeremy J. Shapiro. *Le Monde diplomatique*, December 1998. Retrieved March 27, 2020, from https://mondediplo.com/1998/12/08bourdieu.

Braedly, Susan / Luxton, Meg: *Neoliberalism and Everyday Life*. McGill-Queen's University Press: Montreal 2010.

Bröckling, Ulrich: Das unternehmerische Selbst. Soziologie einer Subjektivierungsform. Suhrkamp: Frankfurt a.M. 2007.

Buggeln, Marc / Wildt, Michael (Eds.): *Arbeit im Nationalsozialismus*. De Gruyter: Berlin 2014.

Campbell, Joan: *Joy in Work, German Work. The National Debate, 1800–1945*. Princeton: Princeton University Press, 1989.

Colin, Nicole / Schößler, Franziska (Eds.): *Das nennen Sie Arbeit? Der Produktivitätsdiskurs und seine Ausschlüsse*. Heidelberg: Synchron 2013.

Cosgrove, Mary: "The Slothful Protest: *Acedia* in Terézia Mora's Darius-Kopp Trilogy and Iris Hanika's *Das Eigentliche*", *German Life and Letters* 74(1), 2021, pp. 47–66.

Cotes, Nicholas/Lauter, Paul (Eds.): *A History of American Working-Class Literature*. Cambridge: Cambridge University Press, 2017.

Crary, Jonathan: *24/7. Late Capitalism and the Ends of Sleep*. London: Verso, 2013.

Dahrendorf, Ralf. "Im Entschwinden der Arbeitsgesellschaft. Wandlungen in der Konstruktion des menschlichen Lebens". *Merkur* 34(8), 1980, pp. 749–60.

Doering-Manteuffel, Anselm / Raphael, Lutz: *Nach dem Boom. Perspektiven auf die Zeitgeschichte seit 1970*. Vandenhoeck & Ruprecht: Göttingen 2010.

Dörre, Klaus et al. (Eds.): *Kapitalismustheorie und Arbeit. Neue Ansätze soziologischer Kritik*. Campus: Frankfurt a.M. 2013.

Erdbrügger, Torsten et al. (Eds.): *Omnia vincit labor? Narrative der Arbeit – Arbeitskulturen in medialer Reflexion*. Frank & Timme: Berlin 2013.

Etzold, Jörn / Schäfer, Martin Jörg (Eds.): *Nicht-Arbeit. Politiken, Konzepte, Ästhetiken*. Bauhaus-Universitätsverlag: Weimar 2011.

Fukuyama, Francis: *The End of History and the Last Man*. Penguin: London 1992.

Goodridge, John/Keenan, Bridget (Eds.): *A History of British Working-Class Literature*. Cambridge University Press: Cambridge 2017.

Graeber, David: *Bullshit Jobs. A Theory*. Allen Lane: London 2018.

Hachtmann, Rüdiger / von Saldern, Adelheid: "Das fordistische Jahrhundert. Eine Einleitung". *Zeithistorische Forschungen* 6(2), 2009, pp. 174–85

Hake, Sabine: *The Proletarian Dream. Socialism, Culture, and Emotion in Germany, 1863–1933*. De Gruyter: Berlin 2017.

Hall, Stuart et al. (Eds.): *After Neoliberalism? The Kilburn Manifesto*. Lawrence & Wishart: London 2015.

Hegel, G. W. F.: *Grundlinien der Philosophie des Rechts*. Suhrkamp: Frankfurt a.M. 1986.

Hegel, G. W. F. / H. B. Nisbet (trans.): *Elements of the Philosophy of Right*. ed. by Allen W. Wood. Cambridge University Press: Cambridge 1991.

Heimberger, Susanne: *Kapitalistischer Geist und literarische Kritik. Arbeitswelten in deutschsprachigen Gegenwartstexten*. Edition Text + Kritik: Munich 2010.

Hennessy, Rosemary: *Profit and Pleasure. Sexual Identities in Late Capitalism*. Routledge: New York 2000.

Herzog, Lisa: *Inventing the Market. Smith, Hegel, and Political Theory*. Oxford University Press: Oxford 2013.

Huws, Ursula: *Labor in the Digital Economy. The Cybertariat Comes of Age*. Palgrave MacMillan: London 2014.

Jaeggi, Rahel/Kübler, Lukas: "Pathologien der Arbeit. Zur Bedeutung eines gesellschaftlichen Kooperationsverhältnisses." *WSI-Mitteilungen* 7, 2014, pp. 521–527.

Johansen, Emily/Karl, Alissa G. (Eds.): *Neoliberalism and the Novel*. Routledge: London 2017.

Kocka, Jürgen: "Mehr Last als Lust. Arbeit und Arbeitsgesellschaften in der europäischen Geschichte." In: Kocka, Jürgen: *Arbeiten an der Geschichte. Gesellschaftlicher Wandel im 19. und 20. Jahrhundert*, Vandenhoeck & Ruprecht: Göttingen 2011, pp. 203–224.

Lemke, Anja / Weinstock, Alexander (Eds.): *Kunst und Arbeit. Zum Verhältnis von Ästhetik und Arbeitsanthropologie vom 18. Jahrhundert bis zur Gegenwart*. Wilhelm Fink: Paderborn 2014.

Lesjak, Carolyn: *Working Fictions. A Genealogy of the Victorian Novel*. Durham: Duke University Press 2006.

Lillge, Claudia: Arbeit. *Eine Literatur- und Mediengeschichte Großbritanniens*. Wilhelm Fink: Paderborn 2016.

Marx, Karl: *Das Kapital Band 1. Der Produktionsprozess des Kapitals*. Dietz: Berlin 1962.

Marx, Karl / Engels, Friedrich: *Über Kunst und Literatur*. 2 vols. Dietz: Berlin 1967.

Mason, Paul: *Postcapitalism. A Guide to Our Future*. Allen Lane: London 2015.

Matthies, Annemarie: Spielbälle. *Neuverhandlungen der Arbeitswelt im Medium Literatur*. Herbert von Halem: Cologne 2016.

Osteen, Mark / Woodmansee, Martha (Eds.): *The New Economic Criticism. Studies at the Intersection of Literature and Economics*. London: Routledge 1999.

Postone, Moishe: *Time, Labor, and Social Domination. A Reinterpretation of Marx's Critical Theory*. Cambridge University Press: Cambridge 1993.

Ring, Annie: "System Error. Complicity with Surveillance in Contemporary Workplace Documentaries." *Seminar. A Journal of Germanic Studies* 52(4), 2016, pp. 465–489.

Röggla, Kathrin: *wir schlafen nicht*. Frankfurt a.M.: Fischer 2004.

Rosa, Harmut: *Beschleunigung. Die Veränderung der Zeitstrukturen in der Moderne*. Frankfurt a.M.: Suhrkamp 2005.

Saller, Reinhard: *Schöne Ökonomie. Die poetische Reflexion der Ökonomie in frühromantischer Literatur*. Königshausen & Neumann: Würzburg 2007.

Schäfer, Martin Jörg: *Die Gewalt der Muße. Wechselverhältnisse von Arbeit, Nichtarbeit, Ästhetik*. Diaphanes: Zürich 2013.

Smith, Steven B.: *Hegel's Critique of Liberalism*. Yale University Press: New Haven 1989.

Solty, Ingar / Stahl, Enno (Eds.): *Richtige Literatur im Falschen? Schriftsteller – Kapitalismus – Kritik*. Verbrecher: Berlin 2016.

Stevanovic, Vid et al. (Eds.): *Literatur und Arbeit*. Frank & Timme: Berlin 2018.

Tate, Dennis / Scriven, Michael (Eds.): *European Socialist Realism*. Berg: Oxford 1988.

Thompson, E.P.: The Making of the English Working-Class. Gollancz: London 1963.

Tinkcom, Matthew: *Working Like a Homosexual. Camp, Capital, Cinema*. Duke University Press: Durham 2002.

Vogl, Joseph: *Kalkül und Leidenschaft. Poetik des ökonomischen Menschen*. Diaphanes: Zürich 2002.

Vogl, Joseph / Wolf, Burkhardt (Eds.): *Handbuch Literatur und Ökonomie*. De Gruyter: Boston 2019.

Waite, Marcus / White, Claire (Eds.): *The Labour of Literature in Britain and France, 1830–1910. Authorial Work Ethics*. Palgrave MacMillan: Basingstoke 2018.

Weeks, Kathi: *The Problem with Work. Feminism, Marxism, Antiwork Politics and Postwork Imaginaries*. Duke University Press: Durham and London 2011.

White, Claire: *Work and Leisure in Late Nineteenth-Century French Literature and Visual Culture. Time, Politics and Class*. Palgrave MacMillan: Basingstoke 2014.

Elena Stingl

Marxian Undercurrents in Bataille's Analysis of Fascism

Abstract: *In this paper, I address George Bataille's observations on the fascism of his age, as well as the controversial reception of his writings on that topic. I argue that most readers have neglected one important aspect of his treatment of fascism. Many critics and commentators have overly focused on Bataille's alleged fascination with the way in which fascist leaders presented themselves on the political stage, and his attempt to describe socially excluded or suppressed elements. At the same time, they have overlooked Bataille's engagement with Marx's critique of political economy in his writings of the early 1930s, particularly with the concepts of "exchange value" and "reduction of concrete to abstract labour". In this chapter, I show how Bataille's account of fascism makes use of these concepts, which are not always obvious on the surface of the text. Furthermore, I argue that without them the discussion of his view of the social developments at the time remains incomplete.*

Keywords: Georges Bataille, Karl Marx, Fascism, Political Economy, Capitalism, Economic Crisis, Interwar Years, Value Theory, Critical Theory.

> *But whoever is not willing to talk about capitalism should also keep quiet about fascism.*
>
> *Max Horkheimer*[1]

Introduction

In one of the most controversial sentences of his essay "The Psychological Structure of Fascism",[2] written and published shortly after the Nazis'

1 Horkheimer, Max / Ritter, Mark (transl.): "The Jews and Europe". In: Bronner, Stephen Eric, MacKay Kellner, Douglas (eds.): *Critical Theory and Society. A Reader*. Routledge: New York et al. 1989, pp. 77–94, p. 78.

2 Bataille, Georges / Lovitt, Carl R. (transl.): "The Psychological Structure of Fascism". In: Bataille / Stoekl, Allan (ed.): *Visions of Excess. Selected Writings 1927–1939*. University of Minnesota Press: Minneapolis 1985, pp. 137–60.

seizure of power in Germany, Georges Bataille argues that fascist leaders present themselves as radically different from all other agents in the political field of society: "Opposed to democratic politicians, who represent in different countries the platitude inherent to *homogeneous* society, Mussolini and Hitler immediately stand out as something *other*." (p. 143).[3] Homogenous, in Bataille's use of the term, denotes something different from what it is generally taken to mean today. He refers it to social phenomena which are in line with the norms of early twentieth-century bourgeois societies and can be appropriated for use by the capitalist mode of production. Heterogenous, by contrast, is used to describe social phenomena that elude productive or scientific appropriation and contravene bourgeois social norms.[4] The *Duce* and the *Führer* appear, according to Bataille, to be endowed with some sort of fundamental 'otherness' ['*tout autres*'], they appear "heterogenous". Like royal sovereigns of the past, he argues, they behave and are treated as if they were situated "above men, parties, and even laws" (ibid).

Critics have often taken such statements, in which Bataille addresses the impression fascism had on many contemporaries, as proof that his own engagement with the topic was colored by a personal admiration for the fascists' uncompromising demeanor. Jürgen Habermas, for instance, raised the question of whether Bataille had fallen for the "the show aspect of fascist leadership",[5] while Carlos Ginzburg claimed that Bataille's texts

---

Quotations from this text from here on directly in the text. All words in *italics* in the original; added emphasis in **bold**. References to this text in the following as 'the essay on fascism'.

3 The French formulation shows that Bataille is concerned with an immediate appearance, not with an essential characteristic: "Mussolini ou Hitler **apparaissent immediatement en saillie comme** *tout autres*". Bataille: "La structure psychologique du fascisme". In: ibid.: *Premiers écrits 1922–1940* (Œuvres complètes 1). Gallimard: Paris 1970, pp. 339–71, p. 348.

4 Bataille's use of these terms is explored in greater detail below.

5 Habermas, Jürgen / Lawrence, Frederick (transl.): *The Philosophical Discourse of Modernity. Twelve Lectures*. Polity Press: Cambridge 1990, pp. 211–37, p. 216. Marcus Coelen has called Habermas' lecture "the most famous non-reading" of Bataille's work ("la plus célèbre non-lecture"); Bataille's writings had been met with reservation on the part of the Frankfurt School since the late 1930s, which had a considerable influence on the perception of Bataille among the adherents of Critical Theory, cf. Coelen: "Une hétérologie de la

exhibit an "extremely equivocal attitude towards Fascist and Nazi ideology".[6] Richard Wolin has gone so far as to reproach Bataille scholarship for having "timidly tip-toed around these potentially compromising political themes."[7]

Readings such as these accuse Bataille of embracing what he merely describes—namely, the manner in which fascist leaders exuded a charisma to which a large part of the European population was immediately receptive. But Bataille's project was by no means a paean to the allure of fascism; it was an attempt to provide a sociological explanation for this common reaction.[8] In the interwar years, Bataille sought to explain the historical

---

réception". In: *Critique* 788-89 (2013), pp. 152–62, p. 157. For an overview of the interrelations between the Frankfurt School and the College of Sociology, founded by Bataille and others in the years prior to the Second World War, cf. Weingrad, Michael: "The College of Sociology and the Institute of Social Research". In: *New German Critique* 84 (2001), p. 129–61.

6 Ginzburg, Carlo / Tedeschi, John & Anne (transl.): *Myths, Emblems, and Clues*. London: Hutchinson Radius 1990, pp. 126–45: 143. Ginzburg specifically refers to a scene in Bataille's novel *Blue of Noon* (written in 1935, published in 1957) in which the protagonist encounters a Hitler Youth gathering that is described as having an "exulting" effect on him, cf. Bataille / Mathews, Harry (transl.): *Blue of Noon*. Paladin Grafton Books: London et al. 1988, p. 154 f.

7 Wolin, Richard: *The Seduction of Unreason. The Intellectual Romance with Fascism from Nietzsche to Postmodernism*. Princeton: Princeton University Press 2004, pp. 153–86, p. 177. According to Habermas, the themes amount to "the cultic honoring of leaders as sacred personages" cf. ibid. 1990, p. 216. Like Wolin, Diedrich Diederichsen observes the risks of a 'critique of reason' especially in the French tradition after (and drawing on) Bataille: "Spiritual Reactionaries after German Reunification: Syberberg, Foucault, and Others". In: *October* 62, 1992, pp. 65–83. In the context of Bataille's alleged 'flirtation' with fascism, cf. Wolin 2001, p. 344 and p. 181, where the latter quotes fragmentarily (and misleadingly) from a text which Bataille co-wrote in 1936, cf. ibid. 1970 (*Œuvres complètes* 1). In my chapter, I refer only to Bataille's 1933/34 essay on fascism, as it was written by him alone for direct publication, has sociological content and is explicitly dedicated to the critical understanding of fascism as social phenomena.

8 According to William Pawlett such "allegations are often simplistic, unsupported and follow predictable and well-worn paths", cf. *Georges Bataille. The Sacred and Society*. Routledge: London et al. 2016, p. 41 f. This issue has been addressed by numerous scholars, e.g. Noys, Benjamin: *Georges Bataille. A Critical Introduction*. Pluto Press: London et al. 2000, p. 8, pp. 43–7; Stoek,

process of social decomposition, a process of which fascist leaders were arguably symptoms. For despite the individual protagonists' psychological appeal to their followers, they hardly of social developments.

In seeking to demonstrate Bataille's alleged admiration for fascist leaders, commentators have often overlooked the importance of the less imposing expression "the platitude inherent to ***homogeneous*** society" in his argumentation. They underestimate Bataille's attempt to not only describe fascist leaders' charisma, but also to explain the supposed "platitude" against which these leaders succeeded in presenting themselves as something 'other' [*tout autre*]. More specifically, as I show in this chapter, Bataille's essay on fascism offers an explanation of how the economic structure of European societies created conditions amenable to the emergence of fascism.

As part of this argument, I propose a re-interpretation of the "The Psychological Structure of Fascism",[9] placing special emphasis on the paragraphs in which he addresses "*homogenous* society". One aspect of Bataille's treatment of fascism which has received little attention amongst scholars of his work is the influence of Karl Marx's critique of political economy on Bataille's writings of the early 1930s.[10] This chapter identifies

---

Allan: „Truman's Apotheosis: Bataille, 'Planisme,' and Headlessness". In: *Yale French Studies* 78, 1990, pp. 181–205; Suleiman, Susan Rubin: "Bataille in the street: the search for virility in the 1930s". In: *Critical Inquiry* 21(1), 1994, pp. 61–79. Bischof, Rita: "'...aus sicherer Quelle...' Wider das Geraune in der deutschen Bataille-Rezeption". In: *Neue Rundschau* 112, 2001, pp. 147–65. Geroulanos, Stefanos: "The Anthropology of Exit: Bataille on Heidegger and Fascism". In: *October* 117, 2006, pp. 3–24. Hewson, Mark and Coelen, Marcus: "Introduction". In: ibid. (eds.): *Georges Bataille. Key Concepts*. Routledge: London et al. 2016, pp. 1–22, p. 8.

9 Although critics have occasionally referred to other texts from Bataille's work of the 1930s for statements they read as reactionary or fascist, no other text has attracted as much attention, or indeed been as frequently misunderstood, as the fascism essay discussed here. For this reason, I concentrate on this text in this chapter.

10 What is meant by 'political economy' or the critique thereof in this chapter is explained aptly by Michael Heinrich: "In the nineteenth century, *political economy* broadly referred to that which we today call economics [Volkswirtschaftslehre oder Wirtschafswissenschaft]. By using the term "critique of political economy," Marx suggests that he is not interested only in a new presentation of political economy, but rather in a fundamental critique of all

the Marxian undercurrents in Bataille's essay on fascism and how he incorporated Marx's concepts into his explanation of the emergence of fascism.[11]

In what follows, I distinguish between 'Marxian' concepts, taken from Marx's writings on political economy, and 'Marxist' ones, referring to the diverse notions of historical materialism, especially among apologists of Marx's philosophy of history as the history of class struggle. Bataille was not a Marxist: Marx's writings do not play as prominent a role in his theoretical work as those, for example, of Durkheim, Hegel or Nietzsche. Nonetheless he dealt with concepts from the first volume of *Capital*, which had an important, but often neglected, impact on his investigation of contemporary political phenomena, especially the rise of fascism.

The Scholarly Consensus

Before unpacking these concepts and their relevance to Bataille's argumentation in his essay on fascism, a remark on the current scholarly consensus on Bataille's economic theory is necessary. His engagement with Marx, I contend, has been neglected by detractors and admirers alike, who generally converge in two points.

First, most scholars readily accept a distinction which Bataille establishes in his 1949 study, *The Accursed Share*, between "restricted" and "general economy".[12] The former adapts a classical understanding of economy

---

established economic science. Marx wants a "scientific revolution," albeit with a political, social revolutionary interest in mind." ibid. / Locascio, Alexander (transl.): *An Introduction to the Three Volumes of Karl Marx's Capital*. Monthly Review: New York 2012, p. 9; emphasis in the text.

11 The material presented here is the result not only of impulses from the conference "Economic Subjects" in Cambridge in July 2018, but also, in particular, of numerous conversations with Daniel Burnfin and Noah Zeldin, with whom I organized a workshop at the Friedrich Schlegel Graduate School at the Free University of Berlin in June 2019 on Bataille's and Alfred Sohn-Rethel's Fascism Analyses. Daniel Burnfin made us aware of the more or less ghostly presence of Marxian concepts in Bataille's essay.

12 See for example: Goux, Jean-Joseph / Aschheim, Katheryn and Garelick, Rhonda (transl.): "General Economy and Postmodern Capitalism". In: *Yale French Studies* 78, 1990, pp. 206–24; Borreil, Jean: "On Georges Bataille: An Escape from Lameness?" In: Boldt-Irons, Leslie-Anne (ed.): *On Bataille. Critical*

as set of social activities related to the production, distribution and consumption of wealth; the latter, in short, includes phenomena of excessive, unproductive expenditure and is based on the idea of a global circulation of energy, rather than inherently social questions.[13] Scholars who engage with Bataille's concept of economy often filter his earlier texts through this distinction, elaborated many years later, and thus are less receptive to more complex layers of his involvement with political economy.[14]

Second, accepting the concept of "general economy", scholars show little patience for differences within the sphere of "restricted economy"; the difference, for example, between productive activity with the purpose of covering an individual's costs of living and industrial production with the purpose of maximizing profits. Instead both are subsumed under the idea of 'productivity' or 'utility', without asking *productive for whom?*, or *useful for what?* Moreover 'capitalist' and 'Marxist' economics are often understood in the same "restricted" way, namely as systems based on

Essays. State University of New York Press: Albany 1995, pp. 129–43; Botting, Fred and Wilson, Scott: "Introduction. From Experience to Economy". In: ibid. (eds.): *The Bataille Reader*. Blackwell Publishing: Oxford et. al. 1997, pp. 1–34; Gerber, Lynn: "Movements of Luxurious Exuberance: Georges Bataille and Fat Politics". In: Biles, Jeremy and Brintnall, Kent L. (eds.): *Negative Ecstasies. Georges Bataille and the Study of Religion*. Fordham University Press: New York 2015, pp. 19–37; Goux: "Georges Bataille and the Religion of Capitalism". In: Biles and Brintnall 2015, pp. 106–22; Winnubst, Shannon: "Sacrifice as Ethics. The Strange Religiosity of Neoliberalism". In: Biles, Brintnall 2015, pp. 123–37; Kendall, Steward: "Expenditure". In: Hewson and Coelen 2016, pp. 75–87.

13 Hewson and Coelen notice a "surprising willingness to take up the wild biophysical speculations on 'general economy' as a means of theorizing the global economy." Ibid. 2016, p. 20.

14 Such genealogical readings usually begin with "The Notion of Expenditure", written just before the essay on fascism, cf. Bataille 1985 (*Visions of Excess*), pp. 116–29. Noys is one of the few to have remarked that this essay, "rather than being a work of 'political economy', as *The Accursed Share* claims to be, is a work of revolutionary critique", cf. Noys 2000, p. 105; other examples of critical approaches to Bataille's economic theory, cf.: Stoekl: *Bataille's Peak. Energy, Religion, and Postsustainability*. University of Minnesota Press: Minneapolis et al. 2007, and Landa, Ishay: "Bataille's Libidinal Economics: Capitalism as an Open Wound". In: *Critical Sociology* 41, 2015, pp. 581–96, and ibid.: "Bataille: The Master, the Slave, and Consumption". In: ibid., pp.1087–102.

productivity. Marx's writings primarily served as an *examination* of capitalism, however, rather than as a model for a new economy that would obey purely rational principles.

In his essay on fascism, Bataille engages with Marxian concepts that go beyond the dichotomy of purposefulness and waste.[15] By highlighting these ideas, my chapter also aims to show that the scope of Bataille's arguments may become clear only at a distance from his more manifest aims. Here, as Jacques Derrida has argued, "we must interpret Bataille against Bataille".[16]

Philological Considerations

In the early 1930s, when Bataille began to elaborate an original set of notions, his peculiar theoretical language was still in an experimental stage of development. His ideas about social transformation and contemporary political upheavals are clothed in an idiosyncratic vocabulary,[17] consisting in part of concepts borrowed from French anthropology,[18] Freudian psychoanalysis,[19] and Marxian

15 For a noteworthy discussion of Bataille's 'general economy' in the context of austerity politics, cf. Dodd, Nigel: *The Social Life of Money*. Princeton University Press: Princeton et al. 2014, pp. 163–210. Linsey McGoey picks up on that connection: "Bataille and the Sociology of Abundance: Reassessing Gifts, Debt and Economic Excess". In: *Theory, Culture & Society* 35(4–5), 2018, pp. 69–91.

16 Ibid.: "From Restricted to General Economy: A Hegelianism without Reserve". In: ibid. / Bass, Alan (transl.): *Writing and Difference*. Routledge: London et al. 2002, pp. 317–60, p. 348.

17 Arppe has characterized Bataille's work as "eclecticism", a "mélange of different disciplines", and his theory as "multi-layered", cf. Arppe, Tiina: *Affectivity and the Social Bond. Transcendence, Economy and Violence in French Social Theory*. Ashgate Publishing: Farnham et al. 2014, p. 105 f.

18 For an overview cf. Falasca-Zamponi, Simonetta: "Sociology and Ethnography". In: Hewson and Coelen 2016, pp. 38–49.

19 The assumption that the essay sets out to describe the *psychological* appeal which individual fascist leaders had on followers seems self-evident, when one considers the essay's title and references to Sigmund Freud's "Group psychology and the analysis of the ego" as "an essential introduction of the understanding of fascism" (p. 160). For Bataille's involvement with psychoanalysis cf. Dean, Carolyn J.: *The Self and its Pleasures. Bataille, Lacan, and the History of the Decentered Self*. Cornell University Press: Ithaca et al. 1992.

economics.[20] The list of books which he borrowed from the Bibliothèque nationale in Paris, where he worked as a librarian, shows that he consulted Marx's works at the time.[21] But it is easy to read over his use of Marxian notions without identifying them, as Bataille rarely links concepts to definite reference points in Marx's work. Tracing their influence is a challenge, because Bataille adapts them to his own purposes. Indeed, they become recognizable, I will argue, only by identifying their conceptual meanings and reconstructing their references.

His essay on fascism was one of a number of texts which Bataille contributed to the review *La critique sociale*.[22] The essay presents an inquiry into different forms of authoritarian rule in the history of European societies that seem for the most part to have disappeared in the modern age, specifically royal, ecclesiastical, and military authority. Once a complex international division of labor had been established over the course of the industrial era, however, a modified version of the old authoritarianism eventually returned in the form of fascism. This 20th century form of authoritarian rule appears, according to Bataille, in response to an "economic danger" (cf. p. 157). He claims that "economic conditions […] serve as [fascism's] base" (ibid.). The social conditions giving rise to the fascist seizure of power were to be found in the "development of economic

---

20 Stoekl calls the years 1932–35 "Bataille's Marxist 'phase' ", Stoekl 1990, p. 195. According to Pawlett, "Marxism, for Bataille, [in the early 1930s, E.St.] is the only revolutionary movement that has freed itself from idealism" ibid. 2016, p. 46. Zeynep Direk notes a technique of inverting Marxian terms in *The Accursed Share*, cf. "Bataille and Kristeva on Religion". In: Biles and Brintnall 2015, pp. 182–201, p. 187.

21 The list indicates that Bataille's more intensive involvement with Marx's writings began around 1930 and it shows that he had borrowed *Le capital* between 1931 and 1932, cf. Bataille: "Emprunts de Georges Bataille à la Bibliothèque Nationale (1922–1950)". In: Bataille: *Articles 2: 1950–61* (*Œuvres complètes* 12). Gallimard: Paris 1988, pp. 549–627, p. 579.

22 The journal's purpose was to "address a non-Stalinist Marxism, rather than serve as intellectual organ for a potential political movement", thus to further Marxist discourse outside the official structures of the French Communist Party, cf. Richman, Michèle: "Fascism Reviewed: Georges Bataille in 'La Critique sociale' ". *South Central Review*, 14(3/4), 1997, pp. 14–30, p. 15.

life" (p. 140). Hence, he sees fascism as a counterreaction against objective economic tendencies.

In order to account for the "economic danger" to which fascism responds, Bataille adopts concepts from Marx's critique of political economy that go beyond the obvious reference to an economic "basis" and ideological "superstructure" (cf. p. 137).[23] In the opening paragraphs of Bataille's essay, he also presents a brief sketch of the economic structure of industrialized countries, in which he makes use of the Marxian concept of the "reduction" of concrete to abstract labor, which occurs in the exchange of products as commodities.[24] Acknowledging the significance of the term "reduction" as used here in relation to its specific meaning in Marx's *Capital*, will be indispensable for understanding Bataille's analysis of fascism as a response to the contemporary economic conditions. Before taking a closer look at Marxian concepts in Bataille's essay, we must recall the historic context in which it was published.

---

23 In the preamble of his essay, Bataille uses the term "infrastructure" in reference to what Marx calls the "economic foundation" or "real foundation" of society. Marx famously argued that "[t]he mode of production of material life conditions the general process of social, political and intellectual life. It is not the consciousness of men that determines their existence, but their social existence that determines their consciousness." Marx, Karl / Sdobnikov, Yuri (transl.): "Preface" to *A Contribution to the Critique of Political Economy*. In: ibid. and Engels, Friedrich: *Marx 1857–61*. (Collected Works 29). Lawrence & Wishart: London 2010, pp. 261–66, p. 263.

24 This is a contentious issue in Marx scholarship. Some argue that the abstraction in question primarily happens in exchange, cf. e.g. Sohn-Rethel, Alfred / Sohn-Rethel, Martin (transl.): *Intellectual and Manual Labor. A Critique of Epistemology*. The MacMillan Press: London et al. 1978, ch. 4 and 6, or Adorno, Theodor W. / Jameson, Fredric R. (transl.): "Society". In: *Salmagundi* 10/11 (1969–70), pp. 144–53; others claim that industrial production plays a more predominant role in rendering labor abstract, cf. e.g. chapter 9 in Postone, Moishe: *Time, Labor, and Social Domination. A Reinterpretation of Marx's Critical Theory*. Cambridge University Press: Cambridge et al. 1993. Bataille's remarks on the structure of industrial societies and his texts written in support for the worker's strikes in France in 1936 provide fertile ground for a more in-depth comparison between these texts and the Marxian analysis of industrial production. Nevertheless, in the context of this chapter, I will only engage with Marx to the extent that it illuminates Bataille's statements on "reduction" in the exchange process.

France in Crisis: The Economic Situation after the Stock Market Crash

Although Bataille sees fascism as a response to the economic threat posed capitalism, nothing in his essay suggests that he regards fascist politics as a solution to the problems arising from social structures. Rather, he suggests that fascist leaders take advantage of people's unease with the economic situation by establishing a new form of authoritarian rule in the political field.

Bataille insists here upon the continued relevance of a claim made by Marx and Engels in the *Communist Manifesto* (p. 139): Liberal-democratic politicians are complicit in the perpetuation of the current mode of production, and thereby in the subordination of human life to the practical constraints which that mode entails. In contrast to those politicians, fascist leaders succeed in presenting themselves as radically different. They are no less complicit in the status quo, but they behave as if none of the rules to which all others are subject would apply to them. The uncompromising, aggressive, "heterogenous" action of fascist agents in the political field, Bataille argues, *seems* to restore human singularity and irreducibility which is diminished by social "homogeneity". Fascist leaders attract attention, according to Bataille, because they embody something that had been eliminated from most people's everyday existence by the logic of commercial society: an existence "valid in itself" (cf. p. 138 f). Adherents of fascism submit to the restoration of human irreducibility despite, or perhaps because of, the fact that rational considerations play no role in it (cf. p. 145). People do not affiliate themselves with fascism after careful consideration, instead this affiliation happens "spontaneously", as Bataille writes, and at a time when society is already in a process of "dissociation" caused by the contradictions arising in the economic sphere (cf. p. 140).

Bataille does not specify which contradictions he has in mind, but rather leaves the conclusions to his readers. The time and place of publication make the exact nature of these unspecified contradictions clear enough, however; indeed, in an essay addressing the current state of disintegration caused by economic developments, published in the early 1930s in a left-wing review, contemporary readers required little further elucidation.

What was meant were the consequences of the global economic crisis caused by the stock market crash of 1929.[25]

Without going into the details of the economic crisis, Bataille's essay registers the 'profound malaise'[26] in which French society found itself at the time. The misery of the workers, especially of the unemployed, and the fear of social decline amongst the petty bourgeoisie, threatened to serve the same radical groups in the seizure of power that had succeeded beyond the Rhine.[27] Bataille's essay sets out to explain how fascist leaders in neighboring countries had succeeded at posing as saviors. His investigation takes it as a premise that they appear in societies that suffer from conflicts which do not arise from the political order but are carried out on the political stage (which is not to suggest that, in Bataille's opinion, the agitation of the fascists in Italy and Germany had merely theatrical effects).

Opposition between Normative Society and Unassimilated Elements

The first section of Bataille's essay contains the principal discussion of relevance in this chapter. Here, he presents the notion of two antagonistic spheres of society, which he calls "homogeneity" and "heterogeneity".[28]

25 According to Noys, "Bataille's energetic reflections on the crisis of value were influenced as much by the 1929 Wall Street crash and the subsequent world depression as they were by the anthropological data on which Bataille drew", cf. ibid. 2000, p. 105. For an overview of the economic crisis in France, cf. Sowerwine, Charles: *France since 1870. Culture, Society, and the Making of the Republic*. Palgrave Macmillan: New York et al. 2009, pp. 133–42. Stovall, Tyler: *Transnational France. The Modern History of a Universal Nation*, Westview Press: Boulder 2015 pp. 306–11. Vigreux, Jean: *Histoire du front populaire. L'échappée belle*. Texto: Paris 2016, pp. 11–40.

26 Vigreux 2016, p. 19.

27 It is safe to assume that Bataille had read the report by Simone Weil (his colleague at *La critique sociale*) on the worker's fight to oppose the NSDAP's rise to power and the systematic dismantling of worker's rights. Cf. Weil, Simone: "The Situation in Germany". In: ibid. / Tuck Mc Farlane, Dorothy, and Van Ness, Wilhelmina (eds. & transl.): *Formative Writings. 1929–1941*. The University of Massachusetts Press: Amherst 1987, pp. 89–147.

28 Bataille italicizes the words "homogenous" / "homogeneity" and "heterogeneous" / "heterogeneity" throughout the essay as a sign that he defines these words in a specific way, with complex ramifications. His use of the term

The former signifies, as mentioned above, regularity and the normative dominance of practical constraints in so-called bourgeois society; the latter denotes elements of social interaction or behavior that refuse assimilation, objects or people who stand out as crude, sacred, or bizarre in contrast to ordinary and conventional, "homogenous" society. He assigns sovereign figures, such as monarchs and the heads of military divisions, to the sphere of "heterogeneity", but also madmen, poets, the lumpenproletariat—and fascist leaders.[29] The common feature of this eclectic group is that they behave or are treated *as though* they were not subject to the rules to which the rest of society is ordinarily subjected.[30] They remain outsiders, pariahs, or heroic figures.

Bataille is generally more interested in describing "heterogeneous" elements of society and spends considerably more time discussing them than political economy or "homogeneity", which he at one point calls "peaceful but fastidious" (p. 143).[31] While some commentators, as I pointed out above, have confused his sociological interest in describing the 'unruly'

"heterogenous" bears similarity to that of Freud and Durkheim. Cf. Freud, Sigmund / Strachey, James (transl.): "Group Psychology and the Analysis of the Ego". In: ibid.: *Beyond the Pleasure Principle Group Psychology and Other Works* (The Complete Psychological Work of Sigmund Freud Vol. XVIII: 1920–1922). The Hogarth Press: London 1955, pp. 65–143, p. 74. Cf. Durkheim, Émile: *The Elementary Forms of Religious Life*. Oxford, Oxford University Press, 2001, p. 42, 85, 198, 218.

29 Significantly, Bataille associates fascism with the notion of Bonapartism (pp. 149, 158), i.e., the view, based on Marx's *18th Brumaire*, that there is a historical affinity between totalitarian leaders such as Louis Bonaparte and the lowest classes of society: "This Bonaparte, installed as chief of the lumpenproletariat, discovering his personal interests here in popular form, perceiving in the dregs, refuse and scum of all classes the sole class that offers unconditional support, here is the real Bonaparte". Marx, Karl: "The Eighteenth Brumaire of Louis Bonaparte". In: Cowling, Mark / Martin, James (eds.): *Marx's Eighteenth Brumaire. (Post)modern Interpretations*. Pluto Press: London et al. 2002, pp. 19–109, p. 63.

30 The concept of "heterogeneity" could be fruitful for current debates on neo-authoritarian leaders, and the popular support they enjoy.

31 After publishing his essay on fascism, Bataille started elaborating his own branch of social science, which he called "heterologie", programmatic notions of which can be found already in this essay, and on which he picked up later in the 1930s when he invented with colleagues a so-called "sociologie sacrée", cf.

elements of society with an endorsement of each of the examples he gives,[32] most Bataille scholars have focused almost entirely on what he had to say about "heterogeneity".[33] To isolate his explanation for the massive popular support for fascism, we must shift our focus to the social processes described in the section on "homogeneity". For it is against the background of 'ordinary' society and in contrast to all other politicians representing the "present [*homogenous*; E.St.] order of things" (p. 138), as Bataille sees it, that the fascist leaders were able to present themselves as 'radically different'.

Truck, Barter, and Exchange: Political Economy beyond the Aspect of Utility

Bataille situates the foundation of "homogeneity" in the mode of production of modern society. At first glance, it may seem as if he is simply discussing a general form of social utilitarianism, or as if he proceeds from the assumption of a classical framework of "productive society", which holds that economic value is measured by the utility that a good provides its user. For instance, he writes:

> *Homogeneous* society is productive society, namely, useful society. Every useless element is excluded, not from all of society, but from its *homogeneous* part. In this part, each element must be useful to another without the *homogeneous* activity ever being able to attain the form of activity *valid in itself*. A useful activity has a *common denominator* with another useful activity, but not with activity *for itself*. (p. 138)

Hollier, Denis (ed.) / Wing, Betsy (trans.): *The College of Sociology (1937–34)*. University of Minnesota Press: Minneapolis 1988.

32 Which he explicitly denies: "*Heterogeneous* fascist action [...] makes an appeal to sentiments traditionally defined as *exalted* and *noble* and tends to constitute authority as an unconditional principle, situated above any utilitarian judgment. Obviously, the use of the words *higher, noble, exalted* does not imply endorsement." p. 145.

33 The concepts of "heterogeneity" or "heterology" continue to preoccupy researchers, as a recent issue of *Theory, Culture & Society* dedicated to "Bataille and Heterology" illustrates. Michèle Richman, in this issue, calls Bataille's essay on fascism "the master text of heterology", cf. ibid.: "Bataille's Prehistoric Turn: The Case for Heterology". In: *Theory, Culture & Society* 35(4–5), 2018, pp. 155–73, p.156.

This seemingly self-evident framework of utility corresponds to what Ellen Meiksins Wood describes as the "commercialization model" of economy, which is often uncritically accepted in economic thought: "With or without a natural inclination to 'truck, barter, and exchange' (in Adam Smith's famous formulation), rationally self-interested individuals [...] sell[] their utilities by selling goods for profit whenever the opportunity presented itself".[34] Similarly, Bataille seems to suggest that the empirical process of production, the production of particular goods or useful objects, in itself is already the cause of social "homogeneity". This would be consistent with the concern that modern society excludes anything that is not a means for the sake of something else (i.e. "*valid in itself*", p. 138).

The statement that "useful activity has a *common denominator* with another useful activity, but not with activity *for itself*" (p. 138), invites many readers to focus almost entirely on the instrumental dimension of useful activity ("not...*for itself*"), while neglecting, although also italicized, the expression "*common denominator*", whose importance I would like to emphasize in the following.[35] Upon closer inspection, this wording suggests that Bataille not only has the particular *utility* of things in mind, but also and importantly their general *exchangeability*. As a reader of *Capital*, Bataille was familiar with Marx' view that one cannot understand the current social mode of production in terms of the "use value" of goods or commodities alone (which includes the labor power of people). The decisive component is their "exchange value". For capitalism is a system

34 Meiksins Wood, Ellen: *The Origin of Capitalism. A Longer View*. Verso: London 2017, pp. 11–33, p. 11, p. 15.

35 For instance, Allan Stoekl accepts a view of "homogenous social structure" as similar to "a bourgeois and finally even a Marxist society erected on the principles of classical utility (that is, on the denial of expenditure without return)", cf. "Introduction". In: Bataille 1982 (*Visions of Excess*), pp. ix-xxv, p. xxii. Although Peter Stallybrass examines commonalities between the notion of "heterogeneity" and Marx' attempts to describe the lumpenproletariat, he does not mention that Bataille echoes Marxian concepts in his presentation of the term "homogeneity", cf. "Marx and Heterogeneity. Thinking the Lumpenproletariat". In: *Representations* 31 (1990), pp. 69–95, p. 81 f., nor does Rodolphe Gasché in his account of the two opposing concepts of "homogeneity" and "heterogeneity" in ibid.: "The Heterological Almanac". In: Boldt-Irons 1995, pp. 157–208, p. 159 ff.

that primarily produces profits ("surplus value"), not goods for people's needs.[36]

In order to exchange things, a medium of comparison or measurement is necessary. Objects must be related to something, and by relating things to each other in a certain proportion of exchange, those who exchange agree, consciously or not, to a shared parameter, the "common denominator" of the acts of exchange. Thereby, the value of the exchanged items is revealed to them. Whatever the use of an activity or object might be, once the process of exchange begins, its value is distinct from its mere use for consumption, its 'utility'. This is how Marx considers the twofold nature of commodities: they possess "exchange value" (i.e. value) in addition to, though in abstraction from, their "use value" (i.e. 'utility') for the producer or consumer.[37] Accordingly, commodities are produced for the sake of exchange, not for direct consumption or private use. They can enter the exchange process only if the equivalent form of their commodities has already been established. At the same time, the exchange process establishes the form of value of commodities by relating them to an equivalent.

Since Bataille's notion of "homogeneity" is fundamentally related to a "*productive* society" in which activities have equivalents or a "common denominator", his essay addresses a society in which products enter the process of exchange. His account moves within the sphere of 'political economy', and does so, moreover, in a manner similar to Marx' critique of political economy. This appears in Bataille's elucidation of what constitutes equivalence:

---

36 Cf. e.g. "Use-value is certainly not *la chose qu'on aime pour lui-même* in the production of commodities. Use-values are produced by capitalists only because and in so far as they form the material substratum of exchange-value, are the bearers of exchange value. [...] [The capitalist's] aim is to produce not only a use-value, but a commodity; not only use-value, but value; and not just value, but also surplus-value." Marx / Fowkes, Ben (transl.): *Capital. A Critique of Political Economy* 1. Penguin: New York et al. 1982, p. 293. Cf. also ibid. p. 254., and Marx on why "use value as such, lies outside the sphere of investigation of political economy", ibid. 2010 (*A Contribution*), p. 270.

37 Cf. e.g. Marx 1982 (*Capital* 1), p. 127, p. 135 f.

> The common denominator, the foundation of social *homogeneity* and of the activity arising from it, is **money**, namely, the **calculable equivalent** of the different products of collective activity. Money serves to measure all work and makes man a function of measurable products. (p. 138)

In a few words, Bataille summarizes here what Marx elaborates over dozens of pages, namely that in more advanced relations of production and exchange one particular form of value has become the "universal equivalent"[38] in which the exchange value of all other commodities is determinately expressed: money. In the circulation of commodities, money has become, according to Marx, the "socially recognized equivalent form"[39] of all commodities, the "crystallization of the exchange value of commodities"[40]. This is the meaning that Bataille takes for granted when he explains the foundation of "social homogeneity": In monetary exchange, qualitatively different commodities (goods or labor) become quantitively commensurable; the quantitative measure of value, the money form of value, rather than purposefulness or utility, is the "calculable equivalent", as he says, of productive activity, including human labor as *value-adding* activity:

> According to the judgment of *homogeneous* society, **each man is worth what he produces**; in other words, he stops being an existence *for itself*: he is **no more than a function**, arranged **within measurable limits**, of collective production (which makes him an existence *for something other than itself*). (p. 138)

When Bataille says that humans are worth the value of that which they produce, he tacitly assumes two things: The human capacity for labor (labor-power), when it enters the process of exchange, is also a commodity; and, like all other commodities, it possesses a twofold character. Whatever the useful purpose of an activity in the private or public realm might be, the value of human labor, under the current mode of production, is decided in terms of exchange, according to Marx. It is coextensive with its function and dependent on collective, measurable units. Individual stakeholders

---

38 Cf. Marx 1982 (*Capital* 1), p. 160 ff.

39 Marx 1982 (*Capital* 1), p. 180.

40 Marx 2010 (*A Contribution*), p. 289. Marx's comments on the physical properties of money (precious metals), resembles Bataille's notion of "homogeneity" as such: cf. ibid.

do not establish these units. They result, as Bataille knows, from "collective production". Production is collective when it appears in the advanced exchange process that Marx calls the capitalist mode of production and orthodox economists call the market economy. By determining the value of human activity in comparison to other commodities, the capitalist mode of production deprives such activity, in Bataille's opinion, of "existence *for itself*". Or, in Marxian terms: Concrete, individual labor is "reduced" to an abstract, measurable quantity, for which money serves as expression.

The Reduction of Human Activity in the Process of Exchange and the Submission of Human Activity to Impersonal Rule

Bataille states that uniform, "homogenous" human relations result from a kind of "**reduction** to fixed rules" (p. 137). By "reduction", for which Bataille provides little context, he means the "commensurability" (ibid.) of all things and people. They become measurable by the same standard through the elimination of differences or individuality. Their commensuration occurs, as demonstrated in the preceding section, through the process of exchange. The reduction of individuality to anonymous fungibility is an effect of *individuals' subsumption under the social process of exchange*. To understand the way in which Bataille employs the concept of "reduction", Marx's analysis of commodity fetishism in *Capital* proves instructive.[41]

Marx explains how in complex economic networks, where many humans work for other humans, the labor of those who work for others itself assumes the form of a commodity. This form, however, does not appear as it is, a social artifact. Rather, it appears to all involved as though it were a natural property of things. Thus, humans 'fetishize' their work relations.[42] In this same context, Marx discusses what he calls a "reduction" of concrete human labor to abstract labor, according to which different kinds of labor count as equivalent. He presents this notion in a passage, first published in the French edition of *Capital* and otherwise found only

41 Marx 1982 (*Capital* 1), pp. 163–77, for the notion of the "fetishism", cf. especially p. 164 f.

42 They appear as material (dingliche) relations instead of social relations: ibid. 1982 (*Capital* 1), p 166.

in his handwritten marginalia, that helps demonstrate what Bataille might have had in mind when he employed the term "reduction": It is the process of abstraction which turns singular actions into measurable entities, effectively homogenizing productive activity *as well as* the producers. The French and English versions of the section read as follows:

> C'est seulement dans leur échange que les produits du travail acquièrent comme valeurs une existence sociale identique et uniforme, distincte de leur existence matérielle et multiforme comme objets d'utilité. [...] L'égalité de travaux qui diffèrent *toto cœlo* les uns des autres ne peut consister que dans une abstraction de leur inégalité réelle, que dans la réduction à leur caractère commun de dépense de force humaine, de travail humain en général, **et c'est l'échange seul qui opère cette réduction en mettant en présence les uns des autres sur un pied d'égalité les produits des travaux les plus divers.**[43]
>
> Equality in the full sense between different kinds of labour can be arrived at only if we abstract from their real inequality, if we reduce them to the characteristic they have in common, that of being the expenditure of human labour-power, of human labour in the abstract. [**And it is only exchange that performs this reduction by putting the one and the other product of the most diverse labors on equal footing.**].[44]

According to Marx, the "reduction" of different kinds of productive activities to abstract, equivalent labor happens in the exchange process ("l'échange seul opère cette réduction").[45] Crucially, this "reduction" does not occur through a 'mental abstraction', but rather by way of a 'real abstraction'.[46] It happens when people sell their labor power for a wage

---

43 Marx: *Le Capital, Paris 1872–1875. 1989.* (Marx Engels Gesamtausgabe II.7). Dietz: Berlin 1987, p. 54 f. For the Pléiade edition cf. ibid. / Rubel, Maximilien (ed.) / Roy, Joseph (transl.): *Économie.* (Œuvres I). Gallimard: Paris 1965, p. 607. The **bold** sentence [**in parenthesis**] appears neither in the English, nor the German edition.

44 Marx 1982 (*Capital* 1), p. 166. "Die Reduktion der verschiednen konkreten Privatarbeiten auf dieses Abstraktum gleicher menschlicher Arbeit vollzieht sich nur durch den Austausch, welcher Producte verschiedener Privatarbeiten thatsächlich gleichsetzt" Marx: *Das Kapital. Kritik der Politischen Ökonomie. Erster Band, Hamburg 1872. 1987.* (Marx Engels Gesamtausgabe II.6). Dietz Verlag: Berlin 1987, p. 41.

45 By "abstract" labor Marx does not mean, as Michael Heinrich argues, a special type of "monotonous" labor, such as assembly-line work in a factory, in contrast to artisanal, allegedly content-rich handicraft: cf. Heinrich 2012, p. 49.

46 Bataille's use of the concept "reduction" comes remarkably close to what Alfred Sohn-Rethel only a few years later would call „Realabstraktion", a

and *through* the selling of it, regardless of whether they are aware of it.[47] According to Marx, as discussed above, under the capitalist mode of production every product of human activity, including productive human activity itself, takes on the form of a commodity as soon as it enters the process of exchange. In this process, different human beings relate their commodities, the various products of their various activities, to each other. Concrete labors and individual products may be naturally heterogeneous, as Bataille would say, but in exchange they effectively become homogenous.

Thus, what Bataille takes from his reading of Marx is that in the system of universalized commodity production, exchange performs the "reduction" of those who produce, i.e. the vast majority of the population. Exchange reduces different kinds of human activity to a social relation in which individuals 'naturally' appear as commensurable, not as "*valid in [them]self*" (p. 138). By way of money, exchange directly 'homogenizes' different products and indirectly 'homogenizes' productive activities, in the specifically Bataillean sense. The daily process of exchange, upon which modern society depends, causes the "homogeneity" of lifeless things as well as of human existence.[48] The "reduction" of which Marx speaks finally reveals why Bataille claims that in capitalism "each man is worth what he produces": The value of human activity emerges from the transformation of singularity into uniformity or fungibility. To that extent, valuable human activity is always already determined by the social conditions that result from the capitalist mode of production. This is why the distinct way in which people produce for exchange, and not just some doctrinaire

---

term which he used to explain the historical genesis of forms of thought on the basis of socio-economic relations of exchange. On this notion cf. Engster, Frank and Schlaudt, Oliver / Blumefeld, Jacob (transl.): "Alfred Sohn-Rethel: Real Abstraction and the Unity of Commodity-Form and Thought Form". Best, Beverley et al. (eds.): *The SAGE Handbook of Frankfurt School Critical Theory*, Sage Reference: Los Angeles 2018, pp. 284–301.

47 Cf. what Marx writes about the reduction of different kinds of labour to simple average labour that goes on behind the backs of the producers, cf. ibid. 1982 (*Capital* 1), p. 135.

48 For Marx on the equivalence with which lifeless things and human existence are treated under capitalism cf. ibid. / Engels (transl.): *Wage-Labor and Capital*. Dodo Press: Gloucester 2009, p. 17.

idea of 'utility', represses activities that refuse assimilation. In other words, when Bataille speaks of "homogeneity", he means, as Slavoj Žižek notes, "the order of exchange" in capitalism.[49]

Before concluding, I would like to focus on one example of how Bataille employs the notion of "reduction" in the course of his argument.[50] Shortly after mentioning the term in the opening sentences, it reappears in the section where he talks about class differences in industrial civilization.

> [I]n the present order of things, the *homogeneous* part of society is made up of those men who own the means of production or the money *destined for their upkeep or purchase*. It is exactly in the middle segment of the so-called capitalist or bourgeois class that the tendential **reduction** of human character takes place, making it an abstract and interchangeable entity: a reflection of the *homogeneous things* the individual owns.
>
> This **reduction** is then extended as much as possible to the so-called middle classes that variously benefit from realized profit. (p. 138)

When Bataille addresses "the middle segment of the so-called capitalist or bourgeoise class" (not to be confused with "the so-called middle classes"[51]), he seems to mean the merchant capitalists who engage in the circulation

49 Žižek, Slavoj: *The Parallax View*. MIT Press: Cambridge et al., 2006, p. 94. William Pawlett's discussion of Bataille's fascism essays is one of the few to acknowledge the presence of "reduction" and "exchange" in the definition of "homogeneity": "The homogeneous sphere reduces human being to a productive function, often measured numerically, such that all beings are, in a sense, interchangeable." Pawlett 2016, p. 49.

50 The term returns in the section on "The State": "The **reduction** of differences through compromise in parliamentary practice indicates all the possible complexity of the internal activity of adaptation required by *homogeneity*." (p. 139), and when he talks about the "principle of all authority: the **reduction** a personal entity, the individualization of power" in contrast to "homogenous society as a **reduction** to the common denominator" (p. 148).

51 Bataille does not describe the characteristics of this class, but he most likely means the petty bourgeoisie, members of which Ellen Meiksin Wood describes as "someone of non-noble status who, while he worked for a living, did not generally dirty his hands and used his mind more that his body in his work. That old usage [...] is likely to refer to a professional, an officeholder, or an intellectual no less than to a merchant" Wood: *The Origin of Capitalism*, p. 14. Cf. also on the difference between the terms 'bourgeoisie' and 'middle-class': Morretti, Franco: *The Bourgeois. Between History and Literature*. Verso: London et al. 2013, pp. 6–12.

of commodities. They are, in his view, no less affected by the process of "reduction" than the wage laborer. According to his definition of "homogeneity", they also participate in the process of exchange. As Marx would have it, they sell the commodities which they possess, not in order to cover their costs of living, but to increase their profits. The "so-called capitalist or bourgeois class" benefits from the uniformity of the vast majority of the population, but they are, by the same token, reduced to their fungibility through the process of exchange. Furthermore, the reduction of human existence to a function of the circulating commodities prevents most people from shaping their productive activity autonomously. The capitalist mode of production suppresses ways of existence that try to resist the submission to exchangeability. Consequently, the meaning of people's lives, across the classes, is restricted to what they have to offer for exchange.

Conclusion: A Case for Confronting Less Glaring Events of Social Life

Earlier in this chapter, I claimed that Bataille's essay on fascism contains, amongst other things, an inquiry into different forms of authoritarian rule in the history of European societies. The population of early 20th century Western nation states no longer lived under the dominance of feudal lords. Most human lives depended on *indirect* "relations of dominance and servitude"[52]. Dominance had shifted from individual figures to the omnipresent, practical constraints of the capitalist mode of production and exchange, which Marx calls "invisible threads".[53] The fact that most people are compelled to work for a living in order to survive, while others unrelentingly increase their profits in order to stay in business, is as involuntary as the fetishization of their working conditions. Marx's description and analysis of this situation in the 19th century holds equally true for century in which Bataille was writing, and in which individuals are less likely to be subjugated by singular masters than by the mastery of a "monstrous

52 Cf. Marx 1982 (*Capital* 1), p. 452.

53 Cf. Marx 1982 (*Capital* 1), p. 719. Heinrich characterizes the form of dominance under capitalism as "the submission to 'inherent necessities,'" [Unterwerfung unter 'Sachzwänge'] cf. Heinrich 2012, p. 75. Also cf. Postone 1993.

accumulation of commodities"[54]. This is precisely the "economic danger" of which Bataille speaks in his essay, I argue, and to which fascism appears as a violent retaliation.[55] Bataille explains fascism as a response to the '*monstrosity*' of the economic structure which subordinates humans to impersonal forces and annihilates their singularity in the omnipresent process of exchange.

Ultimately, Bataille's text seeks to provide an account of the group psychology of mass movements ("affective forces" and social "effervescence") that can explain the appeal of fascism in the 20th century (cf. p. 158 f). For this reason, many scholars have argued that Bataille sees Marxist theory as lacking in concepts capable of explaining the rise of fascism.[56] Indeed, considerations concerning collective affective motives at work in the fascists' seizure of power make up most of Bataille's essay. As I have shown, the Marxian concepts of "exchange value" and "reduction" appear only in the few opening paragraphs of his essay. Nevertheless, they play a crucial role in his account of fascism. Careful examination of the passages in which they appear reveals what many of those who reacted favorably to fascism, in Bataille's view, have reacted *against*. According to his account, followers of fascism were not merely turning against a normative idea of 'utility' or 'productivity', I claim, but rather against the *actual* exchange of products and labor in the market. They reacted against the reality of their everyday work experiences. We can learn from Bataille's essay that not

---

54 Cf. Marx 1982 (*Capital* 1), p. 125, translation amended.

55 In the *Revolt of Reason*, Horkheimer presents a view that comes remarkably close to Bataille's view of fascism as a kind of retaliation against collectively suppressed or excluded remainders of society. Horkheimer argues that, in the course of socialization, humanity and human desires are repressed and subordinated to the demands of social rationalization, in a way that excludes non-instrumental activities. He takes this to result in mounting dissatisfaction, frustration, and resentment, which ultimately culminates in an explosive "revolt of nature", cf. Horkheimer: *The Eclipse of Reason*. Continuum: New York, 1947, p. 109.

56 Cf. e.g. Richman 1997, p. 17, Arppe 2014, Hewson and Coelen 2016, p. 7 f. An assertion that should be questioned, however, if only because Bataille refers to fascism as "bonapartism" (p. 149 and 158), a term with which he deals in an essay written shortly before (yet published posthumously) with reference to Marx's *18th Brumaire*, cf. cf. Bataille 1985 (*Visions of Excess*), pp. 32–44.

only the appearance of fascist agitators is dangerous, but also, long before their appearance, the process in which human existence is reduced from concrete activity to fungible entities.

In order to show the significance of Bataille's analysis the social process of exchange, I have focused almost entirely on the section where he presents his notion of the "homogenous" part of society. Its neglect by scholars and critics may be to some degree indicative of how the subtle processes in the economic sphere received less attention from Bataille himself. From an early stage of his work onwards, Bataille preferred to inquire phenomena that disrupt the ordinary course of human coexistence, including the economic basis of society. What has become ordinary, self-evident, implicit in the era of industrial capitalism, are the seemingly natural, but entirely social relations of subordination that arise when most people have to work for others in order to cover their costs of living. In so doing, they are subjected to the practical constraints of society. Bataille's essay on "The Psychological Structure of Fascism" provides conceptual resources for examining the disruption of these social constraints. But, importantly, it also helps to explain those less conspicuous structures that, despite intermittent disruptions, continue to constitute the largest part of social reality.

References

Adorno, Theodor W. / Jameson, Fredric R. (transl.): "Society". In: *Salmagundi* 10/11 (1969–70), pp. 144–53.

Arppe, Tiina: Affectivity and the Social Bond. Transcendence, Economy and Violence in French Social Theory. Ashgate Publishing: Farnham et al. 2014.

Bataille, Georges: "La structure psychologique du fascisme". In: Bataille, Georges (ed.): *Premiers écrits 1922–1940* (Œuvres complètes 1). Gallimard: Paris 1970, pp. 339–71.

———: "Emprunts de Georges Bataille à la Bibliothèque Nationale (1922–1950)". In: Bataille, Georges (ed.): *Articles* 2: *1950–61* (*Œuvres complètes* 12). Gallimard: Paris 1988, pp. 549–627.

Bataille, Georges / Lovitt, Carl R. (transl.): "The Psychological Structure of Fascism". In: Bataille, Georges / Stoekl, Allan (ed.): *Visions of*

Excess. Selected Writings 1927–1939. University of Minnesota Press: Minneapolis 1985, pp. 137–60.

Bataille, Georges / Mathews, Harry (transl.): *Blue of Noon*. Paladin Grafton Books: London et al. 1988.

Bischof, Rita: "'...aus sicherer Quelle...' Wider das Geraune in der deutschen Bataille-Rezeption". In: *Neue Rundschau* 112 (2001), pp. 147–65.

Borreil, Jean: "On Georges Bataille: An Escape from Lameness?" In: Boldt-Irons, Leslie-Anne (ed.): *On Bataille. Critical Essays*. State University of New York Press: Albany 1995, pp. 129–43.

Botting, Fred and Wilson, Scott: "Introduction. From Experience to Economy". In: Botting, Fred and Wilson, Scott (eds.): *The Bataille Reader*. Blackwell Publishing: Oxford et al. 1997, pp. 1–34.

Coelen, Marcus: "Une hétérologie de la réception". In: *Critique* 788-89 (2013), pp. 152–62.

Dean, Carolyn J.: The Self and its Pleasures. Bataille, Lacan, and the History of the Decentered Self. Cornell University Press: Ithaca et al. 1992.

Derrida, Jacques: "From Restricted to General Economy: A Hegelianism without Reserve". In: Derrida, Jacques / Bass, Alan (transl.): *Writing and Difference*. Routledge: London et al. 2002, pp. 317–60.

Diderichsen, Diedrich: "Spiritual Reactionaries after German Reunification: Syberberg, Foucault, and Others". In: *October* 62, 1992, pp. 65–83.

Direk, Zeynep: "Bataille and Kristeva on Religion". In: Biles and Brintnall 2015, pp. 182–201.

Dodd, Nigel: *The Social Life of Money*. Princeton University Press: Princeton et al. 2014, pp. 163–210.

Durkheim, Émile: *The Elementary Forms of Religious Life*. Oxford, Oxford University Press, 2001.

Engster, Frank and Schlaudt, Oliver / Blumefeld, Jacob (transl.): "Alfred Sohn-Rethel: Real Abstraction and the Unity of Commodity-Form and Thought Form". Best, Beverley et al. (eds.): *The SAGE Handbook of Frankfurt School Critical Theory*, Sage Reference: Los Angeles 2018, pp. 284–301.

Falasca-Zamponi, Simonetta: "Sociology and Ethnography". In: Hewson and Coelen 2016, pp. 38–49.

Freud, Sigmund / Strachey, James (transl.): "Group Psychology and the Analysis of the Ego". In: Freud, Sigmund / Strachey, James (eds.): *Beyond the Pleasure Principle Group Psychology and Other Works* (The Complete Psychological Work of Sigmund Freud Vol. XVIII: 1920–1922). The Hogarth Press: London 1955, pp. 65–143.

Gasché, Rodolphe: "The Heterological Almanac". In: Boldt-Irons 1995, pp. 157–208

Gerber, Lynn: "Movements of Luxurious Exuberance: Georges Bataille and Fat Politics". In: Biles, Jeremy and Brintnall, Kent L. (eds.): *Negative Ecstasies. Georges Bataille and the Study of Religion*. Fordham University Press: New York 2015, pp. 19–37.

Geroulanos, Stefanos: "The Anthropology of Exit: Bataille on Heidegger and Fascism". In: *October* 117 (2006), pp. 3–24.

Ginzburg, Carlo / Tedeschi, John & Anne (transl.): *Myths, Emblems, and Clues*. London: Hutchinson Radius 1990, pp. 126–45.

Goux, Jean-Joseph.: "Georges Bataille and the Religion of Capitalism". In: Biles and Brintnall 2015, pp. 106–22.

Goux, Jean-Joseph / Aschheim, Katheryn and Garelick, Rhonda (transl.): "General Economy and Postmodern Capitalism". In: *Yale French Studies* 78 (1990), pp. 206–24.

Habermas, Jürgen / Lawrence, Frederick (transl.): *The Philosophical Discourse of Modernity. Twelve Lectures*. Polity Press: Cambridge 1990, pp. 211–37.

Heinrich, Michael / Locascio, Alexander (transl.): *An Introduction to the Three Volumes of Karl Marx's Capital*. Monthly Review: New York 2012

Hewson, Mark and Coelen (eds.): *Georges Bataille. Key Concepts*. Routledge: London et al. 2016, pp. 1–22.

Hollier, Denis (ed.) / Wing, Betsy (trans.): *The College of Sociology (1937–34)*. University of Minnesota Press: Minneapolis 1988.

Horkheimer, Max: *The Eclipse of Reason*. Continuum: New York, 1947.

Horkheimer / Ritter, Mark (transl.): "The Jews and Europe". In: Bronner, Stephen Eric and MacKay Kellner, Douglas (eds.): *Critical Theory and Society. A Reader*. Routledge: New York et al. 1989, pp. 77–94.

Kendall, Steward: “Expenditure”. In: Hewson and Coelen 2016, pp. 75–87.

Landa, Ishay: “Bataille's Libidinal Economics: Capitalism as an Open Wound”. In: Critical Sociology 41 (2015), pp. 581–96. Landa, Ishay: “Bataille: The Master, the Slave, and Consumption”. In: Landa, Ishay (ed.), pp. 1087–102.

Marx, Karl: *Das Kapital. Kritik der Politischen Ökonomie*. Erster Band, Hamburg 1872. 1987. (Marx Engels Gesamtausgabe II.6). Dietz: Berlin 1987.

———: *Le Capital, Paris 1872–1875. 1989*. (Marx Engels Gesamtausgabe II.7). Dietz: Berlin 1987.

Marx, Karl / Fowkes, Ben (transl.): *Capital. A Critique of Political Economy* 1. Penguin: New York et al. 1982.

———: “The Eighteenth Brumaire of Louis Bonaparte”. In: Cowling, Mark / Martin, James (eds.): *Marx's Eighteenth Brumaire. (Post) modern Interpretations*. Pluto Press: London et al. 2002, pp. 19–109. Marx, Karl / Engels, Friedrich (transl.): *Wage-Labor and Capital*. Dodo Press: Gloucester 2009.

Marx, Karl / Rubel, Maximilien (ed.) / Roy, Joseph (transl.): *Économie*. (Œuvres I). Gallimard: Paris 1965.

Marx, Karl / Sdobnikov, Yuri (transl.): “Preface” to *A Contribution to the Critique of Political Economy*. In: Marx, Karl and Engels, Friedrich (eds.): *Marx 1857–61* (Collected Works 29). Lawrence & Wishart: London 2010, pp. 261–66.

Meiksins Wood, Ellen: *The Origin of Capitalism. A Longer View*. Verso: London 2017.

McGoey, Linsey: “Bataille and the Sociology of Abundance: Reassessing Gifts, Debt and Economic Excess”. In: *Theory, Culture & Society* 35 (2018), pp. 69–91.

Morretti, Franco: *The Bourgeois. Between History and Literature*. Verso: London et al. 2013.

Noys, Benjamin: *Georges Bataille. A Critical Introduction*. Pluto Press: London et al. 2000.

Pawlett, William: *Georges Bataille. The Sacred and Society*. Routledge: London et al. 2016.

Postone, Moishe: Time, Labor, and Social Domination. A Reinterpretation of Marx's Critical Theory. Cambridge University Press: Cambridge et al. 1993.

Richman, Michèle: "Fascism Reviewed: Georges Bataille in 'La Critique sociale'". In: *South Central Review* 14(3/4), (1997), pp. 14–30.

———: "Bataille's Prehistoric Turn: The Case for Heterology". In: *Theory, Culture & Society* 35 (2018), pp. 155–73

Sohn-Rethel, Alfred / Sohn-Rethel, Martin (transl.): *Intellectual and Manual Labor. A Critique of Epistemology*. The MacMillan Press: London et al. 1978.

Sowerwine, Charles: France since 1870. Culture, Society, and the Making of the Republic. Palgrave Macmillan: New York et al. 2009, pp. 133–42.

Stallybrass, Peter: "Marx and Heterogeneity. Thinking the Lumpenproletariat". In: *Representations* 31 (1990), pp. 69–95.

Stoekl, Allan.: "Introduction". In: Bataille / Stoekl (ed.): *Visions of Excess. Selected Writings 1927–1939*. University of Minnesota Press: Minneapolis 1985, pp. ix–xxv.

———: "Truman's Apotheosis: Bataille, 'Planisme,' and Headlessness". In: *Yale French Studies* 78 (1990), pp. 181–205.

———: *Bataille's Peak. Energy, Religion, and Postsustainability*. University of Minnesota Press: Minneapolis et al. 2007.

Stovall, Tyler: *Transnational France. The Modern History of a Universal Nation*, Westview Press: Boulder 2015 pp. 306–11.

Suleiman, Susan Rubin: "Bataille in the street: the Search for Virility in the 1930s". In: *Critical Inquiry* 21 (1994): pp. 61–79.

Vigreux, Jean: *Histoire du front populaire. L'échappée belle*. Texto: Paris 2016.

Weil, Simone: "The Situation in Germany". In: Weil, Simone / Tuck Mc Farlane and Van Ness (eds. & transl.): *Formative Writings. 1929–1941*. The University of Massachusetts Press: Amherst 1987, pp. 89–147.

Weingrad, Michael: "The College of Sociology and the Institute of Social Research". In: *New German Critique* 84 (2001), p. 129–61.

Winnubst, Shannon: "Sacrifice as Ethics. The Strange Religiosity of Neoliberalism". In: Biles, Brintnall 2015, pp. 123–37.

Wolin, Richard: *The Seduction of Unreason. The Intellectual Romance with Fascism from Nietzsche to Postmodernism*. Princeton: Princeton University Press, 2004, pp. 153–86.

Žižek, Slavoj: *The Parallax View*. MIT Press: Cambridge et al., 2006.

Anat Messing Marcus

The Economic Body and the Incompletion of Time: On Walter Benjamin's "Capitalism as Religion"

Abstract: *The essay demonstrates how the notion of the economic body is conceptualised in Walter Benjamin's posthumously published fragmentary text "Kapitalismus als Religion" (1921). The three sections of the essay extend from this fragment to other areas of Benjamin's thought. The first move links "Capitalism as Religion" to Benjamin's appropriation of myth and shows how the consideration of mythic violence is underlined by the banishment of the maternal-feminine to the domain of the image. In the second move, the concepts of the "dialectical image" and "natural history" are discussed in relation to the indebtedness of having a body. The final section turns to another early fragment, "Wahrnehmung und Leib" (1918/9), in which the distinction between "Schein" and "Sein" is contemplated against the backdrop of the "messianic". Drawing these threads together, the essay uncovers the role of bodiliness, perception and sexuality in Benjamin's critique of secularisation and of myth, released by the formula "capitalism as religion".*

Keywords: Walter Benjamin, dialectical image, capitalism, myth, perception, gender, natural history

> *Wir sollen Ding und Sache sein vor der Kultur*
> *[We ought to be thing and object before culture]*
>
> *Walter Benjamin*[1]

> *The experience of our generation: that capitalism will not die a natural death.*
>
> *Walter Benjamin*[2]

---

1 In a letter to Herbert Belmore, 23 June 1913, see Benjamin, Walter / Adorno, Theodor W.: *The Correspondence of Walter Benjamin 1910–1940*. University of Chicago Press: Chicago 1994, p. 35 (translation modified).

2 Benjamin, Walter / Eiland, Howard / McLaughlin, Kevin (transl.): *The Arcades Project*. Harvard University Press: Cambridge, Mass. 1999, p. 667.

Introduction

In the context of Walter Benjamin's work, knowledge and its critique prefigure a constellation wherein extremities touch, a spatio-temporal set-up governed by a tension between theology and modernity. Through a mode of writing classified as "image-thinking", Benjamin's essays, aphorisms and studies relentlessly aim to capture the ghostly traces of the withdrawal of the sacred within history.[3] It is a thinking that is directed at the exposure of a messianic crack, traceable within historical, capitalist, and also patriarchal, spaces of meaning. This is remarkably evident in his posthumously published fragmentary text "Kapitalismus als Religion", written in 1921. Here too, image, language and body configure in a constellation, one of the most indispensable forms of thought within Benjamin's writings.[4] "Kapitalismus als Religion" begins with the following statement:

> A religion may be discerned in capitalism [Im Kapitalismus ist eine Religion zu erblicken] – that is to say, capitalism serves essentially to allay the same anxieties, torments, and disturbances to which the so-called religions offered answers. The proof of the religious structure of capitalism – not merely, as [Max] Weber believes, as a formation conditioned by religion, but as an essentially religious phenomenon – would still lead even today to the folly of an endless universal polemic. We cannot draw closed the net in which we are caught. Later on, however, we shall be able to gain an overview of it [Später wird dies jedoch überblickt warden].[5]

The relation between theology and modernity, as it has been shown by Giorgio Agamben, can be articulated through the following clarification. Secularisation and profanation, he points out, "are political operations: the

---

3 "My thinking is related to theology as blotting pad is related to ink. It is saturated with it. Were one to go by the blotter, however; nothing of what is written would remain." Benjamin: *The Arcades Project*, p. 471.

4 "Ideas are to things as constellations to stars". Constellation names a spatial, projected figure through which discontinuity, interruption and temporal multiplicity become the origin of philosophical representation. See Benjamin, Walter / Eiland, Howard (transl.): *Origin of the German Trauerspiel*. Harvard University Press: Cambridge, Mass. 2019, p. 10.

5 Benjamin, Walter / Livingstone, Rodney (transl.): "Capitalism as Religion". In: *Selected Writings. Volume 1*, pp. 288–291, p. 288. The German text is found in Benjamin, Walter: *Gesammelte Schriften. Volume VI*. ed. by Tiedemann, Rolf / Sheppenhüser, Hermann. Suhrkamp: Frankfurt a.M. 1986, pp. 100–103.

first guarantees the exercise of power by carrying it back to a sacred model; the second deactivates the apparatuses of power and returns to common use the spaces that power had seized."[6] According to this definition, in sacrifice, profane objects can pass into the sphere of the sacred and an object during the rite can also pass over from the sphere of the divine to that of the profane, a transition enacted through contact, practices of use and touch. Profanation retains the idea of separation from the sacred; it "neutralizes what it profanes. Once profaned, that which was unavailable and separate loses its aura and is returned to use." In secularisation, this separation is repressed, since, as Agamben explains, "the political secularization of theological concepts (the transcendence of God as a paradigm of sovereign power) does nothing but displace the heavenly monarchy onto an earthly monarchy, leaving its power intact."[7] Sigrid Weigel, in explicating Benjamin's dialectical approach to secularisation, shows that this dialectic involves two interrelated tendencies. As she points out, not only that "secularization as a descriptive historical category" means the tracing of "the afterlife of religion in modernity", but that secularisation, in Benjamin's deployment of the concept, acts also as "a method", a way of thinking in images ("Denkbilder") through "scenes into which history has passed."[8] Space and time converge in the image; if history passes into the setting, the place of looking and showing (as glossed in Benjamin's frequently used term "Schauplatz"[9]), history is also inexorably fixed in it, impervious to time and death.

---

6 Agamben, Giorgio / Fort. Jeff (transl.): "In Praise of Profanation". In: *Profanations*. Zone Books: New York 2007, pp. 73–92, p. 74.

7 Ibid.

8 Weigel, Sigrid: "Between Creation and Last Judgement, the Creaturely and the Holy: Benjamin and Secularization", *Paragraph* 32(3), 2009, pp. 359–381, p. 374.

9 See for example the section "Setting" ("Schauplatz") in *Origin of the German Trauerspiel*. In the early fragment "World and Time" Benjamin refers to the world as the "der Schauplatz der Geschichte": "In the revelation of the divine, the world – the theater of history – is subjected to a great process of decomposition [Dekompositionsprozeß], while time – the life of him who represents it – is subjected to a great process of fulfilment [Erfüllungsprozeß]". Benjamin, Walter / Livingstone, Rodney (transl.): "World and Time". In: *Selected Writings vol. 1*, p. 226.

Benjamin's aphoristic text on capitalism as religion is borne by an ambiguity that is inscribed in the German word or concept of "Schuld", meaning at the same time "guilt" and "debt", an ambiguity that he denotes "demonic".[10] Insisting on visuality, as if this relation is produced by appearance, Benjamin writes: "siehe die dämonische Zweideutigkeit dieses Begriffs".[11] According to the *Arcades Project* (1928–1940) linguistic "ambiguity" ("Zweideutigkeit") is the "law" constitutive of the dialectical image, and "language" is considered to be "the place", wherein "[dialectical] images" are encountered.[12] In "Capitalism as Religion", the demonic double-meaning of guilt/debt captures the ceaseless (non-)crossing of meaning between these concepts: debt, in the legal sense, is dissociated from its being a reparation for guilt, guilt is accumulated ad infinitum, (financial) debt is extending beyond the passing of time, etc. The entwinement of (moral) guiltiness and (financial) indebtedness embodies the criss-crossing threads of a *textual* net: a dialectical image, which is Benjamin's critique.

This essay will, firstly, gloss the equation – the similarity and hence the difference – of capitalism and religion, by turning to Benjamin's writings on mythic violence. Secondly, the essay will draw on Benjamin's abbreviated fragment in conjunction with the much later formulations of the epistemological functioning of the "dialectical image" developed in the *Arcades Project*. Thirdly, the aforementioned thinking-image of the net will be extracted as a key figure which resonates with another early fragmentary piece on "Perception and Body" ("Wahrnehmung und Leib", 1918/1920–1921). In this fragment, Benjamin reflects on "the history of perception, which is eventually the history of myth", and binds the empirical sensual semblances subjectively engendered by the human body to language in its highest or purest form. Building on these purviews, the

10 The ambiguity of debt/guilt which extends to that of materiality and spectrality, derived as it is from the logic of mythical or pagan sacrifice and their afterlives, was pointed out by Nietzsche: "[the] central moral concept 'guilt' had its origins in the very material term *Schulden* (to be indebted)". See Nietzsche, Friedrich / Golffing, Francis (transl.): *The Birth of Tragedy; and The Genealogy of Morals*. Doubleday: New York 1956, p. 194.

11 "Kapitalismus als Religion", p. 102.

12 The Arcades Project, p. 462.

emergence of the economic subject asks to be explored through its ties to the complications of its being caught up in a perceptual predicament, the guilt system of the mythical order. Viewed through the figure of the prostitute, central to Benjamin's critique of both capitalism and temporality and history, the idea of the economic body, as it will be discussed, although framed by loss and desire, resists its incorporation into the demonic ambiguity of guilt, to which it is incessantly bound.

Benjamin's enigmatic fragment has been the object of numerous interpretations.[13] Though I cannot rework the many readings this fragment has provoked I will mention the few that I find most relevant to the themes that will be advanced here. Daniel Weidner uncovers the poetic dimension of the fragment and ascribes the double reference to modernity and its primal history to the religious turn in philosophy. Raising the question of Benjamin's "actuality", Weidner notes that while "socialism and revolution seem to have disappeared, capitalism and religion remain."[14] Eric L. Santner employs the early fragment to his ongoing exploration of "creaturely life", emphasising Benjamin's identification of the "bare life" caught in the cult of capitalism.[15] The indivisibility of biological and historical forms of life is central to Samuel Weber's "economic-theological perspective", which he derives from Benjamin's fragment, and to his insight into the cycle of credit and debt as underlined by the ideas of death, life and the biblical myth of Creation.[16] Taking up as well the theme of "the debt of the living", Elettra Stimilli uncovers the theological and philosophical implication of debt in contemporary capitalism. She draws on Benjamin's enactment of the subjectivation of "being in debt", the capitalism that turns

13 Two volumes of collected essays are dedicated to Benjamin's fragment. Baecker, Dirk (ed.): *Kapitalismus als Religion*. Kulturverlag Kadmos: Berlin 2003 and Ponzi, Mauro / Scheibenberger, Sarah / Gentili, Dario / Stimilli, Elettra (eds.): *Der Kult des Kapitals. Kapitalismus und Religion bei Walter Benjamin*. Universitätsverlag Winter: Heidelberg 2017.

14 Weidner, Daniel: "Thinking beyond Secularization: Walter Benjamin, the 'Religious Turn,' and the Poetics of Theory". *New German Critique* 37(3), 2010, pp. 131–148.

15 Santner, Eric L.: *The Weight of All Flesh: On the Subject-Matter of Political Economy*. Oxford University Press: Oxford/New York 2015, pp. 118–120.

16 Weber, Samuel: "The Debt of the Living". *Postmodern Culture* 23(3), 2013, no pagination.

existence into a "lack that is constantly reproduced rather than filled."[17] If this lack is to be annihilated, what would be released, according to Werner Hamacher's illuminative intervention in Benjamin's fragment, is something which is other than "guilt history" ("Schuldgeschichte").[18] In this expression, two interdepended tendencies, substantial to Benjamin's thinking, are condensed: "natural history" ("Naturgeschichte") and "salvation history" ("Heilgeschichte"). In shifting the focus to another concept of history, that of nature, transience appears to be the borderline between temporality and timelessness, as well as the site of their (messianic) commensurability.[19] Put in Hamacher's words, the negation of guilt history "comes about not as reform or reformation, but as the true revolution eliminating at every moment the traces of the guilt system. The nothing of this counterhistory is time itself as the time to come."[20]

The aforementioned assertion near the close of the fragment's first paragraph – that "Wir können das Netz in dem wir stehen nicht zuziehen" – is an expression that is framed within Benjamin's fundamental view that our perception is shaped by historically specific regimes. Samuel Weber has drawn attention to Benjamin's unusual use in this sentence of the verb "stehen", rendered in the English translation of the fragment as "caught". As Weber notes, "We cannot draw closed the net, not because we are trapped in it, but because, more precisely, we are standing in it. We take our stand in the net."[21] Weber's move across the idioms of the German and the English brings to mind the English phrase "take a stand" (against something). And yet, according to Benjamin's postulation, we are always

17 Stimilli, Elettra: *The Debt of the Living: Ascesis and Capitalism*. SUNY Press: Albany 2017.

18 Hamacher, Werner / Wetters, Kirk (transl.): "Guilt History: Benjamin's Sketch 'Capitalism as Religion'". *Diacritics* 32(3–4), 2002, pp. 81–106.

19 The exposure of the concepts of nature and history as overlap and accordingly disavow conceptual stability and identification, was accounted for by Adorno. See Adorno, Theodor W.: "Die Idee der Naturgeschichte". In: Tiedemann, Rolf (ed.): *Philosophische Frühschriften. Gesammelte Schriften. Volume I*. Suhrkamp: Frankfurt a.M., 1973, pp. 345–365.

20 Hamacher, Werner: "Guilt History: Benjamin's Sketch 'Capitalism as Religion'". *Diacritics* 32(3–4), 2002, pp. 81–106, p. 102.

21 Weber, Samuel: *Benjamin's –abilities*. Harvard University Press: Cambridge, Mass. 2008, pp. 250–1.

already standing in the net, projected into the historical and cultural phenomenon of *Schein*, the all-pervasive phantasmagoria, the fetishism and the spectrality – of capitalism. The net enwreathes our bodies as we stand in it; it can be overthrown, in Benjamin's terms, by means of dialectical imaging. This technique is formulated in the preparatory notes to the *Arcades Project* as follows: "the dissolution of historical semblance must follow the same trajectory as the construction of the dialectical image."[22]

Capitalism as Mythic Violence

Benjamin considers capitalism to be a negatively intensified religion; as religion, capitalism is always *more* than the religion it is supposedly equated with. Capitalism is, firstly, "a mere cult" ("eine reine Kultreligion"), an empty shell of conducts and laws, "perhaps the most extreme that ever existed."[23] Religion, in Benjamin's formula, functions at the same time as an origin and a result, and as such, it is only a self-effacing origin: "capitalism has developed as a parasite of Christianity in the West [...] until it reached a point where the history of Christianity became essentially that of its parasite – that is to say, of capitalism."[24] Therefore, although capitalism can be said to have emerged out of the protestant ethic, as Max Weber argued in his seminal study of 1905,[25] it does not comply with Weberian rationality and its underlying idea of the de-spiritualisation of the world. The economic submission to religion under capitalism protracts the archaic moods of anxiety and anguish according to which natural life, framed by the myth of salvation and the prospect of the afterlife, is displaced into guilty life. As Hamacher comments, "The 'capitalist religion' is therefore not a religion, but rather a 'cult-religion', a structure of belief and behaviour, of law and economy, pursuing, like every other cult within the context of myth, the sole aim of organizing" – of what Benjamin defines elsewhere as "fate" or "destiny" – "the guilt- and debt-nexus of the living"

22 The Arcades Project, p. 918.
23 "Capitalism as Religion", p. 288.
24 Ibid., p. 289.
25 Weber, Max: Die protestantische Ethik und der Geist des Kapitalismus. Mohr: Tübingen 1934.

("Schicksal ist der Schuldzusammenhang des Lebendigen").[26] Benjamin's consideration suggests a concept of origin which does not signify an unambiguous historical beginning for capitalism but rather addresses religion as capitalism's "fore- and after- history".[27] For religion or myth, marked as origin within the framework of historical progress or rationality, inescapably points to the incompleteness of myth in modernity.[28]

In capitalism, Benjamin writes, "things acquire immediate [unmittelbar] meaning only in their relation to the cult". This is so because "capitalism has no specific body of dogma, no theology".[29] The cult binds its subjects through the preserving acts of practices and rules dissociated from any spiritual faith. And when the cult is "concretised", a temporal deformation inevitably comes about: the cult becomes "permanence", bereft of the notion of time passing: "there are no 'weekdays', no day that is not a feast day [Festtag]".[30] With the allusion to the Jewish day of Sabbath, the command to remember God's day of rest and inoperativity[31] appears to be forsaken. Moreover, the imbrication of repetition and forgetting together with the word "Festtag" bring to mind the primal sacrificial feast, the sublimation of the primal criminal act of patricide that Freud imagines in *Totem and Taboo* (1912). This was the "act with which so many things began, social organization, moral restrictions and religion"[32] as Freud famously writes. The "primal guilt" ("Urschuld"), in Freud's terms,

26 "Guilt History", p. 86, Benjamin, Walter / Jephcott, Edmund (transl.): "Fate and Character". In: *Selected Writings. Volume 1*, pp. 201–206, p. 204.

27 "The origin, then, does not arise from the facts attested but concerns their fore- and after-history." *The Origin of the German Trauerspiel*, p. 24. As Benjamin states in his conceptualisation of origin in the *Trauerspiel* study, any objective or logic of truth cannot be separated from the conception of the historical time in which it is located.

28 As Horkheimer and Adorno will argue in the *Dialektik der Aufklärung* of 1944.

29 "Capitalism as Religion", p. 288.

30 Ibid.

31 For the idea of non-negating inoperativity, inoperative work and the Jewish Sabbath see Agamben, Giorgio, Kishik / David / Pedatella, Stefan (transl.): *Nudities*. Stanford University Press: Stanford, Calif. 2011, pp.104–105.

32 Freud, Sigmund / Strachey, James (transl.): *Totem and Taboo*. In: *The Standard Edition. Complete Psychological Works of Sigmund Freud*. Volume 13. Hogarth Press: London 1996, p. 142.

informs Benjamin's third thesis, proceeding from the second feature, that of the permanent cult: cultic capitalism produces only guilt/debt: "Dieser Kultus ist zum dritten verschuldend".[33] To the extent that "Capitalism is probably the first instance of a cult that creates guilt, not atonement" ("der erste Fall eines nicht entsühnenden sondern verschuldenden Kultus"),[34] this statement precisely adheres to the critical task of recognising the uncanny workings of guilt/debt in the historically new. The presence of "what has been" in the "now", the temporal key for understanding the nineteenth century, according to the *Arcades Project*, is inscribed in this cultic-capitalist deformation of temporality. Benjamin clarifies this peculiarity of time by evoking two templates, the Nietzschean concept of the eternal return and the Freudian insight into the timelessness of the unconscious.

In regard to Freud, Benjamin notes: "The repressed, the idea of sin" (or rather "the sinful representation", "die sündige Vorstellung"[35]) becomes exchangeable in economic terms. Fused with Marx's identification of time as an abstract exchange value detached from the materiality of the commodity, the repressed sin, which Freud considered the origin of social organisation, is what "pays the interest of the hell of the unconscious".[36] What is intrinsic to hellish time is the unrecognizability of death, or indeed – of debt, and of finitude.[37] According to Freud's plot, the primeval history of the totemic family, the oedipal narrative and monotheism – all originated out of a masculine aggressive struggle over women as objects of exchange, a primal, guiltless father who possessed an unlimited access to sexual jouissance and the patricide that followed. "Im Anfang war die Tat", Freud seals his study, for it was the primal murderous act that has introduced the feeling of guilt. Once "Schuldbewußtsein" was installed by the bans on murder and incest, laws founded on a crime that already took place, "Schuld" obtained its ambivalent undertone through the materialisations of debt and the economy of punishment and retribution.

33 "Kapitalismus als Religion", p. 100.
34 "Capitalism as Religion". p. 288.
35 Ibid. p. 289.
36 Ibid.
37 In "The Debt of the Living", Samuel Weber draws on the near-homophony of "debt" and "death" in order to interpret the inseparability of "guilt" and "debt" accounted for in Benjamin's fragment.

In pointing to the "sinful" character of the Freudian theory, Benjamin also draws attention to the transgression inherent to it, namely, the assignment of myth to the theory regarding the return of the repressed and the working of myth in the symbolic order. In the *Arcades Project*, Benjamin observes in relation to the Nietzschean doctrine of "the eternal return of the same" that in myth there is no reflection: "'Eternal return' is the *fundamental* form [*Grund*form, Benjamin's emphasis] of the prehistoric [urgeschichtlichen], mythic consciousness. (Mythic because it does not reflect.)"[38] Kant, in "Religion within the Limits of Reason Alone" (1793), draws together reason ("Ground") and religion into what he calls "reflective faith",[39] indicating, that is, the monotheistic severance of belief from the body of the sign and the fundamental inscription of the inner moral law. What is projected back from the absent reflection intrinsic to mythic consciousness, we might say, is Freud's "sinful representation". This trope exactly conveys how Freud's version of patriarchy as progressive, intellectual and spiritual development is built around a repressed corporeality and around the refusal of death. This repression is similarly affected by the banishment of the maternal and the restriction of the feminine to the domain of the image.[40]

Helga Geyer-Ryan noted that "the gaze, the image, the body of language, and language itself, are central to Benjamin's thinking. This is

38 The Arcades Project, p. 119.

39 Kant, Immanuel / Greene, Theodore M. / Hudson, Hoyt H. (transl.): *Religion within the Limits of Reason Alone*. Open Court: Chicago 1934.

40 On Freud's erasure the age of the mothers that preceded patriarchal society, see Irigaray, Luce / Gill, Gillian C. (transl.): "Body Against Body: In Relation to the Mother". In: *Sexes and Genealogies*. Columbia University Press: New York 1993, pp. 7–21. Benjamin wrote on Johann Jakob Bachofen's discovery of matriarchal societies and *Mutterrecht* (published 1861), showing how Bachofen's work can be appropriated by both Fascism and by the Marxist imagination of classless society. In this review (written in French in 1935), Benjamin points out that "in that immemorial order, death in no way suggests a violent destruction" and cites Bachofen's phrase "die unbeweinte Schöpfung", a vanishing creation that did not entail lament. Benjamin, Walter / Jephcott, Edmund (transl.): "Johann Jakob Bachofen". In: Eiland, Howard / Jennings, Michael W. (eds.): *Selected Writings. Volume 3*. Harvard University Press: Cambridge, Mass. 1996, pp. 11–24.

why the dominance of (pre-oedipal) space over (oedipal) time is emphasized in his work."[41] This reversal is made explicit when Benjamin chooses a story about a mother to exemplify his definition of mythic violence, an exemplary counterimage to that of divine violence. In the "Critique of Violence" of 1921, Benjamin argues that godly or divine violence ("göttliche Gewalt") is the power or force that annihilates mythic, created formations of exerted power.[42] Divine violence does not shed blood according to Benjamin. This bloodlessness is deeply connected to the fact that it is a form of violence that releases from debt and atonement. Divine violence is "entsühnend",[43] and as such – has nothing to do with the order of guilt and debt.

The "mythic manifestation of immediate violence" to which "divine violence" serves as "its antithesis in all respects"[44] is demonstrated by the legend of Niobe. Niobe, the mother of fourteen children, was punished for her arrogance. She bragged that she was more fertile than Leto, the goddess of fertility. The violence or power ("Gewalt") that was exerted on Niobe, a terrifying transformation into stone, bursts from the "uncertain, ambiguous sphere of fate".[45] The guilt that was imposed on her breaks with the linearity of time and of meaning, for there was no pre-existing law that was transgressed by her. This violence that emerges out of fate stops short of being "actually destructive", as Benjamin comments, for it serves to make guilt history lastingly visible. The punishment that "brings a cruel death to Niobe's children", still "stops short of claiming the life of their mother, whom it leaves behind, more guilty than before through the death of the children, both as eternally mute bearer of guilt and as a boundary stone on the frontier between man and gods."[46] As a gendered allegory coupled with abjection, revulsion and death, Niobe is a border that more than anything else unfolds a threshold in which distinct meanings, such as

41 Geyer-Ryan, Helga: "Effects of Abjection in the Texts of Walter Benjamin", *Modern Language Notes* 107(3), 1992, pp. 499–520, pp. 516–517.
42 Benjamin, Walter / Jephcott, Edmund (transl.): "Critique of Violence". In: *Selected Writings. Volume 1*, pp. 236–252 (p. 250).
43 Ibid., p. 249.
44 Ibid.
45 Ibid., p. 248.
46 Ibid., p. 248.

loss and reparation, are thwarted from crossing into their opposite. Hence the demonic ambiguity that surfaces, a dialectic at a standstill.

The tension between incompleteness and seeking fulfilment in historical time lies at the core of Benjamin's study *The Origin of the German Trauerspiel* (published 1928). In that work, Benjamin examines how in the mourning plays of the German Baroque, deathlessness is relentlessly consigned to a standstill. He demonstrates how these plays render secularisation essentially spatial by presenting the sensuous withdrawal of history into the setting, in the form of the ruin. "In the ruin, history has passed perceptibly [sinnlich] into the setting."[47] What is designated as the "secularisation of time"[48] in space is bound up with melancholy, a reaction to the Baroque's "dark belief" in the subjection of man to fate, his "Schick salsverfallenheit".[49] This awareness informs his definition of mythic violence and is echoed in the story of Niobe. Silent and mute (like a ruin), Niobe is nevertheless mournful over her children. As an attestation of both "pure means" and the law's end, the law that ever preserves and never completely punishes and expiates, she evokes the temporality of eternal return. As a cross-reference of history and nature, she is consigned to "mere life" ("bloßes Leben"),[50] but she is also the imperishable figure of the undead. Transcending the human by the bodily deformation into organic/

47 Origin of the German Trauerspiel, p. 188.

48 Ibid., p. 209.

49 Ibid., p. 141. "Baroque fate", Antonia Birnbaum observes, "deals with a history deprived of divine meaning that arises from an infinite course. The task of the Baroque work will thus be that of dramatizing this privation, of arranging its dynamics and coordinates. Of producing its scene and fulfilment – in a word, of presenting a piece of history become nature. The issue is consequently in fact to render fate perceptible, to represent it". Birnbaum, Antonia: "Variations of Fate". In: Moran, Brendan / Salzani, Carlo (eds.): *Towards the Critique of Violence. Walter Benjamin and Giorgio Agamben*. Bloomsbury: London/ New York 2015, pp. 91–108, p. 93.

50 Benjamin introduces the idea of the naked, mere, or nothing but life, in the *Elective Affinities-essay*: "With the disappearance of supernatural life in man, his natural life turns into guilt, even without his committing an act contrary to ethics. For now it is in league with mere life, which manifests itself in man as guilt". Benjamin, Walter / Corngold, Stanley (transl.): "Goethe's Elective Affinities". In: *Selected Writings. Volume 1*. pp. 297–360, (p. 308).

non-organic mass, she prevails as dead and alienated nature within the historical space of meaning. Significantly, her "eternal downfall" or decline is captured in the word "Untergang", in the literal sense of "going down into", as she is merged into the chthonic realm of the earth.[51]

On the Dialectical Image of the Prostitute

In the *Arcades Project*, Benjamin claims that capitalism "was a natural phenomenon [Naturerscheinung] with which a new dream-filled sleep came over Europe", which occasioned a "reactivation of mythic forces".[52] The nineteenth century's new architectural form, the arcade, housed this dream logic of "latent mythology", enacting its uncanny return. Benjamin saw in the arcades a testimony to the difficulty of the dialectical technique, "the effort to awaken from a dream."[53] In the formulation of the dialectical image, the image is regarded as a site of encounter: "image is that wherein what has been [das Gewesene] comes together in a flash with the now to form a constellation", for "the relation of what-has-been to the now is dialectical: not temporal in nature but figural [bildlich[ ]]."[54] Benjamin designates the "now of recognizability", the epistemological framework of the dialectical image, cognate to "the death of the intention",[55] for what the image consists of is a moment of arrest through which the unworking of time and history in it is substantiated. This temporality is non-diachronic, and as such – not indebted.[56] And yet, this temporality

---

51 For the coinage "the eternity of downfall" ("die Ewigkeit eines Unterganges") see for example "The Theological-Political Fragment" of 1921. The link between messianism and "eternal passing away" appears also in the fragment "Phantasie" of 1921. There, the temporality of "eternal transience" converges on natural historical plane and is evoked by the imagination of ruins, "the world caught in the process of unending dissolution". See Benjamin, Walter, Livingstone, Rodney (trans): "Imagination". In: *Selected Writings. Volume 1.* pp. 280–283, (p. 281).

52 The Arcades Project, p. 391.

53 Ibid., p. 834.

54 Ibid., p. 463.

55 Ibid., p. 462.

56 The idea that the past does not give rise to the future is central to the "Theses on the Concept of History": "Like every generation that preceded us, we have been endowed with a weak Messianic power, a power to which the past has

can only emerge out of myth itself. In an early note (written around 1918/1919) it is commented that "the time of fate" ("die Zeit des Schicksals") signifies the time that "stands under the order of guilt".[57] Negating any temporal discrepancy between past, present and future, guilt decides on the "connection" ("Zusammenhang") that is nevertheless at work in this time. Since this time cannot be present as such, for it is "unselbständig",[58] it is always in a state of debt to the historical world.

The time of fate and the order of guilt enter into the space of the arcade, the historical site of their manifestation. "Ambiguity is the appearance of dialectic in images" ("Zweideutigkeit ist die bildliehe Erscheinung der Dialektik") and "such an image is presented by the arcades, which are a house no less than street. Such an image is the prostitute – seller [Verkäuferin] and sold [Ware] in one."[59] Weigel notes that "it is through his work on the figure of the whore that Benjamin achieved the materialist reversal in his thinking-in-images".[60] Not only is the arcade the social space characterised by the economic powers of the market; it is also a

---

a claim. That claim cannot be settled cheaply." Benjamin, Walter / Zohn, Harry (transl.): "Theses on the Concept of History". In: Eiland, Howard / Jennings, Michael W. (eds.): *Selected Writings Volume 4*. Harvard University Press: Cambridge, Mass. 2003. pp. 389–400, (p. 390).

57 "Zum Problem der Physiognomik und Vorhersagung". In: *Gesammelte Schriften. Volume VI*. Suhrkamp: Frankfurt a.M. 1986, p. 91.

58 Ibid.

59 The Arcades Project. p. 10.

60 Weigel, Sigrid: *Body- and Image- Space. Re-Reading Walter Benjamin*. Routledge: London, New York 1996, p. 87. The interpenetration of gender, aesthetics and the critique of modernity, as well as the position of female sexuality in Benjamin's oeuvre have been widely addressed. To name but a few of these studies, see Rauch, Angelika: "The Trauerspiel of the Prostituted Body, or Woman as Allegory of Modernity". *Cultural Critique* 10, 1988, pp. 77–88, and Geulen, Eva: "Toward a Genealogy of Gender in Walter Benjamin's Writing". *The German Quarterly* 69(2), 1996, pp. 161–180. And although the female flaneur, as a token of female subjectivity, remains invisible in his writings and the objectifications of the female that suffuse them are always attached to an intellectual and cognitive formations of the (male) genius, Benjamin's work is held by several critics to bear on feminist theory by dint of its particular focus on the pre-semiotic enactments of language. Weigel, for example, brings Benjamin's writing into a constellation with Julia Kristeva ("Towards a female dialectic of enlightenment: Julia Kristeva and Walter Benjamin". In: *Body- and*

space organised around the house, the space concerning gender, procreation and sexual difference. Previously a street, the arcades originally serve commercial ends; they were places of habitation for the eternal life of the commodity qua exchange-value. Analogously, the prostitute is a body signifying the exchange-value of the object, an illusion of eternal life. As commodity, she is the reduction of corporeity to an object of use whose use-value is destined to perish.

And yet the prostitute does not function solely as an allegory of modernity, the exemplification of subjects becoming objects under exploiting capitalism. The worker too is forced to sell the commodity of his labour power – and thereby the use of his own body – and the use of that body will also destroy its use value over time, as Marx notes in the analysis of labour in late nineteenth century industrial production.[61] However, as a commodity on the sexual market, the prostitute is the antithesis of sexual reproduction. The prostitute, Benjamin writes, "drives nature from its last sanctuary, sexuality",[62] meaning she expels nature into history, as yet another erasure of the mother. With this, however, the indebtedness of having a body is released, but this awareness, as it were, immediately coalesces – mediated through the figure of the prostitute – into the capitalist form of guilt/debt through the money that is paid to the prostitute. Elsewhere, in relation to Baudelaire, Benjamin notes that "life which signifies death" is what the prostitute stands for but can never sell, what was for Baudelaire "the only thing that matters."[63] In as much as she stands for "life which signifies death" that is not for sale, the prostitute liberates herself from the economic order, and yet her natural historical life is rendered

---

Image- Space, pp. 58–73), as does Geyer-Ryan in "Effects of Abjection in the Texts of Walter Benjamin".

61 See Marx, Karl: *Das Kapital I. Der Produktionsprozess des Kapitals*. Dietz: Berlin 1962, pp. 441–448.

62 Letter to Herbert Belmore, 23 June 1913. *The Correspondence of Walter Benjamin*, p. 35.

63 Benjamin, Walter, Jephcott, Edmund / Eiland Howard (transl.): "Central Park". In: *Selected Writing. Volume 4*, p. 170. As Geyer-Ryan observes, "in his allegorical perception of the allegory, Benjamin associates the body of the sign with the feminine, the meaning of the sign (the allegorical intention, the 'allegory' *tout court*) with the masculine." "Effects of Abjection", p. 114.

incomplete, turning into an image of desire. Benjamin alludes to this nexus of money and life when he writes in the *Arcades Project*: "On the dialectical function of money in prostitution. It buys pleasure, and, at the same time, becomes the expression of shame."[64] In "Capitalism and Religion" he reflects on "the dogma of the dissolving nature of knowledge" and on its link to capitalism by evoking an image: "the balance sheet as a knowledge that both redeems and eliminates". This dissolving nature of knowledge is "redemptive and murderous [erlösend[] und tötend[]]".[65] It is a kind of violence that does not destruct, for it does not leave a remainder; a counterpoise, that is, to mythic violence.

The allegorisation of the figure of the prostitute discloses a twofold obstruction, the (non-) working of passage, the refusal of time, and therefore of meaning – in the image. From the early "Metaphysics of Youth" (1913) to the last "Theses on the Concept of History" (1940), the prostitute lurks in Benjamin's texts. In the section "The Conversation" that appears in that early text, the prostitute is said to thwart understanding by protecting meaning ("Sinn"). She perennially awaits in the "dead field to which he [the male speaker] is straying", consenting, that is, to corporeal existence which is not framed in time, history or language. In the "Theses on the Concept of History" this idea is condensed in the phrasing "der Hure 'Es war einmal' " which also places the prostitute in the direction of myth. The prostitute clarifies the "pictorial nature" of the dialectical image, meaning that the image desires the inanimate while being a phantasmagorical preserver of life. This economy of the image between Eros and death, history and nature, is that which renders the dialectical image as "genuinely historical – that is, not archaic."[66] The image is properly historical since what is recognised in it is "natural history", Benjamin's trope in which the inextricability of nature from history is acknowledged.

---

64 The Arcades Project, p. 492.
65 "Capitalism as Religion", p. 290.
66 The Arcades Project, p. 463.

Perception and Body

Together with Freud and Marx, Nietzsche, according to "Capitalism as Religion", is one of the hegemonic "priests of this cult". The *Übermensch* is the "historical man", "the first to recognise the religion of capitalism and begin to bring it to fulfilment."[67] With the motif of "Umkehr", Benjamin characterises Nietzsche's *Übermensch* as "the man who has arrived where he is without changing his ways." This Nietzschean figure displaces

> the apocalyptic "leap" [*Sprung*, also demanding to be read as "crack"], not into conversion, atonement, purification, and penance [Umkehr, Sühne, Reinigung, Buße], but into apparently steady, though in the final analysis, explosive and discontinuous intensification [sondern in die scheinbar stetige, in der letzten Spanne aber sprengende, diskontinuierliche Steigerung].[68]

"Umkehr", according to this account, is denied from its effective character of change, whereas the leap forward or *Sprung* alludes at the same time to the before and after of an explosive burst. The leap beyond the historical moment is an indication in the direction of this dialectics of "Erfüllung", in drawing God into "human fate" ("Menschenschicksal").[69] And since capitalism is never a religion, only a resemblance of it, it does not involve the "reform of being" ("Reform des Seins"), only its "destruction" ("Zertrümmerung").[70] This disintegration, in which a decimation of matter is intimated, eradicates the view of the divine as an inaccessible abstraction and turns the human gaze to the earthly space of time. If the

67 "Capitalism as Religion", p. 289.

68 Benjamin, as several scholars have suggested, might be drawing here on Hermann Cohen's chapter on "Atonement" in his *Religion of Reason. Out of the Source of Judaism*. In his interpretation of Ezekiel, Cohen stressed the broken link between sin and punishment; instead sin and punishment, what is at stake is sin and turning away from it. In the sinner's turning away, God has no pleasure in its death, but rather in his life. "*Guilt cannot be offence* [...] from every guilt there is a turning away". Cohen, Hermann / Kaplan, Simon (transl.): *Religion of Reason out of the Sources of Judaism*. Fredrick Ungar: New York 1972, p. 193. The term "Umkehr" brings to mind the Jewish concept of penance, the Hebrew *tshuva*, a word whose root means both "return" or "coming back" and "repetition".

69 "Capitalism as Religion", p. 289, translation modified.

70 Ibid.

latter, as indicated, is related to the pre-symbolic, this destruction has to do with the mortification of the subject. Benjamin's critique, we might say, proceeds by exposing that modern, capitalist manifestations of fate, captured as they are in the net of guilt, are interspersed with a conception of fate that can be defined as natural historical ruin.[71]

The net of guilt, as stated, can be "looked over" ("überblickt"). The opening setting through which we enter into Benjamin's dialectical imagining of capitalism as religion, the body standing in the net, the body for whom only "later on" an overview of it can be made possible – this scenography reverberates in the fourth feature of the comparison in question. The God of the capitalist religion, says Benjamin, must be kept hidden and may be addressed "at the zenith" of his "indebtedness" ("Verschuldung").[72] The word "zenith" is telling. It is used, it seems, not only metaphorically in the sense of the highest, most powerful, or crowning point, but also with respect to its meaning as an astronomical term, whereby it denotes the point in the sky vertically above a given position or observer. This point is determined by a vector extending from her feet, not her gaze. With this scenography in mind, Benjamin's account for the capitalist all-embracing "destruction of being" could be said to be guided by a distinction, made in the fragment "Perception and Body" (1918/9), between "Schein" and "Sein", as well as by a distinction between two forms of human corporeality. Of significance to the interwoven net of guilt and debt enwreathing "Capitalism as Religion" is the crossing of meanings between "Leib" and "Körper" (and also between "Geist" and "Sexualität", "Natur" and "Körper"), set out in Benjamin's text "Outlines of the Psychophysical Problem" (1921). On the one hand, there is the historical experienced body, the subjective "Leib" bound to the perceptual faculties, and, on the other, this body's corporeal essence. According to these anthropological or psychophysical reflections, the physical, habitual body, the body which is given in its having is – from the standpoint of the body designated as "Leib" – unimaginable, devoid of semblance.[73] Put in the vocabulary

---

71 For an interpretation of "fate of ruin" see Birnbaum: "Variations of Fate".

72 "Capitalism as Religion". p. 287.

73 Benjamin, Walter / Livingstone, Rodney (transl.): "Outline of the Psychophysical Problem". In: *Selected Writings. Volume 1*, pp. 393–401, (p. 394). With this

of "Body and Perception" – on which the last move of this essay will draw – this discrepancy between corporeality and image is determined by the measure of the messianic figuration: "Schein von Sein nach Maßen der messianischen Gestalt zu scheiden".[74]

The fragment opens by binding the empirical sensual semblances engendered by the human body to language in its highest or purest form: "We are ultimately placed into the world of perception, into one of the highest realms of language, by our bodiliness [Leiblichkeit], our own body."[75] This scenography is informed by the theological idea regarding the fall of language into history. Just as the experience of intransmissibility and incommunicability is recorded in the dialectical image and in the thinking image that is classically constructed around it, here too, Benjamin alludes to the negation of the semiotic functioning of language and to the prevalence of signs over names. With the Fall from the a-temporal site of Creation, as Benjamin interprets the biblical myth, historical time emerges.[76] According to the scenography of body and language, the "natural body" ("Naturleib") is laid bare – being there, it "extends up" ("ragen"); and this occurs in the "most immediate [am unmittelbarsten] fashion". What is significant, in Benjamin's account, is that our body is inaccessible to us in so many ways: "We cannot see our face nor our back, projected into the world with our feet, not our head." Hence the inevitability, Benjamin concludes, that marks "the present moment of pure perception" ("im Augenblick der reinen Wahrnehmung") in which "our body is transformed into us"; thence the "sublime suffering of the eccentric in relation to his body."[77]

---

description, the story of the creation of the human body in the image of God is recalled.

74 Benjamin, Walter: "Wahrnehmung und Leib". In: *Gesammelte Schriften. Volume VI*, p. 67.

75 "Wahrnehmung und Leib", p. 67, my translation.

76 "History becomes equal to signification in human language". Benjamin, Walter / Livingstone, Rodney (transl.): "The Role of Language in *Trauerspiel* and Tragedy". In: *Selected Writings. Volume 1*, pp. 59–61, (p. 60).

77 "Wahrnehmung und Leib", p. 67, my translation. Geyer-Ryan, in clarifying the link between revulsion and the sublime, comments: "The pleasure and fear (Angstlust) of revulsion, the memory of the space of pre-oedipal emptiness in the imaginary, resurfaces in the post-oedipal, symbolic space as the aesthetic experience of the sublime." "Effects of Abjection", p. 502.

Body and language, at their projected origins, share a lack of mediation; the nakedness of being, the (un)embodied "Körper", is analogous to the highest realm of language, its "fore-history".

In the second part of this fragment, Benjamin refers to "the history of perception which is at the end the history of myth",[78] that is, the history of mythically conditioned humanity, subordinated to the ambiguous power of symbolic, fallen language. He describes primordial modes of perception which are not optical in nature: "already man's upright walk, achieved only gradually, allows for earlier different modes of perception".[79] The history of perception "comes into being from the factors of change in nature [Naturveränderung] and change of the body [Veränderung des Leibes];" yet these changes received their "spiritual meaning and their crowning (their mastery, synthesis [Bewältigung, Synthese]) in myth." The mythic essence of perception, the manner in which body and nature "stand" ("stehen") in relation to one another is rendered by its culmination in a "crowning" in the form of a spatial net: "rechts, links – oben, unten – vorn, hinten".[80] "Krönung" here seems to evoke a twofold coronation, two forms of mythic rendition of the body in which the traits of "Leib" and "Körper" become distinct. The intimation of the embodied body, the subjugation of the body to the perceptual mind, immediately coalesces into the category of sovereignty that foreshadows the reduction of the body to its status as a bare object in space.[81] However, to recognise this synthesis as the source of subjection, related to the ideologies of the secular capitalist state and its legal violence, demands to concede to the sheer withdrawal of the body, without a trace, from the "order of the profane" of which Benjamin speaks of in "Theological-Political Fragment" of 1921. As it is stated there, to the extent that the profane is to be "erected" ("hat sich aufzurichten") on the "idea of happiness" ("Glück"), it is in

---

78 "Wahrnehmung und Leib", p. 67, my translation.

79 Ibid.

80 Ibid.

81 For a reading of "Capitalism as Religion" as a "dispositif of guilt-debt" See Ponzi, Mauro: *Nietzsche's Nihilism in Walter Benjamin*. Palgrave Macmillan: Switzerland 2017, pp. 1–20.

"happiness" that the living body finds its "downfall", its "Untergang"[82] or "going down into", the exact spatial polarity to the more upright establishment of the profane. It is life that signifies death, yet this economic body cannot be said to be caught, nor to be enwreathed by the net.

The three sections of this essay, in drawing different threads of Benjamin's thought, have aimed to show the significance of bodiliness, perception and sexuality to Benjamin's counterimage to secularisation and political theology. Once this connection has been laid out, excoriated layers of pre-historical and pre-symbolic forms of life can make visible the crossing over of natural creaturely existence into the historical sphere from which it was originally barred. And once the moment antecedent to the emergence of the law is recognised from the standpoint of the present, the critique of history prefigures the release, and hence the redemption, from the assumption that historical time adheres to completion and hence to progress. In this analysis, the demarcation line between the human and the nonhuman, between the earthly profane and the theologically sacred, is the limit that powerfully intervenes between those domains, but also, that which brings them most closely into accord.[83]

References

Adorno, Theodor W.: "Die Idee der Naturgeschichte". In: *Philosophische Frühschriften. Gesammelte Schriften. Volume I.* pp. 345–365.

Agamben. Giorgio: *Profanations.* Zone Books: New York 2007.

Agamben, Giorgio, Kishik / David / Pedatella, Stefan (transl.): *Nudities.* Stanford University Press: Stanford, Calif. 2011

---

82 Benjamin, Walter, Jephcott, Edmund (transl.): "Theological-Political Fragment". In: *Selected Writings Volume 3*, pp. 305–306, (p. 306).

83 As I revised this paper while the global Covid-19 crisis escalates, a constellation of messianic completion of historical time and the economic body suddenly became charged with an uncanny actuality. Benjamin's terminology of the destruction of the accumulation of capitalist debt resonates prophetic as our biological and symbolic forms of life are exposed as being more dissolvable than ever and as our ways of having/being a body are assailed by possible implications of having and being.

Baecker, Dirk (ed.): *Kapitalismus als Religion*. Kulturverlag Kadmos: Berlin 2003.

Benjamin, Walter: *Gesammelte Schriften, Volume IV*. Suhrkamp: Frankfurt a.M. 1986.

———: *The Correspondence of Walter Benjamin 1910–1940*. University of Chicago Press: Chicago 1994.

———: *Selected Writings*. Volumes 1–4. Harvard University Press: Cambridge, Mass. 1996.

———: *The Arcades Project*. Harvard University Press: Cambridge, Mass. 1999.

———: *Origin of the German Trauerspiel*. Harvard University Press: Cambridge, Mass. 2019.

Birnbaum, Antonia: "Variations of Fate". In: Moran, Brendan / Salzani, Carlo (eds.): *Towards the Critique of Violence. Walter Benjamin and Giorgio Agamben*. Bloomsbury: London/New York 2015, pp. 91–108.

Cohen, Hermann: *Religion of Reason out of the Sources of Judaism*. Fredrick Ungar Publishing: New York 1972.

Freud, Sigmund / Strachey, James (transl.): *Totem and Taboo*. In: *The Standard Edition. Complete Psychological Works of Sigmund Freud*. Volume 13. Hogarth Press: London 1996. .

Geulen, Eva: "Toward a Genealogy of Gender in Walter Benjamin's Writing". *The German Quarterly* 69(2), 1996, pp. 161–180.

Geyer-Ryan, Helga: "Effects of Abjection in the Texts of Walter Benjamin", *Modern Language Notes* 107(3), 1992, pp. 499–520.

Hamacher, Werner: "Guilt History: Benjamin's Sketch 'Capitalism as Religion' ". *Diacritics* 32(3–4), 2002, pp. 81–106.

Irigaray, Luce: "Body Against Body: In Relation to the Mother". In: *Sexes and Genealogies*. Columbia University Press: New York 1993.

Kant, Immanuel: *Religion within the Limits of Reason Alone*. Open Court: Chicago 1934.

Marx, Karl: *Das Kapital I. Der Produktionsprozess des Kapitals*. Dietz: Berlin 1962.

Nietzsche, Friedrich: *The Birth of Tragedy; and The Genealogy of Morals*. Doubleday: New York 1956.

Ponzi, Mauro: *Nietzsche's Nihilism in Walter Benjamin*. Palgrave Macmillan: Switzerland 2017.

Ponzi, Mauro / Scheibenberger, Sarah / Gentili, Dario / Stimilli, Elettra (eds.): *Der Kult des Kapitals. Kapitalismus und Religion bei Walter Benjamin*. Universitätsverlag Winter: Heidelberg 2017.

Rauch, Angelika: "The Trauerspiel of the Prostituted Body, or Woman as Allegory of Modernity". *Cultural Critique* 10, 1988, pp. 77–88.

Santner, Eric L.: *The Weight of All Flesh: On the Subject-Matter of Political Economy*. Oxford University Press: Oxford/New York 2015.

Stimilli, Elettra: *The Debt of the Living: Ascesis and Capitalism*. SUNY Press: Albany 2017

Weber, Max: *Die protestantische Ethik und der Geist des Kapitalismus*. Mohr: Tübingen 1934.

Weber, Samuel: *Benjamin's –abilities*. Harvard University Press: Cambridge, Mass. 2008

———: "The Debt of the Living". *Postmodern Culture* 23(3), 2013.

Weidner, Daniel: "Thinking beyond Secularization: Walter Benjamin, the 'Religious Turn,' and the Poetics of Theory". *New German Critique* 37(3), 2010, pp. 131–148.

Weigel, Sigrid: Weigel: *Body- and Image- Space. Re-Reading Walter Benjamin*. Routledge: London, New York 1996.

———: "Between Creation and Last Judgement, the Creaturely and the Holy: Benjamin and Secularization". *Paragraph* 32(3), 2009.

Simon Godart

The Poet as Speculator: Reading Baudelaire's Economic Subjects with Benjamin

Abstract: *This essay tries to recapitulate how Benjamin's reading of Charles Baudelaire has changed according to his attempt to 'make the economic order' of 19th century France visible – and how his approach of 'motives' and constellations can be put to use in new readings as well. After his first essay on the poet that tried to connect moments of his writing with the social and economic reality in a very direct manner, his exchange with Adorno lead to a remodelling of the methodology for the second text. Here, Benjamin is more interested in the expression of experiences than facts and provides ways to reconstruct the influence the 'age of high capitalism' has had on the subjects literature introduces. In creating moments of choc, Modern literature such as Baudelaire's does not reproduce or imitate topics relevant to the historical context but constructs eruptions and ruptures within the ways time and history themselves are experienced. Transferring these methodological approaches to the prose poems of Baudelaire, I conclude with a reading of "La fausse monnaie" in order to show how the moment of (financial) speculation is mediated in the short narrated scene of Baudelaire's text not only as representation of his everyday experience, but, moreover, as a poetological self-commentary that contributes to what Benjamin called the "authorial plan" of the Modern poet.*

Keywords: Benjamin, Baudelaire, Derrida, Modernity, Speculation, Temporality, poem in prose, Shock, experience

Benjamin reading Baudelaire (twice)

Long before Walter Benjamin dubbed him "the poet in the age of high capitalism," subjectivity and economy were intertwined in the poetry of Charles Baudelaire. The characters he preserves in his short constellations of words and thought were, of course, not only informed by urban life and their industrial surroundings, but were rather *subjected* to them. One can count on the fact that this information is expressed in the oeuvre of Baudelaire, inasmuch as the historical summit of the development of modern capitalism might provide insights into its character and its formative force in society.[1] This is precisely what Walter Benjamin wanted to show in his reading of Baudelaire, a reading that extends beyond pure philology to also include social and historical analysis. Benjamin asks how the experience of the 19th century and, accordingly, the constitution of modern capitalist society in Paris found their way into Baudelaire's writing. In other words, Benjamin read Baudelaire's poetry with an eye to how it can be understood as the literary manifestation of its historical surroundings. He tried, through his criticism, to make both the economic order and the position of the modern subject within it visible. This study was also the groundwork for his monumental *Arcades Project*. Benjamin produced two different essays on Baudelaire that served as foundations for the later project, and each of these essays had a distinct character. The second of these essays, "On Some Motifs in Baudelaire" (1939), constituted a corrective to the first, more ambitious attempt, "Charles Baudelaire: A Poet in the Age of High Capitalism" (1938).[2] Benjamin's methodological self-correction,

1 This is the definition of the epoque of Baudelaire as the title of Benjamin's first essay on him has it. Benjamin addresses this historical summit of high capitalism with regard to Paris as the "capital of the 19th century"; these two moments are already the groundwork for the Arcades-Project. One can only hint at the method of said project here; for more on intrinsic relationship between Baudelaire and the Arcades Project, especially regarding the second outline of the project produced in 1939, the year the Baudelaire-essay was published, see Irving Wohlfarth: "Die Passagenarbeit". In: Lindner, Burkhardt et al. (eds): *Benjamin-Handbuch. Leben — Werk — Wirkung*. Metzler: Stuttgart 2011, pp. 251–274. Following Benjamin explicitly, Berman's history of capitalism also uses both Paris and Baudelaire as paradigms of modern experience. Cf. Berman, Marshall: *All that is Solid Melts into Air. The Experience of Modernity*. Verso: London, 1997. I would like to thank Ben Brewer for helping me with the translation of this text into English; his crucial corrections have not only helped me to adapt the German version of it, but his insightful comments have also shaped my argument. Furthermore, I am very grateful for the help of Johanna Pistorius and Tobias Klein who were assisting me in finding the adequate quotations in the English translations of Benjamin, Baudelaire and Derrida.

2 "Über einige Motive bei Baudelaire" appeared in the *Zeitschrift für Sozialforschung* in 1940. The first version of 1938, "Charles Baudelaire. Ein Lyriker im Zeitalter des Hochkapitalismus", was not published due to criticisms raised by Adorno and Horkheimer. On the genesis and edition of the texts, cf.

in which he moved away from the rather schematic reconstruction of the historical and social reality of nineteenth-century Paris and its unmediated reflection in Baudelaire's poetry, is instructive for contemporary reflections on how to understand and study literature regarding their relationship to their social and economic contexts. Moreover, the differences between the two versions allow us to understand how Baudelaire finally became Benjamin's paradigmatic name for the 19th century. Benjamin's reading of Baudelaire in this latter essay provides indispensable guidelines for probing how literary criticism can use literary texts to make the economic order visible, a task that I endeavour to demonstrate through a reading of Baudelaire's prose poem "La fausse monnaie" in the latter part of this chapter.

In his first essay, Benjamin treats Baudelaire more like character or protagonist than a poet or writer, and the questions that he discusses are accordingly sociological in nature, with the discussion or interpretation of Baudelaire's texts as literary texts playing a far less central role. Presenting something like a socio-historical panorama, the essay provides a detailed survey of Parisian society, with a particular focus on its poorer members, yet includes only a few quotations from the *Fleurs du Mal* and some of Baudelaire's theoretical prose alongside some biographical information about the poet. Baudelaire, Benjamin claims, is writing in (and about) Paris, a city experiencing the upheavals of industrialization in the aftermath of the failed second revolution of 1848. Benjamin situates Baudelaire within this very general setting, alongside numerous other witnesses from the period whom he quotes in his essay. His account is supposed to follow three steps (that were not completed); starting from an introductory study of a particular milieu of the *Bohème*, the second part entitled *The Flâneur* is supposed to show the writer – Baudelaire – in "antithesis." Finally, the third part, *Modern Times*, was intended to mediate between these two. Benjamin aimed to show precisely how the social and economic features of everyday life can be traced in Baudelaire's writing, which is to say, how *bohème* and *flaneur* correspond. Thus, the philological interest is surpassed by the sociological – Benjamin understands poetry as an expression of

Schmider, Christine / Werner, Michael: "Das Baudelaire-Buch". In: *Benjamin-Handbuch*. Metzler: Stuttgart 2011, pp. 567–584, esp. pp. 567–570.

social relations, taking poetry to be a record of its epoch rather than as object of interest for a deeper reflection on itself. This tendency is inspired by his reading of Marx at the time, with the "18th Brumaire" in particular serving as a point of an orientation, which Benjamin treated as a definitive example of the appropriate method for a Marxist examination of the literature of the 19th century.[3] This was a method that painted in rather broad strokes; poetic texts, as part of the superstructure, are taken to be direct results of the social base that Benjamin tries to extract from the passages on the lived reality of the *bohème* in Paris. Neither here nor in his second essay does Benjamin propose to simply deduct poetry from social life in this direct fashion; moreover, one could argue that – with the development of his works on the *Arcades-Project* – it is precisely the relationship between base and superstructure that Benjamin is trying to question through Baudelaire. Benjamin is interested in how Baudelaire could be reconstructed as the hero or the typical historical figure of modernity, and how this model is to be understood in terms of the world that surrounds it. He looks more for a "Ausdruckszusammenhang", a relation of expression, rather than deduction.[4] In this sense, Benjamin treats Baudelaire

3 Benjamin quotes Karl Marx, *Der achtzehnte Brumaire des Louis Bonaparte*. Wien / Berlin 1927. See Marx, Karl / Engels, Friedrich: "Der achtzehnte Brumaire des Louis Bonaparte". In: *Werke*, Bd. 8, Dietz: Berlin 1960, pp. 111–207. He also uses *Das Kapital* and other texts.

4 This discussion on methods goes on in the centre of the *Arcades*. For example, a programmatic stance from convolute N can be understood as the motto of all of Benjamin's work during this time: Benjamin, GS V 1, p. 573 (N 1a 6): "Marx stellt den Kausalzusammenhang zwischen Wirtschaft und Kultur dar. Hier kommt es auf den Ausdruckszusammenhang an. Nicht die wirtschaftliche Entstehung der Kultur sondern der Ausdruck der Wirtschaft in ihrer Kultur ist darzustellen. Es handelt sich, mit anderen Worten, um den Versuch, einen wirtschaftlichen Prozeß als anschauliches Urphänomen zu erfassen, aus welchem alle Lebenserscheinungen der Passagen (und insoweit des 19ten Jahrhunderts) hervorgehen." (Cf. Benjamin, Walter, transl. Eiland, Howard: *The Arcades Project*. Belknap Press of Harvard Univ. Press: Cambridge, Mass. / London 2002, p. 460: "Marx lays bare the causal connection between economy and culture. For us, what matters is the thread of expression. It is not the economic origins of culture that will be presented, but the expression of the economy in its culture. At issue, in other words, is the attempt to grasp an economic process as perceptible Urphenomenon, from out of which proceed all manifestations of life in the arcades [and, accordingly, in the nineteenth century].") Cf.

primarily as a witness to the radical change in society and economics, and his works, quoted just in passing, are treated as circumstantial evidence about the topics and motives they comprise.

For the first essay, however, these relations remain vague, and Benjamin seems to simply assume a correspondence between production in the superstructure with the facts and impressions that Benjamin notes in relation to the base, rather than retracing such lines of correspondence. In line with the text's planned threefold structure, the isolated areas of analysis remain heuristically separated, and the intended synthesis becomes less and less realisable. It seems almost comical when Benjamin tries to bridge the gap between the very thin material taken from the *Fleurs du Mal* and his sociological findings. Time and time again, Benjamin uses formulations that try to establish such relations, but which can barely hide their highly speculative character. His method expresses a "will to *constellation*", which he will execute to great effect in the *Arcades Project* years later, but which is, in this earlier text, only a construction: his extensive quotation of le Play's surveys of 1855, for instance, is meant to provide a differentiated reconstruction of the average budget of the 'ragman' in order to interpret Baudelaire's "Vin des chiffonièrs".[5] This interpretation leaves it at that; all that the essay explains is that the poem "deals, first of all, with the wine tax"[6] whose history and significance he paraphrases directly from Marx's "Die Klassenkämpfe in Frankreich". He then – after the two quartets taken from Baudelaire inserted in isolation – describes that ragman as a figure of general interest for their time; the reading of the poem does little more than point out those vectors and exhibit their presence in Baudelaire, without trying to explain them. The attempt here, however, is not to establish a simple parallel. Benjamin combines diverging sources, Baudelaire and le Play (and others) in order to verify that there has been a widespread fascination with this figure; undoubtedly, he contrasts Baudelaire as voice of the *bohème* and the statistical

Friedlander, Eli: *Walter Benjamin. A Philosophical Portrait.* Harvard University Press: Cambridge, Mass 2012, pp. 179–180.

5 Benjamin, GS I 2, p. 520–523. ("Der Wille zur Konstellation"). He uses Le Play, Fréderic: *Les ouvriers européens*. L'imprimerie impériale: Paris 1855.

6 Benjamin, GS I 2, p. 529.

sociological knowledge of the governmental study by le Play, which, as he writes, aims at the appeasement of "dangerous classes" whose "deep misery appears less appalling when it is neatly rubricated".[7] Benjamin's critical use of this source and its visible tendencies does not affect the representation of Baudelaire, which remains at the level of quotation. In concert with the other voices, Baudelaire's writing is reduced to the status of a mere expression of the *zeitgeist*. This is a representative example of how in "Charles Baudelaire", both author and text are given the status of historical witnesses or documents, and Benjamin treats Baudelaire as a social type, not a literary figure. The surplus of what Benjamin considers to be the expression of the base hinders him from reconstructing the relationship he calls "expression" ("Ausdruckszusammenhang")[8] – he loses sight of the difference between social reality, its attesting documents, and the mode of interplay between these findings and literary texts. When he adopts this method of constellation in the *Arcades-Project* later on, he organises these groups by motifs, rather than by people; in this earlier stage, Benjamin suffers as a result of his choice to take Baudelaire as figurehead of his analysis, making it impossible to "have nothing to say, but only to show".[9] This becomes most obvious in his suggestive attempt to establish that the other sources and description he uses must have had a direct influence on Baudelaire as well. Expressions like "Was Baudelaire aware of this speculation? It is quite possible",[10] remain exactly that: speculations trying to cover up the noticeable lack of connection between his materials, without really aiming for either a philological or philosophical synthesis.

---

7 Benjamin ibid. ("[…] Einfriedung ‚gefährlicher Klassen', deren 'tiefes Elend dadurch weniger anstößig [erscheinen solle], daß es säuberlich rubriziert ist' ".)

8 See fn. 4.

9 Benjamin, GS V, p. 1030. ("Ich habe nichts zu sagen. Nur zu zeigen.")

10 Benjamin, GS I 2, p. 532. ("Hat Baudelaire diese Spekulation gekannt? Es ist leicht möglich.") Benjamin discusses Cassagnac's idea of the proletariat as "race" of its own to illustrate Baudelaire's *Abel et Caïn* – and adds "It is certain that Marx, for whom Ganier de Cassagnac was *the* thinker of the reaction of Bonapartism, has seen these ideas." "Gewiß ist, daß sie Marx, der in Granier de Cassagnac ‚den Denker' der bonapartistischen Reaktion grüßte, begegnet waren." Cf. Marx, "Der 18. Brumaire", p. 207.

These methodological shortcomings provoked prominent and effective criticism that eventually led to the withdrawal of the first Baudelaire essay from the *Zeitschrift für Sozialforschung*.[11] In his correspondence with Benjamin, Adorno leaves no doubt that Benjamin, in his attempt to analyse the relation between the quoted socioeconomic facts and Charles Baudelaire's writing, had not done justice to either. Benjamin's overly direct way of adapting Marxist terminology and methods for his analysis of literature and literary history, Adorno argued, was theoretically unsatisfying. In accordance with Benjamin's relation of expression ("Ausdruckszusammenhang"), Adorno reproached Benjamin for not having treated his objects with the necessary nuance, and demanded that Benjamin readjust his use of Marxist theory. Benjamin's attempts to explain the relationship between elements of the superstructure (poetry) with those of the base (social history) in a "immediate or even causal" way, were too direct, and his understandings, according to Adorno, needed to include a theory of mediation:

> Unless I am very much mistaken, your dialectic is lacking in one thing: mediation. You show a prevailing tendency to relate the pragmatic contents of Baudelaire's work directly and immediately to adjacent features in the social history, and wherever possible, the economic features, of the time.[12]

---

11 For an overview of the complete critical correspondence, see van Reijen, Willem: "Die Adorno-Benjamin-Kontroverse". *Zeitschrift für philosophische Forschung* 60(1), 2006, pp. 99–121.

12 Adorno, Theodor W./Benjamin, Walter, transl. Walker, Nicholas: *The Correspondence 1928–1940*, ed. Henri Lotz, Cambridge, Harvard University Press: Cambridge, Mass. 1999, p. 282. Cf. Adorno, Theodor W./Benjamin, Walter: *Briefwechsel 1928–1949*. Lonitz, Henri (ed.). Suhrkamp: Frankfurt a.M. 1994, p.. 337: "Täusche ich mich nicht sehr, so gebricht es dieser Dialektik an einem: der Vermittlung. Es herrscht durchwegs eine Tendenz, die *pragmatischen Inhalte Baudelaires unmittelbar auf benachbarte* Züge der Sozialgeschichte seiner Zeit und zwar möglichst solche ökonomischer Art zu beziehen." (Brief Adornos an Benjamin vom 10.11.1938). Adorno continues: "[…] [I]ch [halte] es für methodisch unglücklich […], einzelne sinnfällige Züge aus dem Bereich des Überbaus 'materialistisch' zu wenden, indem man sie zu benachbarten Zügen des Unterbaus unvermittelt und wohl gar kausal in Beziehung setzt." ("The reason is that I regard it as methodologically inappropriate to give conspicuous individual features from the realm of the superstructure a 'materialist' turn by relating them immediately, and perhaps even causally, to certain corresponding features of the substructure." *Correspondence*, p. 282) For Adorno, the further elaboration

As the tenor of his argument shows, Adorno finds fault with the very basis of what Benjamin tried to do with Marx and Baudelaire, seeing in the text a juxtaposition of both fields that was unable to shake off the tendentious character of illustrating their mere conjuncture. Base and superstructure remain separated because there seems to be no mediation in Benjamin's construction. This was, as Adorno proceeds to argue, a methodological flaw on both sides, producing neither a panorama of Paris in the 19th century, nor offering further insight into Baudelaire's writing. These concerns ultimately prevented the text from appearing in the *Zeitschrift*.[13]

The Second Reading: Baudelaire's Construction of Empty Experience

Benjamin took those points to heart when he submitted the second version, "Über einige Motive bei Baudelaire", the following year. In this new essay, Benjamin completely reworked the materials from the first, eschewing the earlier essay's threefold structure and anticipated final synthesis for an approach that treated motifs from Baudelaire's poems as the starting point of the interpretation. With this shift, Benjamin overcame the separation between his fields of interest. Without giving up the historiographic demands, the literary form became the focal point of the essay, instead of merely the idea of an all-encompassing panorama of the epoch. Now that these motifs were "no longer merely collected, but, moreover, executed",[14] his constellations gained a necessary distance from the "pragmatic content" and permitted for a reintegration of a concentrated intertext, which, in turn, enabled Benjamin to develop a comparative

---

of a materialistic and dialectic procedure claims that the determination of the materials in poetry can only be thought of as mediated by the "Gesamtprozess", the general process; it remains unclear if the history of motives in Benjamin's second essay can be understood as the corresponding method.

13 Cf. Jennings, Michael W.: *The Writer of Modern Life: Essays on Charles Baudelaire*. Harvard Univ. Press: Cambridge, Mass. 2006.

14 Adorno / Benjamin, *Briefwechsel*, p. 365: "Es werden Motive versammelt aber nicht durchgeführt." [My translation above, S.G.] Later on (p. 368), Adorno stresses that only "theory" might overcome these deductions, but, however, tries to convince Benjamin to use the methods that Benjamin himself had already developed, ("Ihre eigene, rücksichtslose, gut spekulative Theorie.").

history of these moments as well. The introduction of Poe and Proust alongside Baudelaire as central authors for the 19th century provides connecting links for this historical description with regards to how Baudelaire can be understood, as Benjamin argues here and elsewhere, as the last great success of European poetry, revealing much about the *zeitgeist* of literary modernity. Benjamin managed to replace the speculative pairings of the first attempt with stable correspondences between writers and readers. Following Adorno's criticism, this new version examines forms of mediation in literature, transposing the field of interest quite seamlessly to further fields of historical interest. The elements taken from actual texts lose their 'pragmatic' character, and instead allow us to ask how poetic writing in its specificity relates to the surrounding social world, and what role the poet as writer plays within it. Accordingly, Baudelaire is no longer treated merely as a witness of his time, but becomes the subject of its literary expression, whose constitutive moments Benjamin defines as motifs, which are, Benjamin argues, arranged according to an "authorial plan".[15] Thus, a change of perspective is achieved that shifts from the what, the topical or pragmatic contents of his writing, to the how, the reflection on the modality of expression, that is to say, how Baudelaire conceptualizes and executes writing. Now, Benjamin is able to analyse how this century finds in Baudelaire a voice that, by means of lyric, is able to develop model cases of scenes and moments typical of modern day experience, which, in a mediated way, offer far more insight into the workings of the 19th century, whether in images or allegorically.[16] With this rearrangement of

---

15 C.f. for example Benjamin, GS 1,2, pp. 614–15.

16 The vital significance of allegory for Benjamin in general and for his dealing with Baudelaire in particular cannot be discussed in detail here. Even though this concept is present all over the *Arcades Project* as well as in his readings of Baudelaire, a systematic discussion of how allegory is to be understood – apart from the *Trauerspielbuch* – is not to be found here. Cf. Benjamin, GS V 1, p. 412–417. The same formulations return in the *Zentralpark*; Benjamin, I 2, pp. 657–690; he claims that the "Umfunktionierung der Allegorie in der Warenwirtschaft" (p. 671) should be analysed. For the lack of a conception of allegory in the 19th century, cf. Stenzel, Hartmut: "Dekonstruktion der Sinnstiftung und geschichtsphilosophischer Pessimismus". In: Brüggemann, Heinz (ed.): *Walter Benjamin und die romantische Moderne*. Königshausen & Neumann: Würzburg 2009, pp. 299–323, here p. 310.); and in relation to the

his key witness, the second essay avoids the problematic dichotomy – of base and superstructure, of literature and society and, moreover, of form and content – by establishing moments of expression and mediation, which are themselves far better placed to reveal new historical insights. In reconstructing the means or the "plan" visible in the poems, Benjamin demonstrates how to understand and analyse the legible traces that an age leaves in the writing produced within it. This new set of questions, which are also more mediated than those prominent in the earlier essay, make it possible to trace the mediation between experience and expression. This is already part of Benjamin's programme, as evidenced by the essay's title, which limits the scope of the text to just "some motifs" instead of a global explanation of the writer and his times. This restriction is accompanied by a clarification of methods, with the motifs themselves now being treated as that within which the traces of economic and social life become visible.

From the start, Benjamin introduces Baudelaire as speculator confronted with a public which has become "aloof towards lyric poetry"; the exceptional status of the poet who, for some reason, became the "last great mass success of lyric writing"[17] explains not only his position, but also in a broader sense – along with other texts by Benjamin from this time, as the essay on Jochmann and the "Regression of poetry", his *Narrator* or his best-known *Work of Art* essay[18] – how the literary and artistic field is reorganised in the face of the radical changes in society. The interplay between this reluctant public and the poet's plan to write in order to overcome this resistance become the key object of Benjamin's description;[19] he

Task of the Translator, see Menninghaus, Winfried: *Walter Benjamins Theorie der Sprachmagie*. Suhrkamp: Frankfurt a.M. 1995.

17 Benjamin, GS 1,2, p. 607: "Ein zweites Faktum: ein Massenerfolg lyrischer Poesie ist nach Baudelaire nicht mehr vorgekommen. [...] das Publikum wurde spröder auch gegen lyrische Poesie, die ihm von früher her überkommen war."

18 In the same issue of the *Zeitschrift* in which "Über einige Motive" is published, Benjamin also writes a short introduction to a republication of Jochmann's "Rückschritte der Poesie" ("Regression of Poetry"). As an ensemble, both texts bear witness to the decline of lyric poetry in the 19th century, and provide essential key words for the *Arcades Project*. Elsewhere, I have tried to reconstruct this reading and using of Jochmann by Benjamin, the respective article will appear as "Rückschritte, Irrwege. Benjamin, Lecteur de Jochmann" in 2021.

19 Benjamin, GS I 2, p. 607.

sees in Baudelaire the figure of a structural change of poetry.[20] How, in the "inhospitable, blinding epoch of big industry",[21] writing lyric is a form for the expression of these characteristic experiences rather than an attempt to dissolve them in literary form. Drawing on insights gleaned from his exchange with Adorno, Benjamin now approaches Baudelaire's decisions as a plan of expression and shows that this form is, historically speaking and in a mediated fashion, sedimented content.[22]

At the heart of this historical interpretation is the category of temporality as it was theorised and experienced at the end of the 19th century, and as it was described and analysed at the moment that Benjamin himself was writing, in the wake of influential mediations on the topic by Freud, Proust, Bergson, and others. Baudelaire was able to be successful as poet in a world that had ceased to be open to poetry because the end of poetry in his work gives the masses – who will be responsible for his prominence – the expression of precisely their confrontation with new formations of time. The "mass" provides the matrix of modern art and literature, and thus becomes one of his literature's own themes,[23] both as part of the poet's plan and as the background for the *Fleurs du Mal*. By virtue of this "secret present",[24] the mass gradually becomes the acting entity of the texts. This is where Benjamin recognises Baudelaire's "calculation." This

20 He distances himself from Bergson's attempt to reconstruct some kind of 'true' experience. The predominance of this conception in lyric before Baudelaire is precisely what Benjamin observes as a historical shift: (GS 1,2, p. 609), von ihr gekennzeichnet: "Matière und mémoire" bestimmt das Wesen der Erfahrung in der durée derart, daß der Leser sich sagen muß: einzig der Dichter wird das adäquate Subjekt einer solchen Erfahrung sein."

21 Benjamin, GS 1,2, p. 609. (in der "unwirtlichen, blendenden Epoche der großen Industrie.")

22 For this central expression of aesthetic theory of the Frankfurt School, see Adorno, Theodor W.: *Ästhetische Theorie*. Suhrkamp: Frankfurt a.M. 1973, p. 15.

23 The cord / the masses is / are elsewhere defined as "matrix" of modern times. Cf. the third version of the *Kunstwerkaufsatz,* Benjamin GS 1,2, Sp 503. Cf. Neumeyer, Harald: *Der Flaneur: Konzeptionen der Moderne*. Königshausen & Neumann: Würzburg 1999, pp. 108–111.

24 Benjamin, GS 1,2, p. 621–622: "In den *Tableaux Parisien* ist fast überall die heimliche Gegenwart einer Masse nachweisbar."

plan, missing from the first essay, bridges what remained separated there, the economics of Baudelaire's concept and its constitutive connection to the social world of the mass. Baudelaire speculated that modernity finds its most adequate expression in the restructuring of lyric expression in the very moment of its regression, and this provides a much stronger basis for Benjamin's claims about his exceptionality. Baudelaire not only recognises that high capitalism has a general tendency to radically alter time and experience, but discovers the means to manifest and reflect those changes through literature. Its model is the *choc* which is the vital feature of life in the big cities of 19th century France:

> One wonders how lyric poetry can be grounded in experience [einer Erfahrung] for which exposure to shock [Chockerlebnis] has become the norm. One would expect such poetry to have a large measure of consciousness; it would suggest that a plan was at work in its composition. This is indeed true of Baudelaire's poetry [...].[25]

In this understanding, the idea of a conscious plan standing behind the texts leads to the category of expression Benjamin had been looking for; Baudelaire's *spleen* is a lyrical mode to produce those shock-like moments of everyday life, not so much in the form of the representation of a loss of true experience, but rather, on the contrary, by retracing and re-enacting its active destruction – this is how the poetic text can create "the fundamental sensation of modern times".[26] This lived experience of shock is the cornerstone of the motifs. For Baudelaire, it became "facture",[27] the crossing point of his objects and forms. To read him thus would no longer mean trying to identify socio-economically relevant or contemporary economic topics in his poems, but rather to follow Baudelaire's plan

---

25 Benjamin, Walter: *Selected Writings*, Vol. 4. Jennings, Michael W. (ed.). Harvard University Press: Harvard 2006, p. 318. Cf. Benjamin, GS 1,2., p. 614: "Die Frage meldet sich an, wie lyrische Dichtung in einer Erfahrung fundiert sein könnte, der das Chockerlebnis zur Norm geworden ist. Eine solche Dichtung müßte ein hohes Maß von Bewußtheit erwarten lassen; sie würde die Vorstellung eines Plans wachrufen, der bei ihrer Ausarbeitung am Werke war. Das trifft auf die Dichtung von Baudelaire durchaus zu."

26 Witte, Bernd: "Benjamins Baudelaire. Rekonstruktion und Kritik eines Torsos". *Text und Kritik* 31/32, 1979, pp. 81–90, here p. 87.

27 Benjamin, GS I 2, p. 617.

of mediation and expression in their derivate, incomplete moments of sensation in the mode of shock. Above all, this plan constitutes the characteristically modern way of dealing with time and temporal experience that Benjamin wants to reconstruct. In Baudelaire, this epoch has found a medium, or even a translator, whose way of reconfiguring lyric poetry makes visible how the aloof masses of the capital experience their own time and how both its rhythm, and, more importantly, the ruinous state of temporality, the constant and omnipresent lack of a full experience of time, can be traced back to the economic preformation of everyday life. Quoting Nietzsche, Benjamin understands Baudelaire no longer as a spectator, but as the destroyer of the auratic, meaningful and complete:

> This is the nature of the immediate experience [Erlebnis] to which Baudelaire has given the weight of long experience [Erfahrung]. He named the price of which the sensation of modernity could be had: the disintegration of the aura in the immediate shock experience [Chockerlebnis]. He paid dearly for consenting to the disintegration – but it is the law of his poetry. This poetry appears in the sky of the Second Empire as 'a star without atmosphere'.[28]

This usurpation of experience ("Erfahrung") by sensation indeed marks a change, but it soon becomes the 'normal condition' of modernity, and sheds light on the economic structure that leads, above all, to the acceleration and particularization of perceptions of time. To recognise these moments in poetry is vital to Benjamin's concept of mediation as he

28 Benjamin, *Selected Writings* 4, p. 343. Cf. Benjamin, GS I 2, pp. 652–653: "So ist das Erlebnis beschaffen, dem Baudelaire das Gewicht einer Erfahrung gegeben hat. Er hat den Preis bezeichnet, um welchen die Sensation der Moderne zu haben ist: die Zertrümmerung der Aura im Chocerlebnis. Das Einverständnis mit dieser Zertrümmerung ist ihn teuer zu stehen gekommen. Es ist aber das Gesetz seiner Poesie. Sie steht am Himmel des zweiten Kaiserreichs als 'ein Gestirn ohne Atmosphäre'". The final quote is staken from Nietzsche (Nietzsche, Friedrich: *Unzeitgemäße* Betrachtungen II, („Vom Nutzen und Nachtheil der Historie für das Leben",) KSA 1, Colli a., Giorgio/Montinari, Mazzino (eds.) dtv / de Gruyter: Berlin/New York 1988, p. 298: "Alles Lebendige braucht um sich eine Atmosphäre, einen geheimnisvollen Dunstkreis; wenn man ihm diese Hülle nimmt, wenn man eine Religion, eine Kunst, ein Genie verurteilt, als Gestirn ohne Atmosphäre zu kreisen: so soll man sich über das schnelle Verdorren, Hart- und Unfruchtbarwerden nicht mehr wundern."

develops it in the confrontation of shock and mass.[29] In one of his most detailed analyses of the sonnet *À une passante*, he explains that the mass itself has become the secret subject of the text, even though Baudelaire never addresses it directly. The passing movement in the text is constituted by an "amorphous mass,"[30] which offers the persona of the poem the chance of the random and singular constellation of their gazes. The poem can be understood as a trace of the attempt to grasp this constellation as a surplus of the never-ending movement of circulation in the masses of Paris, as trying to generate a moment of experience in writing by way of these masses. Everything passes, the movement overcomes the individuals, but it is gone the next moment. The occurrence remains empty, as the closing lines have it in their speculative way:

> Ne te verrai-je plus que dans l'éternité?
> Ailleurs, bien loin d'ici! trop tard! *jamais* peut-être!Car j'ignore où tu fuis, tu
> ne sais où je vais,Ô toi que j'eusse aimée, ô toi qui le savais! [31]

This confrontation with the random and futile encounter produces a moment of shock for a subject constrained between the irrevocable glimpse of

29 This is how Marx is reintroduced into the second essay as source for the new interpretation of Baudelaire, although in a far less important position. Benjamin, GS I 2, p. 618–619: "Die Menge – kein Gegenstand ist befugter an die Literaten des 19. Jahrhunderts herangetreten. […] Kein Zufall, daß der junge Marx Anlaß fand, mit den 'Mystères de Paris' ins Gericht zu gehen. Aus der amorphen Masse, der damals ein schöngeistiger Sozialismus zu schmeicheln suchte, die eherne des Proletariats herauszuschlagen, stand ihm als Aufgabe früh vor Augen."

30 Benjamin, GS I 2, p. 618.

31 Baudelaire, Charles: *Les fleurs du mal*. Reclam: Stuttgart 1998, p. 192. Cf. Baudelaire, Charles / Wagner, Geoffrey (transl.): *Selected Poems of Charles Baudelaire*. Grove Press: New York 1974. "Shall I see you again only in eternity? / Somewhere else, very far from here! Too late! Perhaps never!/ For I do not know where you flee, nor you where I am going,/ O you whom I would have loved, O you who knew it!"; "Wird in der Ewigkeit ich dich erst wiedersehen? | Woanders, weit von hier! zu spät! soll's *nie* geschehn / Dein Ziel ist mir und dir das meine unbekannt, / Dich hätte ich geliebt, und du hast es geahnt." This German translation by Monika Fahrenbach-Wachendorf resembles the one Benjamin wrote himself to some extent. Sadly, I cannot discuss his translation of Baudelaire at length here; cf. Benjamin, Walter: *Charles Baudelaire Tableaux Parisiens*. In: Birnbaum, Antonia/Métayer, Michell (eds.): *Walter Benjamin: Kritische Gesamtausgabe*, vol. 7. Suhrkamp: Berlin 2017.

an eye (Augenblick) and the ongoing current of the urban crowd. Unable to halt, to interrupt this stream of situations, movements and encounters, every such glimpse of an eye can, in its literary reproduction, only be correctly described in a form of conditional, potential language; the subjunctive form, as expression of vague speculations unfulfilled in the situation itself, becomes the natural way of speaking for the poem's voice. According to his 'plan', Baudelaire manages to present the failure of lived experience (Erlebnis) to become experience (Erfahrung) without nostalgically mourning that loss; on the contrary, this slipping away of the present and the shock experience are presented with relish:

> The delight of the urban poet is love – not at first sight, but at last sight. It is an eternal farewell, which coincides in the poem with the moment of enchantment. Thus, the sonnet deploys the figure of shock, indeed of catastrophe.[32]

The connection of the eternity (v. 9) of the farewell and the speculation with which the poem ends evaporates all of the narrative and sensible material the street scene would have provided. The poem itself becomes the scene of this revocation of experience, using the same gesture in both the poem's commencement and its petering out. The "catastrophe" lies not in what happens, but rather in the impossibility of anything happening at all, in the mere passing of the situation already present in the poem's title. That this love is both "at first and last sight" exemplifies the detached relationship of the man of the crowd to his surroundings and his sense of time; farewell for eternity, which is itself just a matter of seconds, a flash. This combination of finitude and infinity stands in direct contrast to the models of the experience of time in modernity that Benjamin sketches in "On Some Motifs", especially Bergson's.[33] What happens in these poems is precisely

---

32 Benjamin, *Selected Writings* 4, p. 324. Cf. Benjamin, GS I,2, p. 623: "Die Entzückung des Großstädters ist eine Liebe nicht sowohl auf den ersten als auf den letzten Blick. Es ist ein Abschied auf ewig, der im Gedicht mit dem Augenblick der Berückung zusammenfällt. So stellt das Sonett die Figur des Chocks, ja die Figur einer Katastrophe."

33 Benjamin GS I 1, p. 644: "Daß in Bergsons durée der Tod ausfällt, dichtet sie gegen die geschichtliche (wie auch vorgeschichtliche) Ordnung ab. [...] Die durée, aus der der Tod getilgt ist, hat die schlechte Unendlichkeit eines Ornaments." ("The fact that death has been eliminated from Bergson's *durée* isolates it effectively from a historical [as well as prehistorical] order. [...] The

the construction of these untimely combinations as shocks; in this sense, the loss of a relation to time finds 'expression' in the rigorous sense of the word – Benjamin now calls it "Entsprechung", which could be translated as 'equivalence' or, in the own words of his poet, 'correspondences.'[34] Thus, lyric poetry can express an estranged relationship to time that lies somewhere between the gambler and the worker:

> The shock experience [Chockerlebnis] which the passer-by has in the crowd corresponds to the isolated 'experiences' of the worker at his machine. [...] He [Baudelaire]was, however, captivated by a process in which the reflexive mechanism that the machine triggers in the workman can be studied closely, as in a mirror, in the idler. To say that this process represented in games of chance may appear paradoxical. [...] But it certainly does not lack futility, emptiness, an inability to complete something – qualities inherent in the activity of a wage slave in a factory.[35]

---

durée from which death has been eliminated has the bad infinity of an ornament." [Benjamin, *Selected Works* 4, p. 336].) Cf. further, Benjamin, *Passagen-Werk*, GS V, p. 969: "Der Müßiggang hat die Anweisung auf unbegrenzte Dauer, die dem bloßen Sinnengenuß, von welcher Art er auch sei, grundsätzlich abgeht. (Ist es richtig, daß die "schlechte Unendlichkeit", die im Müßiggang vorwaltet, als Signatur der bürgerlichen Gesellschaft bei Hegel vorkommt?) (M 5,1)". ("Idleness has in view an unlimited duration, which fundamentally distinguishes it from simple sensuous pleasure, of whatever variety. [Is it correct to say that the 'bad infinity' that prevails in idleness appears in Hegel as the signature of bourgeois society?]". Benjamin, *The Arcades Project*, p. 806, m 5,1).

34 It goes without saying that "*Entsprechung*" is directly connected with what Baudelaire calls "correspondences"; one of the most programmatic poems within the *Fleurs du mal* thus entitled gives way for Benjamin's reading of Baudelaire as allegorist. Schlossman, Beryl: "Benjamin's *Über Einige Motive bei Baudelaire*: The Secret Architecture of Correspondences". *Modern Language Notes*, 107 (3) 1992, pp. 548–579, here p. 556: "Benjamin uses the correspondences to develop the connection between secret architecture [by which Schlossmann describes in other words what I have identified with Benjamin as "plan" here, S.G.] and the objects of loss-. His reading of the image of 'secret architecture' displays the question of the structure of the *Fleurs du mal* by evoking the structuring net of experience."

35 Benjamin, *Selected Writings* 4, pp. 329–330. Cf. GS 1,2, pp. 632–633: "Dem Chockerlebnis, das der Passant in der Menge hat, entspricht das 'Erlebnis' des Arbeiters an der Maschinerie. [...] Er [Baudelaire] ist aber von einem Vorgang gefesselt worden, in dem der reflektorische Mechanismus, den die Maschine am Arbeiter in Bewegung setzt, am Müßiggänger wie in einem Spiegel sich näher studieren lässt. Diesen Vorgang stellt das Hasardspiel dar. [...] was ihr durchaus

This futility comprises the whole scope of Baudelaire's writing – but it is by no means a relapse into an unmediated form of representation that sees flaneur and gambler as direct images of the worker, nor a simplistic identification of the subjects in the economic entanglements with these types. They are understood as motifs that express something common to each of them: the poverty of experience. Everything passes, goes on, but nothing comes to happen; all that remains are manifold options, speculations, which are, in their sheer abundance, consigned to futility. The painful shock is, in this sense, not so much a painful experience *per se* as it is demonstration of the rupture of experience itself in the subjects.

Speculations. Reading "La fausse monnaie" with Benjamin

Benjamin only gestures towards Baudelaire's prose, mainly reading parts of the *Fleurs du Mal.* The collection of the *Petites Poèmes en Prose*, however, also treats this conception of shock, and indeed goes even further in the direction of a speculative dispossession of time. Particularly with regard to Benjamin's theory of the relation of prose and lyric in the wake of modernity, discussed at length in his essay on Jochmann, an exploration of how he would have interpreted these short prose pieces is called for. It comes as no surprise when Benjamin quotes from the dedication letter of prose poems and finds that this letter mirrors the decisive categories of his reading:

> Who among us has not dreamed, in his ambitious moments, of the miracle of a poetic prose, musical, yet without rhythm and without rhyme, supple and resistant enough to adapt to the lyrical stirrings of the soul, the undulations of reverie, and the sudden leaps of consciousness. This obsessive ideal is born, above all, from the experience of giant cities, from the intersecting of their myriad relations.[36]

---

nicht abgeht, das ist die Vergeblichkeit, die Leere, das Nicht-vollenden-Dürfen, welches vielmehr der Tätigkeit des Lohnarbeiters in der Fabrik innewohnt."

36 Benjamin, *Selected Writings* 4, p. 320. Cf. Benjamin, GS I 2, pp. 617–618: "Wer unter uns hätte nicht schon in den Tagen des Ehrgeizes das Wunderwerk einer poetischen Prosa erträumt? sie müßte musikalisch ohne Rhythmus und Reim sein, sie müßte geschmeidig und spröde genug sein, um sich den lyrischen Regungen der Seele, den Wellenbewegungen der Träumerei, den Chocks des Bewußtseins anzupassen. Dieses Ideal, das zur fixen Idee werden kann, wird vor allem von dem Besitz ergreifen, der in den Riesenstädten mit dem Geflecht ihrer

One of those fifty prose poems is especially apt for asking how these texts should be read according to the method of plan and motifs as the idea of expression of the economic order of modern times. Moreover, the notion of dispossessing speculation introduced above can be further clarified here. In "La fausse monnaie", together with "Les yeux des pauvres",[37] a piece of some six hundred words, poetry becomes a kind of involuntary, perhaps inevitable speculation that, in the end, leaves one destitute. The motif of the poet as speculator is already evoked in the title by the unmistakable symbol of capitalist relations: the coin. This invites a reading that offers new insights into how this writing makes the economic order visible. This becomes even clearer as the text explores exceptional cases of economic exchange—alms and forgeries, both of which are liminal cases of the circulation of goods and values in the proper sense.

This micro-narrative can be summarized as follows: leaving a tobacco store, the narrator and his companion give some small change they have just received to a beggar. The narrator is startled by the high value of the coin his friend gives to the beggar and admires his generosity. Upon being asked about it in a fragment of a dialogue, the other then "excuses" himself by explaining that the coin was a forgery.

Jacques Derrida dedicated a well-known monograph to this short text. For him, it is vital that apart from this very short exchange of words, the text remains an "inner monologue" by the narrator.[38] He does not

---

zahllosen einander durchkreuzenden Beziehungen zu Hause ist." In the original text by Baudelaire, the quote is slightly different: "Quel est celui de nous qui n'a pas, dans ses jours d'ambition, rêvé le miracle d'une prose poétique, musicale sans rythme et sans rime, assez souple et assez heurtée pour s'adapter aux mouvements lyriques de l'âme, aux ondulations de la rêverie, aux soubresauts de la conscience?". Dedication letter by Baudelaires to Asène Houssaye (1862), quoted in Bunzel, Wolfgang: *Das deutschsprachige Prosagedicht: Theorie und Geschichte einer literarischen Gattung der Moderne*. Niemeyer: Tübingen, 2005, p. 65.

37 This is the title of poem 16; Baudelaire, *Vingt poèmes en prose*, pp. 62–68. Berman uses this text for an elaboration on the modes of experience in post-Haussmann Paris that shares many features with the one introduced here. Berman, *All That Is Solid Melts into Air*, pp. 148–155.

38 Derrida, Jacques: *Donner le temps*, vol. 1, *La fausse monnaie*. Galilée: Paris 1991, p. 152. For the English translation, cf. Derrida, Jacques: *Given time, 1,*

give away his thoughts in the scene, but transforms them only into the written form the readers are presented with; which means that he does not, in a strong sense, tell us anything, or, put differently, he tells far too much. The text consists of nothing but the escalating daydreams initiated by said scene which the narrator shares with us: futile nonsense that he is somehow forced to think by nature, because it has given him the gift of a thus formed mind ("nature m'a fait cadeau"). All the poem does is reflect on the motifs and results of the forged coin changing hands:

> Mais dans mon misérable cerveau, toujours occupé à chercher midi à quatorze heures (de quelle fatigante faculté la nature m'a fait cadeau!), entra soudainement cette idée qu'une pareille conduite, de la part de mon ami, n'était excusable que par le désir de créer un événement dans la vie de ce pauvre diable, peut-être même de connaître les conséquences diverses, funestes ou autres, que peut engendrer une pièce fausse dans la main d'un mendiant. Ne pouvait-elle pas se multiplier en pièces vraies ? ne pouvait-elle pas aussi le conduire en prison ? Un cabaretier, un boulanger, par exemple, allait peut-être le faire arrêter comme faux-monnayeur ou comme propagateur de fausse monnaie. Tout aussi bien la pièce fausse serait peut-être, pour un pauvre petit spéculateur, le germe d'une richesse de quelques jours. Et ainsi ma fantaisie allait son train, prêtant des ailes à l'esprit de mon ami et tirant toutes les déductions possibles de toutes les hypothèses possibles. [39]

This short passage is rich in a logic dominated by the economics that arise inside the core of the little story. But, as Derrida points out, the emblem of the false coin and the strange circularity of the gift produce a surplus

Counterfeit Money. University of Chicago Press: Chicago and London 1992, p. 119.

39 Baudelaire, Charles: *Vingt poèmes en prose*. dtv: Munich 1973, pp. 71–73. Translation by Kamuf, Peggy in: Derrida, *Given time, 1, Counterfeit Money*, p. 96: "But into my miserable brain, always concerned with looking for noon at two o' clock (what an exhausting faculty is nature's gift to me!), there suddenly came the idea that such conduct on my friend's part was excusable only by the desire to create an event in this poor devil's life, perhaps even to learn the varied consequences, disastrous or otherwise, that a counterfeit coin in the hands of a beggar might engender. Might it not multiply into real coins? Could it not also lead him to prison? A tavern keeper, a baker, for example, was perhaps going to have him arrested as a counterfeiter or for passing counterfeit money. The counterfeit coin could just as well, perhaps, be the germ of several days' wealth for a poor little spectator. And so my dance went its course, lending wings to my friend's mind and drawing all possible deductions from all possible hypotheses."

of results, motives and consequences that exceeds the normal cases of exchange of the market. Baudelaire takes us somewhere else, the situation of buying and selling does not take place within the framework of the story, and all that is left are the remains, the small change of the transaction before the scene.[40] The trigger of all that follows is the constellation of the false coin and the beggar who stands – in contrast to the ragman of Benjamin's first essay[41] – completely detached from the workings of supply and demand; he has no services nor goods to offer, and his earnings are neither wages nor profits. In this sense, the whole situation stands outside an economic order, being understood as a system of exchanges of goods and values and the assumption of some equivalence in this exchange – or, as it stands, that it produces some returns. Even the honest donation of the narrator – in real money, as one must suppose – has already left the logic of economics behind, since his motivation for giving alms does not add up to bartering with the beggar. Being nothing but a gift, the matter of possible countervalues is excluded from this transaction, or at least the narrator leaves it at that. The false money doubles this effect of distance, inasmuch as it introduces unsecured coins into this particular shadow economy. He neither exchanges nor invests, and, even still, the circulation of the coin produces a whole series of speculations, all of them without any sound ground. The coin is seen as it changes hands, and thereby alone, the narrator is given the doubtful present of future or possible results, and the object of speculation introduces its own logic or calculation.

Baudelaire's narrator is at the mercy of the situation in two ways; his over-potent phantasy takes this little episode of which he had been

---

40 Derrida, *Donner de Temps*, p. 133: "Ils viennent d'acheter — de se payer — du tabac et toute l'économie du récit, comme le récit de l'économie, procède d'un reste, de la monnaie rendue, de la monnaie qui reste de cet achat." Cf. the translation by Kamuf, Peggy in: Derrida, *Given time, 1, Counterfeit Money,* pp. 102–103: "They have just bought - offered themselves - some tobacco: The whole economy of the narrative as well as the narrative of the economy, proceeds from a *remainder,* from the change returned, from the change that remains from this purchase."

41 In their correspondence, Adorno hints at this moment explicitly when he invites Benjamin to understand the ragman as moment in which "capitalism even subjugates the beggar under the exchange value" (Adorno / Benjamin, *Briefwechsel*, p. 369: "noch den Bettel dem Tauschwert […] unterwerfen").

nothing but an idle witness and unleashes an antithetical series of hypotheses, asking which one of them might be valuable. This opening of idle speculations resembles the unsecured value of the false coin that seems to produce an income of too many moral possibilities. Derrida describes how the economy of the poem itself becomes a forged one; one reads nothing but wild speculations, none of which are the real thing. Under the unsecured title[42] promising us to tell the story of the false coin, Baudelaire just collects all of the eventualities that could arise from the scene. No one does anything beyond speculating, and, for that matter, there are too many ways to think further, and all of the personae seem to take part. When Baudelaire calls the beggar a *petit pauvre speculateur*, he addresses not only the beggar, but also himself as the author or the narrator who keeps on imagining what could happen now, and even the friend himself as well, whose momentary calculation at the doorstep of the store might well have been directed towards eternal reward for his generosity. The risk of these investments that only lends (*prêter*) these ideas to his companion remain on the side of the narrator, and all he does is pile up unsecured storylines. To operate with false money initiates an empty or cyclic circulation that does not have a common ground in an equivalent value, but exchanges the positions of those taking part in it. All of the persona in the prose text are contaminated by the falseness of the coin and its shadow economy:

> The speculation of the narrator who speculates on the probable speculation of his friend on the subject of the possible speculation of the poor devil passes by way of counterfeit money as ovular or seminal capital engendering true money. In principle, without assignable limit. What takes shape here is the infinity or rather the indefiniteness of the "bad infinite" that characterizes the monetary thing (true

---

42 Derrida, *Donner le temps*, p. 114: "Ce texte est aussi la pièce, une pièce de fausse monnaie provoquant un événement et se prêtant à toute cette scène de leurre, de don, de pardon ou de non-pardon. Tout se passe comme si le titre était le texte même dont le récit ne serait en somme que la glose ou une longue note sur la fausse monnaie du titre, en bas de page." Translation by Kamuf, Peggy in: Derrida, *Given time,* p. 86: "This text is also the coin, a piece of counterfeit money provoking an event and lending itself to this whole scene of deception, gift, forgiveness, or non-forgiveness. It is as if the title were the very text whose narrative would finally be but the gloss or a long note on the counterfeit money of the title, at the bottom of the page."

> or counterfeit money) and everything it touches, everything it contaminates (that is, by definition, everything).[43]

In his further reflections, Derrida mainly deals with the logic of the gift that, in this case, is as gratuitous as it is futile, while nonetheless producing too many effects without determining their (moral, pragmatic, financial etc.) value in the moment of their donation. What strikes him as most important is the general notion of something non-present in the moment of giving presents, so to speak; the exchange of the false coin as gift or donation is a model case for its special temporality. In the moment of handing over the false coin, it is undecidable whether it will wander on as true or false, and hence if its effects will be useful or harmful for its new owner; in the present of the story, the gift remains itself unsecured. The narrator explicitly states that the question of the honesty or goodwill of his companion that marks out the realm of the text's speculations cannot be answered within the situation; something remains unsecured, or, temporally speaking, unfulfilled.

It is not necessary to reconstruct everything that Derrida takes from the offers of Baudelaire's text here. What is vital for us is the observation of "La fausse monnaie" itself becoming an unsecured speculation, the traces of which constitute the text itself. This falseness contaminates the text: there might be a narration and a fiction here, but it seems to be just an act of a subject. Appearing as the narration of a short episode, the text introduces the chance to go on telling what follows, what actually, eventually, will have happened, without fulfilling any of these possibilities. Even in the moral deliberations of the narrator, a final judgment is yet to be found when the text reaches its end.

It may appear to be only natural that this dissolution of agency and its subject takes place in this storyline, dictated by the prose poem's topic

---

43 Derrida, *Given time,* p. 158. Cf. Derrida, *Donner de temps*, p. 199–200: "La spéculation du narrateur qui spécule sur la spéculation probable de son ami au sujet de la spéculation possible du pauvre diable passe par la fausse monnaie comme capital ovulaire ou séminal engendrant de la vraie monnaie. En principe sans limite assignable. Ici s'annonce l'infinité ou plutôt l'indéfinité de « mauvais infini » qui caractérise la chose monétaire (vraie ou fausse monnaie) et tout ce à quoi elle touche, tout ce qu'elle contamine (c'est-à-dire, par définition, tout)."

and form. As consummation of the economy of the gift, Baudelaire's text could do nothing but let its hero and his stories disappear into thin air. To ask how this could be read as a mediation of experience and, further, how the economic subjects are represented, only leads us back to the "bad infinity"[44] which the text unleashes. This phrase, already present in Benjamin and also adapted by Derrida, explains the condensation of temporal experience in the moment; the speculations that arise from the motifs and sensations of the big city, both in prose and lyric, develop a rapid sequence of possible futures, which appear only in the form of a flash. Needless to say, both thinkers allude to the conception of bad infinity by Hegel, but they transform the notion, or one could say, they coin it anew. For Hegel, the term designates the futile, fruitless and never-ending which follows from abstract negations, and which, therefore, is to be avoided at all costs. For the life world of modern times, however, and in the mediated depiction of it in Baudelaire, this bad infinity become the name of the rule, being the source of the proliferating speculations as seen in "La fausse monnaie". The "desire to produce an event"[45] – observed in the silent companion of the narrator – leads nowhere and remains hypothetical. No possible sublation or reconciliation, no closure of experience; the motifs of the lyrical subjunctive and the empty fantasies of prose connect the singular and the instantaneous with its counterpart, a sinister infinity (*éternité*) that remains forever indeterminable. One might thus summarize the 'plan' of Baudelaire, or what he explicitly coins as a poetic of modernity: he wants – if one is brave enough to speculate here: *ex negativo* – to find traces of said infinite in the transitory of the mere moment, the blink of an eye or flash of sensation.[46] In contrast to experience, this sensation

44 Derrida, *Donner de Temps*, p. 200: "Ici s'annonce l'infinité ou plutôt l'indéfinité de « mauvais infini » qui caractérise la chose monétaire (vraie ou fausse monnaie) et tout ce à quoi elle touche, tout ce qu'elle contamine (c'est-à-dire, par définition, tout)."

45 Cf. above, désir de créer un événement.

46 Cf. the *Salons*; Baudelaire, Charles: "Le Peintre de la Vie modern". *Figaro* 26(11), 1863, p. 5: "Il cherche ce quelque chose qu'on nous permettra d'appeler la modernité; car il ne se présente pas de meilleur mot pour exprimer l'idée en question. Il s'agit, pour lui, de dégager de la mode ce qu'elle peut contenir de poétique dans l'historique, de tirer l'éternel du transitoire. [...] La modernité,

is haunted by the bad infinity that demonstrates the incapacity for closure in subjective time: what is happening remains unsecured. The speculative is thus a vital part of the plan or poetics of the poet. Without refusing Derrida's reading of "La fausse monnaie", one can, according to Benjamin's *Motifs*, resituate this effect of speculative dissolution within the plan: the false gift of the false coin in the text participates in the relation of expression, and, therefore, can be understood not merely as a textual effect, but instead as part of the system of motifs and moments which Benjamin calls 'the plan'. In other words, there is an attempt to make the economic order visible in "La fausse monnaie", however mediated and indirect that attempt may be. To reconstruct this together with the global "plan", it would be necessary to explain how the futile speculations are mirrored by the reduction of agency in the poem, showing more loss than giving of presents. The narrator does not simply lose his position over the false coin, and, therefore, the chance to tell its story conclusively to its end; the situation itself is lost, this narrator can no longer tell a story at all, which would mean, as Benjamin defines it elsewhere, to "das pure An-sich des Geschehens [...] dem Leben des Berichtenden [einsenkt], um es als Erfahrung dem Hörenden mitzugeben."[47] "La fausse monnaie" is a story of the end of narration,[48] a development that for Benjamin goes along the

---

c'est le transitoire, le fugitif, le contingent, la moitié de l'art, dont l'autre moitié est l'éternel et l'immuable." Cf. further Berman, *All that's solid*, p. 133.

47 Benjamin, *Selected Writings* 4, p. 316. Cf. Benjamin, GS I 2, p. 611: "[...] das pure An-sich des Geschehens [...] dem Leben des Berichtenden [einsenkt], um es als Erfahrung dem Hörenden mitzugeben."

48 In "Der Erzähler" (Benjamin, GS II 2, p. 438–464), Benjamin says (p. 439) "daß es mit der Kunst des Erzählens zu Ende geht." ("[...] that the art of storytelling is coming to an end." (*Selected Writings* 3, p. 142). One could conceptualize the speculation in Baudelaire's prose as opposed to the concept of mere information as Benjamin illustrates it in contrast to narration; ibid., pp. 444–445: "Diese neue Form der Mitteilung ist die Information. [...] Die Information hat ihren Lohn mit dem Augenblicke dahin, in dem sie neu war. Sie lebt nur in diesem Augenblick, sie muß sich gänzlich an ihn ausliefern und ohne Zeit zu verlieren sich ihm erklären." "This new form of communication is information. [...] The value of information does not survive the moment in which it was new. It lives only at that moment; it has to surrender to it completely and explain itself to it without losing any time." (*Selected Writings* 3, pp. 147–148). In contrast to this, the little speculator is interested in nothing but his futile thinking to pass

decline of lyric poetry in the 19th century, but sheds light on the aforementioned plan of Baudelaire, who does not only acknowledge this diagnosis for his time, but, moreover, actively searches for the literary means of this destruction of experience.

In spite of all economics of the gift, Benjamin allows for a reading that retraces the textual effects not to the structure of giving presents in general, but to the historic loss of experience as part of subjective life under the conditions of modernity – it is in his way of dealing with temporality that Baudelaire's narrator comes to terms with the *pauvre petit speculateur*. His 'gifted mind' is not able to ignore the episode and the dreams and possibilities it sets into motion; everything happens as if the narrator had read Benjamin's Freud from *Jenseits des Lustprinzips*, when he describes how he is, painfully and without alternative, forced to speculate after the little scene in front of the tobacco shop.[49] His surplus of impressions transforms, turned around by the poem, into a deficit of experience, too little of an event. The presumed speculative profit offered by the contingency of the situation fizzles out, and the desired event is not produced. The abundance of his register of possibilities is not only to be understood as an effect of the text; here, Baudelaire achieves a demonstration of the modern subject's painful knowledge of their inability to come to an end. The text does not so much represent this as shock, as much as it reproduces it as such; under the circumstances of life in the big city, as part of the ongoing, everchanging masses, the text piles up all the stories it is unable to tell, in a fast sequence of diametrically opposed possibilities that might stand for the everyday experience of small but constant shocks. The flaneur and the speculator share this ruptured relationship to time with the worker or the gambler mentioned above. Given that in this permanent exchange

---

the time, which means – to lose it. The withdrawal of the instantaneous in the moment of speculative possibilities could be a form of reaction to the crisis of narration as well as experience.

49 In "Über einige Motive", Benjamin underlines the compulsive moments as described by Freud in the repetition compulsion. The idea that neurotics have typical dreams that reproduce "the catastrophe that had harmed them ("die Katastrophe, von der sie betroffen worden, [reproduzieren]". Benjamin, GS I 2, p. 613.) Cf. Freud, Siegmund: "Jenseits des Lustprinzips". In: *Gesammelte Werke*. Vol 13. Fischer: Frankfurt a.M. 1967, pp. 5–69, p. 10.

everything is possible, time and event are estranged as they simply appear to be nothing but endless possibilities, missed chances, speculations.

The methodological shift between Benjamin's first and second essays on Baudelaire thus shifts from topics to motifs in order to highlight these moments of mediation. 'Expression' and 'correspondence' are not to be taken as a zero-sum-game, but develop a representational economy of their own. The motifs do not stand for themselves like the moments Adorno called "pragmatic",[50] but are instead configurations of this understanding of temporality brought to life by modernity. Shocks are not told as they happened but created by the means of lyric and prose; and it is only by tracing their construction that the 'expression' of his time becomes visible in Baudelaire. Thus, it is in the motifs that one finds the structuring and informing effects that the order of high capitalism has on the subjects of 19th century Paris. What is gained by this reading is the image of the poet as speculator whose 'plan' or, in other words, calculation, enables him to show the effects of the economic order by way of motifs and scenes that are at first glance detached from it. That Baudelaire "counted on" such readers,[51] and had to find a way to overcome their reluctance towards poetry, presents a vivid image of the effects the social and economic re-structuring of this time, which must be addressed in modes such as the shock that literature is able to produce.

References

Adorno, Theodor W. / Benjamin, Walter: *Briefwechsel 1928–1949*. ed. Lonitz, Henri. Suhrkamp: Frankfurt a.M. 1994.

50 Cf. fn. 12.

51 Benjamin, GS I 2, p. 607: "Baudelaire hat mit Lesern gerechnet, die die Lektüre von Lyrik vor Schwierigkeiten stellt. [...] Es ist befremdend, einen Lyriker anzutreffen, der sich an dieses Publikum hält, das undankbarste." Baudelaire envisaged readers to whom the reading of lyric poetry would present difficulties. (Benjamin, *Selected Writings* 4, p. 313: "Baudelaire envisaged readers to whom the reading of lyric poetry would present difficulties. [...] It is strange to come across a lyric poet who addresses himself to such readers-the least rewarding type of audience.")

Adorno, Theodor W. / Benjamin, Walter / Walker, Nicholas (transl.): *The Correspondence 1928–1940*. ed. Lotz, Henri. Harvard University Press: Cambridge, Mass. 1999.

Adorno, Theodor W.: *Ästhetische Theorie*. Suhrkamp: Frankfurt a.M. 1973.

Baudelaire, Charles: "Le Peintre de la Vie moderne". *Figaro* 26(11), 1863.

Baudelaire, Charles : *Vingt poèmes en prose*, Munich: dtv 1973.

Baudelaire, Charles: *Les fleurs du mal*. Reclam: Stuttgart 1998.

Baudelaire, Charles / Geoffrey Wagner (transl.): *Selected Poems of Charles Baudelaire*. Grove Press New York: 1974.

Benjamin, Walter: *Selected Writings*. ed. Michael W. Jennings, Harvard University Press: Harvard 2006.

Benjamin, Walter: *Charles Baudelaire Tableaux Parisiens*. (*Kritische Gesamtausgabe*, vol. 7), eds. Birnbaum, Antonia / Métayer, Michel. Suhrkamp: Berlin 2017.

Benjamin, Walter/ Eiland, Howard (tranls.): *The Arcades Project*. Belknap Press of Harvard Univ. Press: Cambridge, Mass. / London 2002.

Berman, Marshall: *All That Is Solid Melts into Air: The Experience of Modernity*. Verso: London 1997.

Bunzel, Wolfgang: *Das deutschsprachige Prosagedicht: Theorie und Geschichte einer literarischen Gattung der Moderne*, Niemeyer: Tübingen 2005.

Derrida, Jacques : *Donner le temps*, vol. 1, *La fausse monnaie*. Galilée: Paris: 1991.

Derrida, Jacques: *Given time, 1, Counterfeit Money*. University of Chicago Press: Chicago and London 1992.

Freud, Siegmund: "Jenseits des Lustprinzips." In: *Gesammelte Werke*. Vol 13. Fischer: Frankfurt a.M. 1967, pp. 5–69.

Friedlander, Eli: *Walter Benjamin. A Philosophical Portrait*. Harvard University Press: Cambridge, Mass. 2012.

Jennings, Michael W.: *The Writer of Modern Life: Essays on Charles Baudelaire*. Harvard Univ. Press: Cambridge 2006.

Le Play, Fréderic: *Les ouvriers européens*. L'imprimerie impériale: Paris 1855.

Marx, Karl / Engels, Friedrich: "Der achtzehnte Brumaire des Louis Bonaparte", in: *Werke*. vol. 8, Dietz: Berlin/DDR 1960, pp. 111–207.

Menninghaus, Winfried: *Walter Benjamins Theorie der Sprachmagie*. Suhrkamp: Frankfurt a.M. 1995.

Neumeyer, Harald: *Der Flaneur: Konzeptionen der Moderne*. Königshausen & Neumann: Würzburg 1999.

Nietzsche, Friedrich: *Unzeitgemäße* Betrachtungen II, ("Vom Nutzen und Nachtheil der Historie für das Leben",) KSA 1, ed. Giorgio Colli a. Mazzino Montinari, dtv / de Gruyter: Berlin / New York 1988.

Schlossmann, Beryl: "Benjamin's *Über Einige Motive bei Baudelaire*: The Secret Architecture of Correspondences". *Modern Language Notes* 107(3), 1992, pp. 548–579.

Schmider, Christine / Michael Werner.: "Das Baudelaire-Buch". In: Lindner, Burkhardt (ed.): *Benjamin-Handbuch*. Metzler: Stuttgart 2011, pp. 567–584.

Stenzel, Harmut: "Dekonstruktion der Sinnstiftung und geschichtsphilosophischer Pessimismus". In: Brüggemann, Heinz (ed.): *Walter Benjamin und die romantische Moderne*. Königshausen & Neumann: Würzbur 2009, pp. 299–323.

van Reijen, Willem: "Die Adorno-Benjamin-Kontroverse". *Zeitschrift für philosophische Forschung* 60(1), 2006, pp. 99–121.

Witte, Bernd: "Benjamins Baudelaire. Rekonstruktion und Kritik eines Torsos". *Text und Kritik* 31/32, 1979, pp. 81–90.

Wohlfarth, Irving: "Die Passagenarbeit". In: Lindner, Burkhardt (ed.): *Benjamin-Handbuch*. Metzler. Stuttgart 2011, pp. 251–274.

Nora Weinelt

Bartleby, or How Not to Be a Failure: The Malfunctioning Subject in 19th Century Work Environments

Abstract: *This paper examines a figure of thought that emerged in many Western capitalist societies in the mid-to-late 19th century: the idea that it is possible for the subject to 'be a failure'. Looking at the English expression as well as at its German and French equivalents, I attempt to show how the concept of 'being a failure' – in contrast to the potentially transcendent quality of tragic failure – implies a mode of non-fulfilment that is informed by contemporary thermodynamic, biological, and economic discourse. 'Failure' originally meant the sudden omission or cessation of an expected performance, usually by a machine, a technical device, or a tool. By the end of the 19th century, however, 'being a failure' had also come to characterize individuals, thus describing the failing subject as a technically non-functioning or malfunctioning one. This semantic extension first occurred in the context of work, particularly in the context of white-collar work. In this paper I will compare two mid-to-late 19th-century narratives whose protagonists perform (or rather fail to perform) one specific historical form of such work that seems especially designed to engender the subject as failure, that of the handwriting copyist. Italo Svevo's* Una vita *insists on Alfonso's being a failure, whereas Herman Melville's short story about* Bartleby, the Scrivener *explicitly refuses to portray Bartleby as a failure, even though he does not perform his given tasks. Both texts, however, employ notions of de-subjectification, (in)transitivity, and ascription in order to articulate what it might mean for the subject not simply to fail but to 'be a failure', an articulation that is all the more interesting because it seems largely inconceivable within current discourses about work, subjectivity, and failure.*

Keywords: Failure, being a failure, office workers, Italo Svevo, *Una vita*, Herman Melville, *Bartleby, the Scrivener*

Fail Better, Fail Faster, Fail Forward

In business, "nothing fails like success", as an American saying goes, but for the last two or three decades especially, the opposite seems to be true: nothing succeeds like failure. Failure, so the neoliberal metanarrative suggests, is not only an acceptable stage of the work process – it is *needed* in order to make progress, a prerequisite for creativity and productivity. Bill Gates, a Harvard dropout, founded his first business Traf-O-Data in the 1970s – but with "virtually no customers"[1] in the history of its existence, it didn't last very long. Steve Jobs, another college dropout and Gates' life-long rival, shared a similar fate: He was famously fired from his own company in the 1980s. Both Gates and Jobs succeeded regardless of their failures, or, as many would argue, precisely because of them. In the last thirty years, the business model of the start-up – typically scalable, technology-based companies with high failure rates – has become the epitome of a new concept of 'failing better' that has infiltrated the way we look at success, most prominently in the United States, but also, although maybe to a lesser extent, in the UK and throughout Europe.

Creating a master narrative around one's own failure seems to be the most important cultural technique of 'failing better', judging from the trillions of FailCons, Pep Talks, and failure affirming self-help books. Successful entrepreneurs speak about their rocky road to the top, necessarily in hindsight. It is not without irony that the allegedly self-empowering gesture of embracing failure is only available to those who have not failed, at least not for good. The voices of those who have never made it very far, on the other hand, by definition cannot be heard – 'true' or persistent failures know nothing of success. The neoliberal concept of failure that has been so prevalent in recent years thus creates a dialectic of reassurance: the more failure is talked about, the less it is unamendable failure that is being talked about. The voices within this discourse of failure might have failed at some point in their lives, but in the end, they are no total failures. Zach Klein, co-founder of the video platform Vimeo and one of many tech entrepreneurs who like to talk about failure, seems to confirm this observation, at least judging from a well-known quote that is attributed to him: "When something you make doesn't work, *it* doesn't work, not

1 As described by Traf-O-Data co-founder Paul Allen in *Newsweek*. Allen, Paul: "My Favorite Mistake. Paul Allen". *Newsweek*, 24.4.2011, retrieved 4.4.2020, from https://www.newsweek.com/my-favorite-mistake-paul-allen-66489.

you. *You*, you work. You keep trying."[2] As comforting as this assertion may be, its plausibility remains uncertain. My paper will examine a figure of thought that suggests otherwise and has been thoroughly neglected in contemporary discourses of failure: the idea that it is in fact possible for a subject to *be a failure*, in and of itself, irredeemably and hopelessly so.

Being a Failure, *versagen*, *rater*

The concept of a kind of failure that is deeply and irreducibly tied to the subject itself is, as I want to argue, specific to Western capitalist societies and thus specifically modern. The English expression 'to be a failure' (as opposed to 'to fail') as well as the corresponding German verb *versagen* (as opposed to *scheitern*) and the French verb *rater* (as opposed to *échouer*) imply a decidedly unheroic, banal mode of non-fulfilment that doesn't allow for second chances. While this can also be said about the more ancient idea of tragic failure, the idea of 'being a failure' defies any potential for an epistemological surplus value, any notion of transcendence.[3] On the contrary, this modern idea, whose origins are to be found in 19th century mechanical and thermodynamic thought, perceives the failing subject as a technically non-functioning or malfunctioning one. The term 'failure' originally described a sudden break from what was to be expected, in mechanical contexts ("a total defect", as Noah Webster's 1828 dictionary put it) and with respect to biological events (for example the "*failure* of crops").[4] In the early 19th century, failure was seen as an "omission" or a "non-performance"[5] rather than a poor performance in a work environment – or, for that matter, in life. Consequently, the expression 'to be a

2 As cited in Christensen, Tanner: "What it really means to fail". *Creative Something*, 29.8.2013, retrieved 4.4.2020, from https://creativesomething.net/post/59676599532/what-it-really-means-to-fail.

3 For a more in-depth discussion of tragic failure and its epistemological value in the ancient tragedy, see Schmitt, Arbogast: "Menschliches Fehlen und tragisches Scheitern. Zur Handlungsmotivation im Sophokleischen 'König Ödipus'". *Rheinisches Museum für Philologie* 131, 1988, pp. 8–30.

4 Webster, Noah: *Webster's Dictionary 1828. Online Edition*. Retrieved 4.4.2020, from http://webstersdictionary1828.com/Dictionary/failure. Italics in the original.

5 Ibid.

failure' is never mentioned in Webster's first dictionary edition, nor is its potential opposite: to be a success.

A similar semantic history can be traced for the German *versagen* and, albeit in a far more specific way, the French *rater*. Up until the middle of the 19th century, *versagen* primarily meant 'to refuse',[6] thus referring to both the act of speaking itself (*sagen*) and a notion of free will, which seems to be absent from today's idea of being a failure. One of the expressions in which the verb *versagen* was most often used was *den Dienst versagen* – to deny service. While *den Dienst versagen* almost exclusively described a voluntary refusal in Middle High German and up until around 1800, it slowly grew to extend its meaning over the course of the 19th century – and was soon applied to failing technical devices and/or energetic systems such as explosives or, first and foremost, rifles.[7] In this context, *den Dienst versagen* did not connote a wilful denial. To the contrary, *versagen* was used to underscore the inexplicability of the rifle's failure to carry out the service for which it had been designed. The rifle failed for reasons unknown to the men who had been relying on its proper functioning. Soldiers in particular were confronted with a sudden non-performance of devices that were expected to work yet simply did not. The idea of a rifle that fails is also at the etymological root of the French term *rater*, even if in a rather curious way: *rater*, from the corresponding noun *le rat*, originally referred to the unexpected non-functioning of a weapon because of rats that were suspected to have done unnoticeable damage in the storage room.[8]

---

6 Cf. Grimm, Jacob and Wilhelm: *Deutsches Wörterbuch*. Vol. 25. Ed. Deutsche Akademie der Wissenschaften Berlin. dtv: München 1984, col. 1031.

7 Compared to other potentially failing devices or systems, failing rifles are mentioned disproportionately often in 19th century functional texts – possibly because they pose a much greater threat to personal and national safety. For a contemporary example, see Rüstow, Caesar: *Die Kriegshandfeuerwaffen. Eine genaue Darstellung ihrer Einrichtung in den europäischen Armeen, ihrer Anfertigung, ihres Gebrauchs und ihrer allmäligen Entwickelung*. Vol. 2. Bath: Berlin 1864, S. 171.

8 "On dit, qu'une arme a pris un Rat, lorsque le Chien s'est abattu, & que l'arme n'a pas pris feu." Cf. Backer, Georges de: *Dictionnaire de Proverbes François, avec l'Explication de leur Significations, et une partie de leur Origine*. George de Backer: Bruxelles 1710, lemma *rater*.

All of these examples, a failing rifle as well as a failure of crops and, more broadly, a total defect, in one way or another represent closed energetic systems that are subject to the first law of thermodynamics, one of the most important scientific discoveries of the 19th century. Conceptualized by Robert Mayer in 1842,[9] it asserted that the total energy of a system (plus its surroundings) is conserved at any time, thus allowing one to quantify and determine the energy level within a closed system – energy input generally equals energy output. Failure, or *Versagen*, however, described something inexplicable and, according to the laws of thermodynamics, downright impossible: systems in which energy had been inserted did not work as expected, despite all efforts to calculate cause and effect or to foresee the way the system was going to behave. The events (or rather: non-events) to come could neither be predicted nor prevented or controlled. The thermodynamic worldview soon started to expand to fields other than physics themselves, most notably to the science surrounding the energetic system that is the human body. Until today, terms such as 'heart failure' (*Herzversagen*) or 'kidney failure' (*Nierenversagen)* describe the sudden omission of an expected bodily function, for reasons unknown. From there, the concept slowly started to apply to the subject as such: functional failure transitioned into a constitutional failure, the constitutional failure we speak of today when we say that somebody *is* a failure.

While the idea of technical, mechanical, or biological failure is not mysterious per se, let alone metaphysical, it did have a certain unexplained quality in the 19th century. Even though none of the above-mentioned systems or devices showed visible outer signs of dysfunction, they did not work, and even though a seed had been planted or a trigger pulled, the expected outcome was inexplicably not met. This is not to say that there was no way of understanding the cause of failure at all; there might very well have been one – retrospectively and in a more advanced scientific setting. In the immediate situation and for the naked eye, however, there was

---

9 James Prescott Joule and Ludwig August Colding worked out equivalent findings simultaneously. For a more comprehensive discussion of thermodynamics, see Müller, Ingo: *A History of Thermodynamics. The Doctrine of Energy and Entropy*. Springer: Berlin 2007, pp. 9–46.

none. Failure, therefore, seemed to originate from within a flawed system or device itself rather than from an external mishandling or mistake.

The English term 'failure' in particular referred to one very specific flawed system from early on: to the financial system. Other than the failure of crops or a total defect, Webster's 1828 dictionary mentioned a "breaking, or becoming insolvent"[10] that implied the sudden cessation of cash flow. In his study *Born Losers. A History of Failure in America*, Scott A. Sandage has shown how in the early 19th century, failure was thought of as "an incident, not an identity".[11] The omission of performance or the cessation of supply was a singular event, not a state or, even worse, a character trait. The Panic of 1819, the first major financial crisis in the United States, and the second crisis of 1837, which hit even harder, unmistakably showed that failures could occur unpredictably – and to anyone. "Earlier economic dips had obvious, tangible causes like drought, revolution, or wartime embargoes",[12] Sandage writes, but the unprofitable years following the Panic of 1819 seemed to "mysteriously come from within the economic system itself. Without obvious reasons, processes of production and exchange went awry."[13] Financial failure just happened, all of a sudden and seemingly out of nowhere, and most importantly with no one to blame.

At the same time, however, the problem of financial failure turned out to be of ever-increasing importance within a society that unconditionally believed in entrepreneurship, competitive effort, and economic growth. The so-called Market Revolution, which began after the British-American War of 1812 and picked up speed in the 1820s, led to the development of a relatively differentiated national economy, fuelled by the Industrial Revolution (of which the Market Revolution was a result), the war that had brought imports from Europe to a halt, and ongoing westward expansion. In the Land of Opportunity, which based its identity on the spirit of

10 Webster 1828.

11 Sandage, Scott. A.: *Born Losers. A History of Failure in America*. Harvard UP: Cambridge, London 2006, p. 11.

12 Ibid., p. 29.

13 Rothbard, Murray N.: *The Panic of 1819. Reactions and Policies*. Columbia UP: New York, London 1962, p. ii.

discovery and adventure, the dream of rising from rags to riches and, more generally, the pursuit of happiness were increasingly seen as an obligation rather than an option, and the 'self-made man', a phrase and myth coined by Henry Clay in a speech before the Senate in 1832, came to epitomize the good American citizen.[14] In this regard, business performance emerged as a pars pro toto for life performance, and accordingly, financial failure, as little as it may have had to do with personal mistakes in the first place, quite literally started to compromise a man's value and valuation.

While *losing* money was an acceptable risk that was riding on every business adventure, the possible consequence of *not having* any money fundamentally contradicted the American doctrine of "the duty of the individual toward the increase of his capital".[15] In a society that was, probably more than any other, impregnated by both a *Protestant Ethic and the Spirit of Capitalism*, as Max Weber famously claimed, financial failure posed not only an economic problem, but also an ethical and even a juridical one: wealth was interpreted as a sign of predestination, while bankruptcy, the most detrimental outcome of financial failure, constituted a criminal offence that lead to substantial prison time until 1833.[16] "The merchant obviously believes the State street proverb that nobody fails who ought not to fail", Ralph Waldo Emerson wrote in his journal in 1842, "[t]here is always a reason, *in the man*, for his good or bad fortune, and so in making money."[17] And a later edition of Noah Webster's dictionary, published posthumously in 1857, offered an adjusted definition of

14 Outlined in greater detail in Irvin G. Wyllie's pivotal study on *The Self-Made Men in America. The Myth of Rags to Riches*. Rutgers UP: New Brunswick 1954.

15 Weber, Max: *The Protestant Ethic and the Spirit of Capitalism*. Routledge: London, New York 2005, p. 17.

16 Over the course of the 19th century, a number of bankruptcy acts were approved and repealed shortly afterwards. It was not until the Act of 1841 that entrepreneurs were granted the right of voluntary bankruptcy and debt relief for the first time, a possibility that had not existed previously as legislation had mainly been focusing on creditors' rights. Cf. Campbell Black, Henry: *A Treatise on the Law and Practice of Bankruptcy. Under the Act of Congress of 1898*. Vol. 1. Beard Books: Washington, D.C. 2000, p. 1.

17 Emerson, Ralph Waldo: *Journals and Miscellaneous Notebooks of Ralph Waldo Emerson*, quoted after Sandage, p. 46. Italics Sandage's own.

failure: "some weakness in a man's character, disposition, or habit".[18] In the early 1800s, Americans 'made failures', as Sandage[19] points out – an expression that implied a potential individual contribution, a mistake for example, but did not extend to the subject as such. By the end of the century, however, '*being* a failure' had become a metaphor for financial fiasco and total loss, for a profound and irredeemable ineptitude.

Failures in the Office

It is not surprising, then, that the semantic shift from a term for a sudden omission or cessation to an idiom describing a person that doesn't work properly occurred in the context of – work. Stripped off its original meaning, 'to be a failure' is today, more than anything, a biographical category, but it still implies the unexplained absence of a performance that was expected: performance in life and, inseparably, always also performance at work.[20]

Although the risk of underperforming (or not performing at all) is not limited to a specific professional field, there is a certain type of worker that is, at least as far as 19th century literature is concerned, especially likely to think of himself or herself (typically 'himself') or to be thought of by others as a failure: the white-collar worker, the office clerk, or the worker who is included in the notoriously difficult to translate German term *Angestellte*.[21] Until today, people who do not 'work' but

18 Webster, Noah: An Explanatory and Pronouncing Dictionary of the English Language, with Synonyms, quoted after Sandage, p. 12.

19 Sandage, p. 11.

20 As a biographical category, the concept of 'being a failure' does not follow any objective standards of judgment. Whether or not someone's life might be seen as a failure very much depends on social circumstances (financial background, family education level etc.) and on goals and expectation that are being set accordingly. While not getting into a top school, for example, might lead to a feeling of 'being a failure' for some, for many first-generation academics it most likely will not.

21 Generally speaking, *Angestellte* are private-sector employees whereas *Beamte* work in public institutions, although the two do intersect frequently. While there has been an ever-continuing sociological discussion around defining characteristics of *Angestellte* – they tend to be middle-class brain workers, yet a High Street sales assistant is *angestellt*, too –, there seems to be quite a clear cultural iconography surrounding the term: In films or TV series (*The Office*

'labour'[22] are less prone to 'being a failure' – thanks to what Marx called the alienation from the products of their labour and, ultimately, from their labour as activity itself:

> Labour's realisation is its objectification. Under these economic conditions this realisation of labour appears as *loss of realisation* for the workers; objectification as *loss of the object and bondage to it*; appropriation as *estrangement*, as *alienation*. [...] [T]he worker is related to the *product of his labour* as to an *alien* object. [...] Whatever the product of his labour is, he is not.[23]

While labourers are, according to Marx, indeed instruments used for production, and therefore much more closely related to the idea of a dysfunctional tool or device than office clerks are, they generally do not identify with their work or its product. *Being* a failure in its most literal sense, however, requires just that: a good amount of personal (yet often involuntary) involvement with one's own work, so much so that professional failure extends to every other aspect of life, and eventually to one's whole existence as such.

It is striking how often early literary texts that centre on their protagonist's being a failure, usually from the second half of the 19th

---

and its German adaption *Stromberg* come to mind), *Angestellte* work in an office, usually wearing some sort of business attire and being concerned with a more or less intellectual type of task. For a more detailed description, see Siegfried Kracauer's famous 1930 study on *Angestellte* as a then (relatively) novel group of workers: Kracauer, Siegfried: *Die Angestellten. Aus dem neuesten Deutschland.* Suhrkamp: Frankfurt a. M. 1971.

22 Raymond Williams describes how 'labour', a term that originally referred to all kinds of productive work, "came to mean that element of production which in combination with capital and materials produced commodities" in the 19th century. Until today, terms and expressions such as 'labour costs' or 'labour movement', which go back to the Marxist tradition, imply "the specializations of the capitalist period". Williams, Raymond: *Keywords. A Vocabulary of Culture and Society.* Oxford UP: Oxford, New York 2015, pp. 128, 131. In more recent academic critiques of work in contemporary society, however, some authors have opted to use 'work' and 'labour' interchangeably in order not to essentialize the very conception of work they want to call into question. Cf. Weeks, Kathi: *The Problem with Work. Feminism, Marxism, Antiwork Politics, and Postwar Imaginaries.* Duke UP: Durham, London 2011, p. 15.

23 Marx, Karl: *Economic and Philosophic Manuscripts of 1844.* Progress Publishers: Moscow 1974, pp. 63–64. Italics in the original.

century, are concerned with the specific work environment of the office and the specific form of subjectification it entails. Alfonso Nitti, for example, the protagonist of Italo Svevo's 1892 novel *Una vita* ("A life"),[24] whose being a failure is already alluded to through his last name,[25] leaves his rural hometown to pursue a career in a bank in Trieste, one of the most important commercial cities of the Habsburg Empire. As a small accountant, Alfonso has to copy balance sheets and letters day in and day out, lacking both talent and interest for his job. He is physically unable to write for as long as he is expected to. His hand gets tired quickly, and, what is more, he is intellectually unable to focus on his copy and to keep copying without making mistakes. His failure to do so is often referred to in stunningly mechanistic terms. The narrator, who is especially critical of his main character's undertakings, affirms that Alfonso "did not know how to copy mechanically",[26] but also connects his (non-)achievements at work to a more fundamental problem, akin to Webster's "total defect": his body, the alleged cause of his poor performance, is described as inexplicably

24 Svevo, Italo: *Una vita*. In: *Opera Omnia II. Romanzi*. Ed. Maier, Bruno. Dall'Oglio: Milano 1969, pp. 131–426. Indicated pages will refer to the Italian edition, all translations my own.

25 'Nitti' is reminiscent of both the Italian word *niente* ('nothing') and its German equivalent *nichts* or *nix*, as Victor Brombert has pointed out, cf. Brombert, Victor: *In Praise of Antiheroes. Figures and Themes in Modern European Literature 1830–1980*. University of Chicago Press: Chicago 2001, p. 62. The fact that Alfonso's name relates to both languages is no coincidence: Svevo, born to a Jewish family as Aaron Hector Schmitz in the then Habsburgian town of Trieste, grew up with the local Venetian dialect as his mother tongue. At the age of twelve, he was sent to a boarding school near Würzburg (Bavaria) in order to learn German, a language his father considered important for his future career in trade. He did not speak Standard Italian, the language he would eventually write his three novels in, until he was an adult – a fact he acknowledged in his pseudonym Italo Svevo, which translates to 'Italian Swabian'. Svevo's literary work famously combines the various linguistic and cultural influences he encountered, to the point of being deemed an outsider within Italian literature itself. In this respect, his take on office workers may be seen as representative for Central Europe in a broader sense, not just for one specific country. For a more in-depth account of Svevo's intellectual formation, see Camerino, Giuseppe A.: *Italo Svevo e la crisi della Mitteleuropa. Edizione ampliata e completamente riveduta*. (Critica e letteratura 34). Liguori: Napoli 2002, pp. 9–76.

26 Svevo 1969, p. 140.

weak,[27] and even though Alfonso spends most of his free time trying to strengthen it, the results of his efforts leave much to be desired. There is no diagnosable illness and therefore no cure: "It wasn't the good will that he was lacking", the narrator states, "it was the capacity; his defect was an organic one".[28] Alfonso does not fail – he *is* a failure in his very existence.

Consequently, what started off as a very specific form of non-performance – as the failure to copy mechanically –, soon expands to Alfonso's whole life. Despite his obvious lack of talent and the fact that he dreads his job, Alfonso is left with no other choice than continuing to do it; for financial reasons on the one hand, but also and more importantly because it seems to be critical to the future he envisions for himself within Triestine bourgeois society. He must succeed at his role in the bank in order to one day be able to do a more suitable kind of work, preferably as an author. In the meantime, his only chance to not only progress within the hierarchy of the bank, but to eventually progress *out of* the hierarchy of the bank is Signor Maller, his employer and only connection to the city's upper class, who regularly invites his employees to his salon events, weekly gatherings from which Alfonso hopes to benefit in his attempt to climb the social ladder. In the beginning, the evenings at Casa Maller do indeed work in Alfonso's favour, so much so that Annetta, Maller's daughter, wants him to marry her. At least at this point of Alfonso's 'career', the comparison the text draws on several occasions between Alfonso and some of literature's greatest parvenus – Stendhal's Julien Sorel, for example – seems apt.[29] Over the course of the novel, however, it becomes increasingly clear that Alfonso's failure to perform his tasks in the office results in his failure to ascend not only in the bank, but also in society more generally: Maller and Annetta as well as most of his colleagues and salon acquaintances have eventually come to think poorly of him and his capacities, and the only way left

---

27 Cf. ibid., p. 181.

28 Ibid., p. 180.

29 Besides Stendhal's *Le Rouge et le Noir*, *Una vita* also references Maupassant's *Bel Ami*, cf. Micali, Simona: *Asceso e declino del "uomo di lusso". Il romanzo dell'intellettuale nell'Italia Nuova e i suoi modelli europei*. Le Monnier: Firenze 2008, esp. pp. 194–196.

for Alfonso to redeem himself is through the work he has already been doing unsuccessfully. Alfonso, who finally accepts his being a failure in the eyes of the Triestine bourgeois society, ends up killing himself; he dies an *inetto*, an inapt person, a term so fitting for Alfonso's fate that Svevo originally wanted to use it as the title of his novel.[30]

Copyists like Alfonso may be the quintessential incarnation of the office worker. Their work mainly consists of handwriting copies, an inherently unoriginal activity that is at the same time an inherently unique manifestation of the subject itself. In other words, it is a form of alienated labour that tends to disrupt any alienation between the worker and his work: a failure to copy documents adequately despite one's best efforts is almost automatically also a failure of the subject, and all the more so because the task does not require the subject to author anything original on his own. Even though Alfonso does not like his job and has never really wanted it in the first place, he actually does, at least to a certain extent, identify with it. His failure to copy is *not just* a failure of his tired hands; rather, his poor performance at work is seen as a symptom of a more general and more fundamental ineptitude, not only by his boss or colleagues, but eventually also by himself. At the same time, however, the work Alfonso – or any office worker – is supposed to be doing is always imposed upon him from the outside. Office workers by definition deal with institutional requirements and restraints; they always live up to or fall short of external expectations, and while every failure is perceived as the failure of the worker himself, success is never his own but the success of the company. The concept of being a failure is thus based on a peculiar relation between personal input and impersonal output, a specific form of subjectification that makes the worker invest more and more personal effort, that makes him get better at what he is doing, while only offering the prospect of not being socially negated as a reward.

30 Cf. Svevo, Italo: *Opera Omnia III: Racconti, Saggi, Pagine Sparse*. Ed. Maier, Bruno. Dall'Oglio: Milano 1968, p. 802. The word *inetto* shares its etymology with the English 'inapt'; both are derived from the Latin *in-aptus*.

Bartleby's Non-Functioning, Bartleby's Non-Failing

Alfonso Nitti, the unlucky accountant who would rather not copy, has a famous ancestor: Bartleby, the scrivener who "would prefer not to".[31] Herman Melville's short story was first published in 1853, some forty years before Svevo's *Una vita*, and prefigured, maybe even established a whole genre of literature centring on white-collar workers, office clerks, and small accountants that was to become popular in the decades to follow. Just like Alfonso, Bartleby works in finance (or, more precisely, at a law office on Wall Street), just like Alfonso he is a copyist – and just like Alfonso, he does not perform as expected. Over the course of the story, Bartleby simply ceases to write, explained only by the notorious formula he recites with a stoic politeness and "in a singularly mild, firm voice",[32] until he eventually ceases to do anything at all and starves to death. But while Alfonso's suicide acknowledges and reaffirms his being a failure, Bartleby's death seems to belong to a whole different order of resistance, one to which Alfonso never gains any access. Bartleby is not a failure in the sense that is discussed in this paper, a fact which is almost unnecessary to point out in light of his recent lionization by anti-capitalist groups.[33] At the same time, however, the story of Bartleby, who works under circumstances that are extremely similar to those of Alfonso, still articulates the modern idea of 'being a failure' – even more so, perhaps, by playfully disrupting it.

At the outset of the story, even before addressing the title character's arrival at the office and the strange events it brings, the lawyer, who serves as a first-person narrator, spends several paragraphs musing on the inadequacies and incapacities of his regular staff, thereby establishing the problem of his employees' functioning and functionality as one of the text's central concerns. Turkey, an elderly Englishman, is unable to work

---

31 Melville, Herman: "Bartleby, the Scrivener. A Story of Wall Street". In: *The Piazza Tales and Other Prose Pieces 1839–1860*. Ed. Hayford, Harrison / Macdougall, Alma / Tanselle, Thomas. Northwestern UP: Evanston, Chicago 1987, pp. 13–45. Bartleby recites his formula as many as seventeen times.

32 Ibid., p. 40.

33 Occupy Wall Street, for example, based many of their claims on Melville's short story, cf. Edelman, Lee: "Occupy Wall Street. 'Bartleby' against the Humanities". *History of the Present* 3(1), 2013, pp. 99–118.

in the afternoon, as the lawyer points out using diction that is strikingly informed by discourses of thermodynamics and energy:

> In the morning, one might say, his face was of a fine florid hue, but after twelve o'clock, meridian – his dinner hour – it blazed like a grate full of Christmas coals; [...] exactly when Turkey displayed his fullest beams from his red and radiant countenance, just then, too, at that critical moment, began the daily period when I considered his business capacities so seriously disturbed for the remainder of the twenty-four hours. [...] The difficulty was, he was apt to be altogether too energetic. There was a strange, inflamed, flurried, flighty recklessness of activity about him. [...] [H]is face flamed with augmented blazonry, as if cannel coal had been heaped on anthracite.[34]

While Turkey's performance cannot be trusted in the afternoon (a fact that is not unrelated to his wine consumption during lunch break, as the narrator later concedes), his ambitious younger colleague Nippers is being tormented by the opposite problem. Because of digestive issues he is unable to function properly in the mornings; unlike Turkey, he does not suffer from a "strange, inflamed, flurried, flighty recklessness of activity" but rather from a complete lack of any (bowel) activity whatsoever. As neither of the two copyists is able to perform to the lawyer's full satisfaction and the uncopied documents keep piling up, the lawyer-narrator decides to hire a third[35] clerk: Bartleby, who, "[i]n answer to [an] advertisement", stands "upon the threshold of [his] office"[36] one morning and will not leave.

During his first few days at the office, Bartleby lives up to the lawyer's expectations, copying at an unmatched pace, unceasingly and tirelessly so:

> At first, Bartleby did an extraordinary quantity of writing. As if long famishing for something to copy, he seemed to gorge himself on my documents. There was no pause for digestion. He ran a day and night line, copying by sun-light and by candle-light. I should have been quite delighted with his application, had he been cheerfully industrious. But he wrote on silently, palely, mechanically.[37]

34 Melville 1987a, p. 15.

35 In fact, there is a third employee from the beginning: Ginger Nut, a twelve-year-old who runs errands – and is not given any copying assignment.

36 Melville 1987a, p.15.

37 Ibid., p. 19.

This passage, the first one to describe Bartleby's performance at work, implicitly compares the three clerks to each other. As opposed to his colleagues, Bartleby seems to be functioning flawlessly, "mechanically" even, and as opposed to his colleagues he seems to be enjoying good health, displaying no symptoms of inebriety or digestive problems. Quite to the contrary: his new employee, who lives on a handful of ginger nuts a day and never leaves his desk to eat or sleep, "seemed to gorge himself on my documents", as the lawyer recalls in noticeable disbelief, "famishing for something to copy". As a figure of thirdness, Bartleby compensates Turkey's and Nippers' incapacities through his own efficiency; his "application" – a term that is often used in connection with devices or tools – is carried out without any human trace, but also, as the narrator states, without any hint of emotion or joy. Bartleby acts, quite literally, as a copying machine. In his writing, the difference between life and work and between man and machine is suspended; his whole life is subjected to the logic of mechanical function – he himself *has become* that very function.

It is no coincidence, then, that he works as a copyist, of all professions. While in Svevo's *Una vita*, the literary trope of copying is used to negotiate matters of originality and, more precisely, the complex tension between personal input and impersonal output that comes with being a clerk, Bartleby withdraws from the idea of the original (the opposite of imitation or duplication, and the very premise of copying) as such. It is only once mentioned in the story – in its most crucial moment: just when the lawyer asks his scrivener to "verify the accuracy of the copy, word by word",[38] making him compare his work to the original, Bartleby utters his famous formula for the first time. He might be copying with the utmost precision and efficiency, but, in accordance with his "application", he simply does not do anything else. He is so profoundly immersed in his self-sufficient activity, which is not based on anything and not aimed at anything either,[39] that the original needs to be omitted in order for him to perform.

This first "I would prefer not to" is followed by multiple other occasions in which Bartleby does not perform the tasks he is given – usually tasks

38 Ibid., p. 20.
39 Cf. Mainberger, Sabine: Schriftskepsis. Von Philosophen, Mönchen, Buchhaltern, Kalligraphen. Fink: München 1995, p. 192.

that go beyond sheer copying –, until he ceases to work altogether, without any further explanation. On a linguistic level, the machine-like nature of his failure is reflected by the intransitivity of his formula, which seems to constitute a refusal at first glance, but in fact suspends any grammatical or semantic reference, as Gilles Deleuze has pointed out:

> It has been noted that the formula, I prefer not to, is neither an affirmation nor a negation. […] The attorney would be relieved if Bartleby did not want to, but Bartleby does not refuse, he simply rejects a nonpreferred (the proofreading, the errands…). And he does not accept either, he does not affirm a presence that would consist in continuing to copy, he simply posits its impossibility. […] [T]he formula that successively refuses every other act has already engulfed the act of copying, which it no longer even needs to refuse. The formula is devastating because it eliminates the preferable just as mercilessly as anything non-preferred. It not only abolishes the term it refers to, and that it rejects, but also abolishes the other term it seemed to preserve […]. All particularity, all reference is abolished.[40]

Bartleby's "I would prefer not to" turns out not to be a refusal or a preference, which would have indicated a personal affectedness or involvement. He does not prefer one thing over the other but omits the grammatical object which the transitive verb 'to prefer *to*' requires – he just prefers, intransitively. Bartleby, who seemed to be the epitome of a clerk who does what is expected from him in the beginning, now exhibits what it means to radically stay true to this demand. In the extent to which Bartleby is equivalent to his function, his failure is that of a function or a machine as well: as a copying machine that fails inexplicably (or so it seems), he exposes the intransitive logic of functioning behind the transitive logic of employed, dependent work.

In this sense, Bartleby's not *being* a failure is facilitated by his almost non-human demeanour – and, paradoxically, by the fact that he does indeed fail in the way a tool, a device, or a machine would. After Bartleby has uttered his "I would prefer not to" for the first time, the lawyer asks "You *will* not?",[41] and Bartleby replies, in what Giorgio Agamben has

---

40 Deleuze, Gilles: "Bartleby; or, The Formula". In: *Essays Critical and Clinical.* University of Minnesota Press: Minneapolis 1997, pp. 68–90, here p. 70–71. Deleuze's reading of *Bartleby* is based on Phillipe Jaworski's study on *Melville. Le désert et l'empire.* Presses de l'École Normale Supérieure: Paris 1986, esp. p. 19.

41 Melville 1987a, p. 35. Italics in the original.

described as an effort to "eliminate all traces of the word 'will' ",[42] and therefore all traces of desire, emotion, or transitive action: "I prefer not." In his machine-like intransitivity, he cannot become affected by any sort of external expectation, or, for that matter, by the disappointment of not meeting it. It seems impossible to attribute any intrinsic quality or attitude to this pale, nondescript scrivener: no preference or refusal, and no individual incapacity or failure either.

Yet the lawyer-narrator is trying to do just that, in a desperate attempt to explain his employee's startling behaviour. Asked about the reasons for his sudden non-copying, Bartleby says: "Do you not *see* the reason for yourself?"[43] The narrator thereupon concludes his scrivener might suffer from eye problems:

> I looked steadfastly at him, and perceived that his eyes looked dull and glazed. Instantly it occurred to me, that his unexampled diligence in copying by his dim window for the first few weeks of his stay with me might have temporarily impaired his vision.[44]

Bartleby does not comment on the lawyer's hermeneutical short circuit or the bodily disfunction it alleges. When the narrator finally has to concede that his interpretation is as inaccurate as all the others he has already come up with before, he is left with one last default explanation: "Bartleby was billeted upon me for some mysterious purpose of an all-wise Providence, which it was not for a mere mortal like me to fathom."[45] Bartleby's monolithic formula is so unfathomable to the lawyer that not only do the events in his office start to slip out of his control, their interpretation does as well. At one point, he realizes that Bartleby's "I would prefer not to" has infiltrated the way he and his other clerks speak ("Somehow, of late I had got into the way of involuntarily using this word 'prefer' upon all sorts of not exactly suitable occasions"[46]), yet at the same time, the formula

42 Agamben, Giorgio: "Bartleby, or on Contingency". In: *Potentialities. Collected Essays in Philosophy*. Ed. Heller-Roazen, Daniel. Stanford UP: Stanford 1999, pp. 243–271, here p. 254.
43 Melville 1987a, p. 32. Italics my own.
44 Ibid.
45 Ibid., p. 37.
46 Ibid., p. 31.

remains mysterious and indistinct to him and thus triggers a "congestion of signifiers".[47] Bartleby's failure to copy and the lawyer's failure to understand its reasons eventually result in an even more fundamental semiotic failure that disrupts the relation between the signifier and the signified, voiding all conventional mechanisms of signification and compromising the lawyer's ability to tell the story of what happened in his office as a consequence.

In this respect, it is ultimately the lawyer-narrator himself who is pushed to the brink of failure in the modern sense of the word, not only regarding the way he is dealing with Bartleby's non-copying, but also and above all in the act of narrating as such. He is constantly struggling to find the right words to make sense of something that cannot be made sense of. And while in Svevo's novel the story of Alfonso Nitti's unremarkable life is being told, as the title *Una vita* already indicates, almost nothing is known about Bartleby's biography. "While of other law-copyists I might write the complete life", the narrator admits at the very beginning of the text, "of Bartleby nothing of that sort can be done. I believe that no material exists for a full and satisfactory biography of this man."[48] This confession underscores the most radical consequence of Bartleby's "I would prefer not to": impervious to any attribution or ascription, impervious even to any description, he undermines all attempts of a *biographein*, all attempts to write his life and, therefore, all attempts to judge his life as well. As a figure of "universal suspension",[49] Bartleby escapes all biographic paradigms of success and failure.

Yet while *Bartleby, the Scrivener* might not be a text that centres on its protagonist's being a failure (quite the opposite, in fact), it certainly is a text that was written against the backdrop of mid-19th-century failure discourse in America – a discourse Melville was observing avidly, as another short prose piece of his shows. *The Happy Failure*, published one year after *Bartleby* in 1854, is a parable revolving around success and failure in

47 Matala de Mazza, Ethel: "Angestelltenverhältnisse. Sekretäre und ihre Literatur". In: Siegert, Bernhard / Vogl, Joseph (eds.): *Europa. Kultur der Sekretäre.* diaphanes: Zürich, Berlin 2003, pp. 127–146, here p. 145. Translation my own.
48 Melville 1987a, p. 13.
49 Mainberger, p. 193.

life.[50] The first-person narrator, a teenage boy, joins his uncle to witness the debut of an invention the elderly man had been working on for the past ten years: the "Great Hydraulic-Hydrostatic Apparatus for draining swamps and marshes".[51] Through this machine, the uncle hopes to finally gain the "immortal renown" he has been striving for all of his life, maybe even "the glory denied to a Roman emperor. He tried to drain the Pontine marsh, but failed."[52] In order to prevent "some malignant spy [to] steal from me the fruits of ten long years of high-hearted, persevering endeavor",[53] the uncle has his slave Yorpy and his teenage nephew ship the apparatus to a remote river island, where he wants to unveil his invention for the first time. But once the uncle tries to set the machine in motion, it does not work as expected: "Nothing could be more sure than that some anticipated effect had, as yet, failed to develop itself", the first-person narrator states; "it was plain something or other was going wrong".[54] They try again,

> and as no perceptible effect yet followed, I was each moment looking for the previous command to tip the box over yet more, when, glancing at my uncle's face, I started aghast. It seemed pinched, shriveled into mouldy whiteness, like a mildewed grape. I dropped the box, and sprang toward him just in time to prevent his fall.[55]

Yet on their way back from the island, the narrator suddenly realises how "swiftly the current now swept us down" compared to "[h]ow hardly before [we had] striven to stem it", while the uncle, devasted at first, eventually acknowledges he had been striving for the wrong thing all along ("Boy, take my advice, and never try to invent anything but – happiness") and concludes: "I'm glad I've failed. I say, boy, failure has made a good old man of me."[56]

---

50 Melville, Herman: "The Happy Failure. A Story of the River Hudson". In: *The Piazza Tales and Other Prose Pieces 1839–1860*. Ed. Hayford, Harrison / Macdougall, Alma / Tanselle, Thomas. Northwestern UP: Evanston, Chicago 1987, pp. 245–261.

51 Ibid., p. 255.

52 Ibid., p. 256.

53 Ibid.

54 Ibid., p. 259.

55 Ibid., p. 260.

56 Ibid.

Melville's parable about a failing machine and failure in life condenses and continues one of the key themes of *Bartleby, the Scrivener*: the tension between ambition and the desire to renounce. For while Bartleby has mastered the art of renunciation in the most refined way, the lawyer-narrator himself, who is weirdly fascinated by his new scrivener's behaviour, seems to be secretly dreaming of doing the same thing. His law office is concerned with "rich men's bonds and mortgages and title-deeds".[57] Therefore, he is surrounded by successful businessmen, the late John Jacob Astor being one of them, as he mentions several times, and although he does not want to "speak in vanity" about his relationship to his famous acquaintance, he does "love to repeat" his name, "for it hath a rounded and orbicular sound to it".[58] Right at the beginning of the text, he also complains about the abolition of the New York Court of Chancery at which he had held the office of a Master of Chancery: "It was not a very arduous office, but pleasantly remunerative."[59] He makes it very clear that he had "counted upon a life-lease of profits, whereas I only received those of a short few years".[60] At the same time, the lawyer introduces himself as "a man, who, from his youth upwards, has been filled with the profound conviction that the easiest way of life is the best" and claims to be "one of those unambitious lawyers who never addresses a jury, or in any way draws down public applause".[61] While he is certainly "not insensible"[62] to money and may even be eager to succeed, he cannot help but admire Bartleby's non-performance.

Being a failure in neoliberal societies

When we talk about somebody being a failure today, we do not think of copyists or scriveners, and probably not even of clerks or employees in general. Yet the idea of 'being a failure' is still very much connected to the concept of work – albeit to a concept of work that has changed

---

57 Melville 1987a, p. 14.
58 Ibid.
59 Ibid.
60 Ibid.
61 Ibid.
62 Ibid.

and broadened over the last century, and within the last three decades especially. The German sociologist Ulrich Bröckling has identified what he calls a "hegemony of entrepreneurial subjectification"[63] in contemporary Western societies. Being an entrepreneur, he claims, has developed into far more than just a profession – rather, it is seen as a prerequisite for any kind of (social) success:

> An entrepreneur is something we are supposed to become. The call to act as an entrepreneur of one's own life produces a model for people to understand what they are and what they ought to be, and it tells them how to work on the self in order to become what they ought to be.[64]

According to Bröckling, an entrepreneurial mindset is something we are set to strive for, regardless of our actual day jobs: As entrepreneurial subjects, we weigh every potential action in terms of revenue and expenses and 'work' every waking hour – on our careers first and foremost, but also on romantic relationships[65] and friendships, on health and appearance, on well-being and relaxation, on our very bodies.

The discursive shift from focusing on the "entrepreneur within the enterprise" to "presenting the individual *as* the enterprise"[66] can be traced back to the 1990s, when self-help books with titles such as *You & Co* or *Life Entrepreneur* propagated entrepreneurship as the only viable "attitude to life".[67] It is no coincidence, then, that the 1990s also saw the individualization of the corporate 'failure culture' I described at the beginning of this paper. People who think like entrepreneurs have got to fail like them, too: nothing ventured, nothing gained, neither in business nor in life.

Contrary to what Silicon Valley start-up founders want to make us believe, though, in contemporary Western societies individual failure is rarely perceived as being connected to productivity or creativity, and it has little to do with the heroic fight against all odds which they claim to

---

63 Bröckling, Ulrich: *The Entrepreneurial Self. Fabricating a New Type of Subject.* Sage: London 2015, p. ix.

64 Ibid., p. iix.

65 For a closer look on how love has become subject to capitalist ideas of success, see Illouz, Eva: *Cold Intimacies. The Making of Emotional Capitalism.* Polity: Cambridge 2007.

66 Bröckling, p. 31.

67 Ibid., p. 32.

have fought. Instead, it is more often perceived as the banal but all the more existential kind of failure to which I dedicated the bigger part of my paper: as an underperformance, an underachievement, a non-functioning even in the most basic areas of life. This is mostly due to the very nature of today's broadened scope of 'work' and the notions of subjectification, in(transitivity), and ascription it carries: We work *on* our selves, our work is, similarly to that of Alfonso Nitti, an inherently unique manifestation of subjectivity, something we are inseparably intertwined with and defined by, yet something that is at the same time – in one way or the other – imposed upon us from the outside. Apart from just professional work, then, there are many other fields in which a person may fail – dating, or parenting, or ultimately also just living as such. More often than not, 'failing' today still implies 'not working properly', both in the early mechanistic sense of the expression and in the contemporary sense of modelling one's own self. And even though successful entrepreneurs like Zach Klein promise it will always be *it* that fails, not *us*, our contemporary conception of work suggests that we through our selves and in ourselves might be the ones who do not work or cannot work, the ones who *are failures*. While our idea of 'work' may have changed, our idea of *not working* has largely remained the same.

References

Agamben, Giorgio: "Bartleby, or on Contingency". In: *Potentialities. Collected Essays in Philosophy*. Ed. Heller-Roazen, Daniel. Stanford UP: Stanford 1999, pp. 243–271.

Allen, Paul: "My Favorite Mistake. Paul Allen". *Newsweek*, 24.4.2011, retrieved 4.4.2020, from https://www.newsweek.com/my-favorite-mistake-paul-allen-66489.

Backer, Georges de: *Dictionnaire de Proverbes François, avec l'Explication de leur Significations, et une partie de leur Origine*. George de Backer: Bruxelles 1710.

Böckling, Ulrich: *The Entrepreneurial Self. Fabricating a New Type of Subject*. Sage: London 2015.

Brombert, Victor: *In Praise of Antiheroes. Figures and Themes in Modern European Literature 1830–1980*. University of Chicago Press: Chicago 2001.

Camerino, Giuseppe A.: *Italo Svevo e la crisi della Mitteleuropa. Edizione ampliata e completamente riveduta*. (Critica e letteratura 34). Liguori: Napoli 2002.

Campbell Black, Henry: *A Treatise on the Law and Practice of Bankruptcy. Under the Act of Congress of 1898*. Vol. 1. Beard Books: Washington, D.C. 2000.

Christensen, Tanner: "What it really means to fail". *Creative Something*, 29.8.2013, retrieved 4.4.2020, from https://creativesomething.net/post/59676599532/what-it-really-means-to-fail.

Deleuze, Gilles: "Bartleby; or, The Formula". In: *Essays Critical and Clinical*. University of Minnesota Press: Minneapolis 1997, pp. 68–90.

Edelman, Lee: "Occupy Wall Street. 'Bartleby' against the Humanities". *History of the Present* 3(1), 2013, pp. 99–118.

Grimm, Jacob and Wilhelm: *Deutsches Wörterbuch*. Vol. 25. Ed. Deutsche Akademie der Wissenschaften Berlin. dtv: München 1984.

Illouz, Eva: *Cold Intimacies. The Making of Emotional Capitalism*. Polity: Cambridge 2007.

Jaworski, Phillipe: *Melville. Le désert et l'empire*. Presses de l'École Normale Supérieure: Paris 1986.

Kracauer, Siegfried: *Die Angestellten. Aus dem neuesten Deutschland*. Suhrkamp: Frankfurt a. M. 1971.

Mainberger, Sabine: *Schriftskepsis. Von Philosophen, Mönchen, Buchhaltern, Kalligraphen*. Fink: München 1995.

Marx, Karl: *Economic and Philosophic Manuscripts of 1844*. Progress Publishers: Moscow 1974.

Melville, Herman: "Bartleby, the Scrivener. A Story of Wall Street". In: *The Piazza Tales and Other Prose Pieces 1839–1860*. Ed. Hayford, Harrison / Macdougall, Alma / Tanselle, Thomas. Northwestern UP: Evanston, Chicago 1987, pp. 13–45.

Melville, Herman: "The Happy Failure. A Story of the River Hudson". In: *The Piazza Tales and Other Prose Pieces 1839–1860*. Ed. Hayford, Harrison / Macdougall, Alma / Tanselle, Thomas. Northwestern UP: Evanston, Chicago 1987, pp. 245–261.

Matala de Mazza, Ethel: "Angestelltenverhältnisse. Sekretäre und ihre Literatur". In: Siegert, Bernhard / Vogl, Joseph (eds.): *Europa. Kultur der Sekretäre*. diaphanes: Zürich, Berlin 2003, pp. 127–146.

Micali, Simona: Asceso e declino del "uomo di lusso". *Il romanzo dell'intellettuale nell'Italia Nuova e i suoi modelli europei*. Le Monnier: Firenze 2008.

Müller, Ingo: *A History of Thermodynamics. The Doctrine of Energy and Entropy*. Springer: Berlin 2007.

Rothbard, Murray N.: *The Panic of 1819. Reactions and Policies*. Columbia UP: New York, London 1962.

Rüstow, Caesar: *Die Kriegshandfeuerwaffen. Eine genaue Darstellung ihrer Einrichtung in den europäischen Armeen, ihrer Anfertigung, ihres Gebrauchs und ihrer allmäligen Entwickelung*. Vol. 2. Bath: Berlin 1864.

Sandage, Scott. A.: *Born Losers. A History of Failure in America*. Harvard UP: Cambridge, London 2006.

Schmitt, Arbogast: "Menschliches Fehlen und tragisches Scheitern. Zur Handlungsmotivation im Sophokleischen 'König Ödipus' ". *Rheinisches Museum für Philologie* 131, 1988, pp. 8–30.

Svevo, Italo: *Opera Omnia III: Racconti, Saggi, Pagine Sparse*. Ed. Maier, Bruno. Dall'Oglio: Milano 1968.

Svevo, Italo: *Una vita*. In: *Opera Omnia II. Romanzi*. Ed. Maier, Bruno. Dall'Oglio: Milano 1969.

Weber, Max: The Protestant Ethic and the Spirit of Capitalism. Routledge: London, New York 2005.

Webster, Noah: *Webster's Dictionary 1828. Online Edition*. Retrieved 4.4.2020, from http://webstersdictionary1828.com/Dictionary/failure.

Weeks, Kathi: *The Problem with Work. Feminism, Marxism, Antiwork Politics, and Postwar Imaginaries*. Duke UP: Durham, London 2011

Williams, Raymond: *Keywords. A Vocabulary of Culture and Society*. Oxford UP: Oxford, New York 2015.

Wyllie, Irvin G.: *The Self-Made Men in America. The Myth of Rags to Riches*. Rutgers UP: New Brunswick 1954.

Aileen Behrendt

Against the Capitalist Narrative of Success and Failure – the Precarious Lives of Jean Rhys's Interwar Women

Abstract: *Rhys's interwar novels all portray the lives of destitute women, populating the big European cities in the 1930s. Constantly pressed for money, her heroines are forced to occupy precarious social positions as vagabonds, which only perpetuates their emotional and economic bankruptcy. As a result, they lack the resources to resist such injustice. Unimpressed by capitalist promises of work and wages as the bringer of happiness, her texts reveal the significant constructivist efforts behind this ideology. In this paper, I explore how Rhys's interwar novels thus challenge the capitalist narrative of success and failure, the economic imperative of growth and progress as well as the concept of rewarding work.*

Keywords: Jean Rhys, liquid modernity, Zygmunt Bauman, tourists and vagabonds, precarious work, women and work, interwar years, British women writers.

In the nineteenth-century, working women, especially factory girls, captured the imagination of Victorian writers and social critics like Charles Dickens or Elizabeth Gaskell. These women were often portrayed either as the tragic victims of labour conditions, or as low-lives and prostitutes. Early twentieth-century literature continued this exploration of women and work, but the concerns went beyond questions of morality when women started entering a more middle-class labour market. This proved to be a potential threat to the social status quo, which established working women as a new figure in modern literature and produced different representational strategies and tropes to contain them. Female characters who worked were often portrayed as a curious but marginal phenomenon, at odds with the social as well as with the economic world. Therefore, these representations can be used to interrogate gendered social and economic constructions of (paid) labour. In her monograph *Femina Oeconomica*, Franziska Schößler writes:

> Zwar bleibt weibliche Arbeit insbesondere in der kanonischen Literatur der bürgerlichen Moderne bis in das 20. Jahrhundert hinein häufig ein Randphänomen, weil die Grenzziehungen des binären Gender-Programms fortgeschrieben und der Ausschluss von Frauen aus der Lohnarbeit reproduziert werden. Nicht zuletzt dadurch aber geben literarische Texte Aufschluss über die Vergeschlechtlichung von Tätigkeiten sowie die Asymmetrien in der Verteilung von Kapital und Anerkennung, die sich mit der Ideologie der bürgerlichen Geschlechterordnung und dem Siegeszug der Lohnarbeit im 19. Jahrhundert einstellen.[1]

In contrast to Hermann Melville's famous short story "Bartleby, the Scrivener: A Story of Wall Street" (1853), whose deliberate non-engagement gives him significant agency when he refuses to perform his duties as law office clerk and thus disrupts the run of the entire workplace, female employees seem to face different struggles in literature. It is striking that even though after World War I female typists largely replaced male office clerks,[2] there seem to be no female Bartlebian typists in literature. Instead one encounters such characters as the bored secretary Pompey in Stevie Smith's *Novel on Yellow Paper* (1936) and *Over the Frontier* (1938) or Irgmgard Keun's diligent Gilgi, the titular character of *Gilgi – Eine von Uns* (1948).

The middle-class occupation of office clerk afforded a male employee respectability and stability, which are often presented as undesirable in male narratives, such as George Orwell's *Keep the Aspidistra Flying* (1936), or Anthony Powell's *Afternoon Men* (1931). Yet this narrative is rarely available to women. The male protagonists of these stories fail in their endeavour to escape the drudgery of the office, and either end up where they started from or they face financial and emotional destitution. Women, on the other hand, are not meant to succeed in their occupations in the first place. Their rejection of economic imperatives works differently, because they are subjected to them differently. There are no possibilities for them to advance their careers or escape to go on ill-fated

1 Schößler, Franziska: *Femina Oeconomica: Arbeit, Konsum und Geschlecht in der Literatur von Goethe bis Händler*. Peter Lang: Frankfurt am Main et al. 2017, p. 28.

2 Grandy, Christine: "Paying for Love: Women's Work and Love in Popular Film in Interwar Britain." *Journal of the History of Sexuality*, 19(3), 2010, pp. 483–507, p. 489, retrieved 19.11.2019, from https://www.jstor.org/stable/40986336.

adventures, and they often end up with unwanted pregnancies that put an end to their occupation as office clerks, and sometimes even their lives. While they might suffer the same boredom as their male counterparts, their work does not provide them with respectability and stability. Regardless of the potential of newfound freedom, the only socially acceptable success remains marriage.

Precarious Lives: Women and Work

Middle-class female employment gained greater visibility after World War I, but suspicions of prostitution lingered. Cultural texts, from literature and film to advertising, cast the spotlight on the bodies and sexuality of women who work. Schößler demonstrates how literature persistently portrays working women as morally ambiguous characters and often embeds them in sensationalist stories about prostitution.[3] In her essay on gender and work in interwar cinema, Christine Grandy finds that films popular among British audiences featured storylines across diverse social positions and settings in which women temporarily enter working environments, but ultimately abandon them for love, so that the male hero's position as breadwinner – and thereby also the conventional gender order – is restored.[4] The cultural pushback against female employment was aided by the economic devaluation of it. A woman's wage often did not suffice to cover her expenses. The resulting precarious living conditions served as a fertile ground for inscribing suspicions against working women. Literature of the interwar years reflects this, prominently featuring female characters suffering from financial strains who are struggling to make ends meet. As Schößler puts it: Women, upon first entering the labour market, as artists, maids, waitresses or clerks, were confronted with the pauperizing effect of their labour and can thus be understood as the 'avant-garde of precarity.'[5] Apart from gaining insufficient wages, middle-class women who entered the work place in the early 20th century also strayed from the prescriptive gender order and were thus disqualified from the tenuous security this

3 Schößler, p. 21.
4 Grandy, p. 487.
5 Schößler, p. 23.

order provided for them. As a consequence, they were even more at risk of exploitation, poverty and social exclusion, ultimately rendering their lives precarious.

It is precisely this intersection of social and economic precariousness that resonates with today's readers, almost a century later. Arne Kalleberg and Steven Vallas define precarious work as uncertain, unstable, and insecure, arguing that employees bear the risks of work (as opposed to business or the government) and receive limited social benefits and statutory protections.[6] The fictional women who enter the labour market during the interwar years struggle with a similar experience of work, which is further complicated by the added vulnerability of their bodies and sexualities, as well as their decreased social status. Precarious labour conditions and (unpaid) care work are also at the centre of current debates about a gendered economy and precarity is therefore a striking aspect of the literary representation of women and work. One broad sociological research trend even places "the concept of precarity at the center of their conceptions of modernity."[7] In his theory of labour movements, Zygumt Bauman takes this approach when he distinguishes between solid and liquid modernity in capitalist nations,[8] the first encapsulating Fordism, while the latter is chiefly characterized by "uncertainty, fragility and precariousness."[9] Whereas in the Fordist model, a particular form of capitalism that dominated labour and social relations in the decades following the Second World War, the mass production of goods went hand in hand with waged workers that are able to afford them, the economy in liquid modernity from roughly the 1970s onwards relies on the exploitation of the masses for the sole benefit of the privileged.

---

6 Kalleberg, Arne L. / Vallas, Steven P.: "Probing Precarious Work: Theory, Research, and Politics." In: Kalleberg, Arne L. / Vallas, Steven P. (eds.): *Precarious Work*. Emerald Publishing Limited: Bingley, UK 2018, p. 1.

7 Kalleberg / Vallas, p. 3.

8 As Bauman argues in *Liquid Modernity*, one of the reasons for liquid modernity, occasionally referred to as light modernity, is the emergence of light-speed travel in the software universe that cancels out spatial distance, Bauman, Zygmunt: *Liquid Modernity*. Polity Press: Cambridge 2000, p.117.

9 Beilharz, Peter: "Zygmunt Bauman." In: Jon Simmons (ed.): *From Agamben to Zizek*. Edinburgh University Press: Edinburgh 2011, pp. 45–59, p. 57.

Even though Bauman's concept of liquid modernity tries to capture contemporary life shaped by global economy, I want to show how the concept, primarily by dint of Bauman's focus on movement within it, can be useful when addressing the precarious working lives of women in interwar literature. While the spatial component of Bauman's theory is tied to software development, which does not apply to this era, interwar literature nonetheless shares similar concerns about mobility. These concerns largely derive from new technological advances in an age fascinated by new means of travel, like cars and airplanes, and more generally by border crossings, bohemian lives and cosmopolitanism. This period saw the renaissance of the flâneur as literary figure, who first emerged in 19th century writing in France. This city-wanderer observes the masses and takes his inspiration from aimlessly drifting in and out of the city's streets, cafés, and arcades. The flâneur stands in stark contrast to the worker, whose routine movements follow the logic of a work schedule. He stands out because he is not part of the masses. But what does this constellation mean for women? The division between home and work with its underlying gendered implications for spaces means that women stand out in the work space and they stand out if they roam the city, unattached and therefore conspicuous, trying and failing to find their footing in public spaces. Their presence in urban spaces is continuously questioned, especially if they cannot be identified as commodities or objects to be gazed upon by street-roaming men.[10] Women cannot claim the same iconic visibility of the flâneur, a welcome figure woven into the narratives of the modern city. While many scholars have striven to remedy this gendered bias,[11] and

10 Dreyer, Elfriede / McDowall, Estelle: "Imagining the *flâneur* as a woman." *Communicatio: South African Journal for Communication Theory and Research* 38(1), 2012, pp.30–44.

11 See Parsons, Deborah L.: *Streetwalking the Metropolis: Women, the City, and Modernity*. Oxford University Press: Oxford 2000, or D'Souza, Aruna / McDonough, Tom: *The Invisible Flâneuse?: Gender, Public Space, and Visual Culture in Nineteenth-Century Paris*. Manchester University Press: Manchester 2006, as well as Balducci, Temma: *Gender, Space, and the Gaze in Post-Haussmann Visual Culture: Beyond the Flâneur*. Routledge: New York et al. 2017.

writers like Jean Rhys have been understood as flâneuses,[12] I am interested in refining these approaches by looking at the tenuous relationship between roaming and loitering. To use Bauman's metaphors for modern life, the flâneur is a tourist, not a vagabond.

I find it productive to work with Bauman's theory because his metaphors of the tourist and the vagabond can be used to characterise interwar literature's depiction of working women and amateur prostitutes. Bauman argues that tourists are wanderers who are financially secure enough to enjoy the benefits of a global economy and trade, whereas the vagabonds are forced to move according to a market logic. As Bauman maintains: "if the tourists move because they find the world irresistibly *attractive*, the vagabonds move because they find the world unbearably *inhospitable*."[13] I want to use these metaphors with which Bauman tries to describe new, global class hierarchies and show how literature creates similar figures in the bourgeois *Weltenbürger* or the city flâneur and the less famous, displaced female vagabond that can be read as an intersectional criticism of gendered and classist social structures.

In Jean Rhys's fiction, vagabonds abound. Financially struggling to the extent that they have to prostitute themselves, the fictional women follow popular tropes of the interwar years and thus join the ranks of the long and troubled depiction of working women. The sensationalist narratives that frame them often undermine the social critique these amateur prostitutes of literature embody. Doubly tainted by the assumed (sexual) liberties of financially independent women and the unseemly relationship between women and money, it is not surprising that working women are an integral part of the cultural imaginary of their time. And yet, Rhys's novels also speak to modern readers. The descriptions of uprooted, precarious modern life, of insecurity, forced mobility and the lack of social security networks, have gained renewed currency. Thus, Rhys's novels bridge the modern and the postmodern world, exploring the struggle of disenfranchised characters who fail to find their place in a capitalist society and consequently cannot recover from financial ruin.

---

12 See Elkin, Lauren: *Flaneuse: Women Walk the City in Paris, New York, Tokyo, Venice and London*. Penguin Random House: London 2016.

13 Bauman 1997, p. 92 (emphasis in the original).

Rhys's interwar novels all portray the lives of destitute women, populating the big European cities in the 1930s. Constantly pressed for money, her heroines can only occupy socially insecure positions that perpetuate their emotional and economic bankruptcy. As a result, they lack the resources to actively resist such injustice. While they resign themselves to failure, the novels also show how failure can throw a spanner in the works. In a Bartlebian sense, Rhys's novels refuse to swallow the company line, they, like Melville's protagonist, 'would prefer not to.' Unimpressed by capitalist promises of work and wages as the bringer of happiness,[14] her texts reveal the significant constructivist efforts behind this ideology. In *Good Morning, Midnight* (1939), the protagonist, Sasha, outlines the personal vulnerability that goes hand in hand with the manifold pitfalls of earning wages and workplace hierarchies as she compares the dependency on one's employer to mutilation. Similarly, Rhys's other heroines investigate their dependence on dresses and make-up for potential fixed-term contracts as mistresses in *After Leaving Mr Mackenzie* (1930) and *Voyage in the Dark* (1934). The devaluation of them as economic subjects and the commodification of their bodies highlight the gendered demands of employees. The novels also show that there is a fluid border between respectable working women and prostitution, which renders both ends of the spectrum unstable. Focusing on the portrayal of precariousness, I want to explore how Rhys's interwar novels thus challenge capitalism's narrative of success and failure and the concept of rewarding work. I argue that these texts challenge the economic imperative of growth and progress by depicting how women are placed at the margins of production, constantly under surveillance, interrogated and ultimately blamed by society for their precarious positions as vagabonds.

My focus on failure and its intersection with gender invites a discussion of the heroine's actions or non-actions within a system that constantly

14 For an in-depth discussion of the relationship between love and work and the capitalist strategies to create a more intimate relationship to one's work and find happiness there, see Weeks, Kathi: "Down with Love: Feminist Critique and the New Ideologies of Work." *WSQ: Women's Studies Quarterly. The Feminist Press* 45.(3&4) 2017, pp. 37–58, retrieved 8.12. 2020, from DOI: 10.1353/wsq.2017.0043.

commodifies them. This complicates other critical readings of Rhys's puzzlingly passive protagonists, who seem to have little survival instincts in a capitalist system, unable to hold down a job or hold onto a man – a parallel that speaks volumes about their outlook on life. They are often presented as failing characters whose profound indifference, inaction, alcoholism, or lack of future plans and ambitions stand in the way of their common sense. However, I want to show how capitalist society translates common sense into business sense, which then follows a gendered market logic, and as such mostly benefits the male characters. In the following paragraphs, I will read Rhys's three 1930s novels side by side to highlight the relationship between money, business logics, and the commodity of female bodies. This reading puts Bauman's metaphor of vagabonds and tourists into a conversation with the precarious relationship between women and work.

Invisible Vagabonds: The Fixed-Term Contract of the Mistress

After Leaving Mr Mackenzie complicates ideas of agency. While the title implies that Julia has ended the relationship with Mr Mackenzie, the narrative suggests the opposite. Although the narrated situations repeatedly victimise Julia, the narrative allows tiny ruptures that question such unambiguous roles of winners and losers. While the male characters are men of leisure, ambling about the city, or in Bauman's terms, tourists, they are constantly confronted with their Other, the vagabond Julia, who forces them to acknowledge her. Despite their contempt and their hierarchical power over Julia and despite even Julia's seeming incompetence at extracting money from her affairs, all men eventually relent. They do so mostly to get rid of her; Mackenzie offers her money hoping she will not cause a public scene after their break-up, and Julia's first lover quickly dismisses her with some money, relieved he can handle this at his private club. This implies that it is her visibility that threatens not only their reputation, but also their comfortable lives. Their lives only remain morally and economically comfortable so long as the exploitation remains invisible. Bauman describes the vagabond as "the dark background against which the sun of the tourist shines so brightly that the spots are hardly seen […] The more repulsive and abhorrent the lot of the vagabond, the more bearable are the minor discomforts and major risks of the tourist life."[15] Therefore one can read Julia as a vagabond, who refuses to be invisible or cater to the tourist, which upsets the social structure of the invisible precarious lives of mistresses that underpins the glamorous life of the gentleman. Yet, Julia does not profit from her visibility to the extent that she can overcome her precariousness, but only so that she can remain in this ambivalent realm of former mistress – a realm that, despite being subject to a market logic, is less clearly defined and regulated.

The narrative strategy mirrors the precarity it describes, and destabilises social and spatial certainties. Like Rhys's other interwar heroines, Julia has a complex relationship to the hotel rooms she inhabits. In fact, the novel's chapter titles reflect the central themes of men and hotel rooms, as the chapters about 'Mr Mackenzie,' 'Mr Horsefield' and 'Mr James' are complemented by locations, starting with the 'Hotel on the Quay' she chooses once Mackenzie has left her, then 'London' in general, 'Notting Hill,' and finally Paris again with the 'Ile de la Cité.' These titles evoke the struggle to gain social visibility because they suggest that unless Julia's identity is tied to a man, she is shut away in the neither private nor public space of the hotel room, seemingly unable to fully occupy either space on her own. In the middle of the narrative, a chapter is titled 'Change of Address' and towards the end, as her economic destitution becomes more pronounced, the vague chapter reference reads 'It might have been anywhere.' These chapter titles are misleading in so far as that Julia is not moving in 'Change of Address,' only taking a walk and going to the cinema and therefore occupying transitory public spaces, like the streets, restaurants and cinemas of Paris. This amplifies her sense of dislocation, as these liminal spaces seem to be the only ones she can inhabit – a contradiction that dislodges meaningful social structures. In contrast, 'It might have been anywhere' is set in her London hotel room, into which Horsefield invites himself. The deliberate vagueness of the title indicates that these encounters have lost all specificity and stress Julia's status as a vagabond, not only in Bauman's metaphorical sense, but also in a literal one. While her vagabond status renders her economically and socially vulnerable and

15 Bauman 1997, p. 94

displaces her according to a (sexual) market logic, her refusal to remain invisible ruptures the logic of this system.

Julia faces the interchangeable men in her life with a radical passivity that seems almost like a Bartlebian attempt at failure. Mackenzie considers her a paradox: "She was too obvious and too obscure. The really incredible thing was that she did not seem to want to get away with it, that she did not seem to understand the urge and the push to get away with it at all costs."[16] In other words, while she submits to her sexual exploitation, she does not deny her status as mistress and thus avoids complicity with a system that hypocritically renders them invisible. Business logics and metaphors dominate all of Julia's social interactions, especially those with the titular character. Mackenzie is alarmed when she returns his final pay-off, realising that she has left the realm of "common sense",[17] or capitalist logic, and is therefore unintelligible and dangerous to that system. When confronting her first lover, she reflects on the injustice of their social positions, entirely determined by the logic of money: "Because he has money he's a kind of god. Because I have none I'm a kind of worm. A worm because I've failed and I have no money."[18] As Rebecca Colesworthy observes, in *After Leaving Mr Mackenzie,* begging becomes the trope of women's paradoxical relation to a fraternal social order that renders them always already guilty for failing to be either a man or an object of male desire.[19]

Mr Mackenzie is established as a figure of privilege within the system that denies Julia a place. Colesworthy, in her reflection on the social implications of the gift, argues that capitalism depends on the circulation of gifts but systematically disavows this, modifying that in Julia's case, her male benefactors deny their dependence on gifts but blame Julia for hers.[20] This reading identifies the double standard of measuring success

16 Rhys, Jean: *After Leaving Mr Mackenzie*. (1930). Penguin Books: London 2000, p. 20.

17 Rhys 1930, p. 23.

18 Rhys 1930, p. 81.

19 Colesworthy, Rebecca: "Jean Rhys and the Fiction of Failed Reciprocity." *Journal of Modern Literature* 37(2), 2014, pp. 92–108, p., retrieved 20.09.2018, from DOI: 10.2979/jmodelite.37.2.92, 101.

20 Rhys 1930, p. 96

according to material wealth without acknowledging privilege or inequalities. Mackenzie is described as "comfortably off, but no millionaire",[21] which allowed him to retired at the age of forty-eight. Instead of reflecting on this privilege, he attributes his wealth mostly to "a certain good luck which had always attended him."[22] His background makes clear that he owes most of his fortune, in both senses of the word, to his father's business venture, meaning he came into wealth not by his own action but through inheritance, or succession. His example shows the lingering feudal structure of capitalism, where some people are born into privilege while others are forever excluded, as well as the effort invested to sustain these structures.[23] With Mackenzie, this becomes apparent because he distracts from his arbitrary luck of birth, his succession to the business throne, to focus on a more general good luck, which he frames as his personal achievement feeding into the capitalist myth of personal responsibility. This liberates him from honestly reflecting on his image as a successful capitalist. He can therefore conveniently pretend that capitalism is a fair system so that he does not have to take social responsibility for anyone, including his mistresses. None of Rhys's heroines could fall back on such a fortune. Even though Sasha in *Good Morning, Midnight* inherits a moderate income, she cannot build upon this in any way to multiply the sum and establish herself as a successful capitalist, so she uses her inheritance to hide away from the world. Reading Rhys's novels in relation to each other therefore suggests that there is a marked and emphatically gendered difference not only based on the size of the inheritance, but also on the possibilities to do something with it.

The comfort of Mackenzie's solid upper-middle class position intersects with his masculine privilege, which is governed by "a certain code of morals and manners, from which he seldom departed. He did depart

21 Rhys 1930, p. 18.

22 ibid.

23 Several studies on neo-feudalism have been published over the course of the last decades, many inspired by Jürgen Habermas's concept of 'refeudalisation', introduced in his seminal work *The Structural Transformation of the Public Sphere* (1962). See Neckel, Sighard: "The refeudalization of modern capitalism." *Journal for Sociology* 56(3), 2020, pp. 472–486, retrieved 8.12.2020, from DOI: 10.1177/1440783319857904.

from it, but only when he was practically certain that nobody would know that he had done so. His code was perfectly adapted to the social system."[24] This 'code of morals and manners' alludes to another instance of the feudal structure of capitalism as it harks back to presumed codes of chivalry, likening Mackenzie to a capitalist 'nobleman.' To put it another way: Mackenzie's vision of capitalism installs him, the businessman, as a knight, but one whose chivalry can be abandoned so long as there are no witnesses. This double standard unmasks the code as a farce. It evokes the cynical image of knights publicly rescuing the damsels in distress but privately ravishing the kitchen maids. As such, the code works at the intersection between class and gender. Mackenzie utilizes the loophole of this code for his affairs with women and admonishes himself for his occasional impulsiveness which had led him to relationships that "he had regretted bitterly afterwards, though when it came to getting out of these affairs his business instinct came to his help, and he got out undamaged."[25] Once again, Mackenzie interprets the events of his life according to a capitalist rhetoric with which he can celebrate his business instinct as his personal achievement that ensures his protection from any inconvenience without having to reflect on his predatory behaviour towards others, whose lack of privilege does not grant them the same protection.

In the novel, female success is reduced to the seduction of men, suggesting that there is no reward for any other avenue of femininity within the capitalist system. Though a pillar of respectability, Julia's counter-image, her poor middle-class sister Norah, leads an equally precarious life as she is buried by the burden of taking care of her ill mother. As Arnold E. Davidson observes, the novel dramatizes the difference between the two sisters to show how little difference it makes.[26] Anne Cunningham reads Norah as the example of the cost one nonetheless incurs when living

24 Rhys 1930, p. 18.
25 Rhys 1930, p. 19.
26 Davidson, Arnold E.: "The Art and Economics of Destitution in Jean Rhys's 'After Leaving Mr Mackenzie'." *Studies in the Novel* 16(2), 1984, pp. 215–27, pp. 224–25. retrieved 20.09.2018, pp. 224–5.

with the approval from God and society.[27] In contrast to Julia, Norah has internalised the capitalist and patriarchal ideology, "trained to certain opinions which forbid her even the relief of rebellion against her lot",[28] and is therefore as disadvantaged and confined as Julia. But their confinement differs. Rhys shows how through her actions of sacrificing herself, Norah validates the norms that confine her, whereas Julia resists the prescribed respectability, able to identify the sexism to which they are subjected and liberate herself in so far as she does not quietly accept the status quo. Though financially and socially more secure, Norah's envy of her sister's perceived liberties overshadows their relationship. Julia's resistance threatens to expose the hypocrisy of Norah's respectable life so that the two sisters cannot acknowledge their intersecting disenfranchisements at the hands of a patriarchal capitalist structure, and this lack of solidarity is constitutive of that system. To ensure that Julia's threatening presence cannot damage Norah's sense of self, she enlists the help of their uncle as the family patriarch, counting on his ability to ward off Julia. He does not disappoint as he measures her experience against his own, without acknowledging that he received more privileges while hers were bound to an unhappy marriage: "everybody has to sit on their own bottoms. I've found that out all my life. You mustn't grumble if you find it out too."[29] In his function as the family patriarch, he denies all financial and social responsibility for her. He represents the contempt against women for their social and economic vulnerability while denying any responsibility in contributing to it.

Julia upsets the social order because she insists on her social independence and refuses to return to her husband – an option that seems only plausible to other, respectable characters in the novel who ignore the reality of her situation and are blind to the fragility of this system of dependency. At the same time, Julia leads a precarious life, in which her small degree of social independence rests on her financial dependency on other men and

---

27 Cunningham, Anne: "'Get on or Get Out': Failure and Negative Femininity in Jean Rhys's 'Voyage in the Dark'." *Modern Fiction Studies* 59(2), 2013, pp. 373–94, retrieved 20.09.2018, from DOI:10.1353/mfs.2013.0022, p. 384.
28 Rhys 1930, p. 51.
29 Rhys 1930, p. 61.

thus remains, apart from small ruptures into which she had invested emotionally or economically, invisible.

Commodification of Female Bodies

In *Voyage in the Dark* (1934), Anna Morgan is thrown into the world of the disenfranchised and is repeatedly abandoned and exploited, but her failure to survive in London can be read as a critique of colonial and sexist practices. Anna's cyclical experience of loss showcases the roots of exploitation on which the capitalist system is built, but whose existence it seeks to disguise.

Like Rhys's other novels, money becomes a central theme as the quest for money, which secures her protagonists' lodgings and satisfies their alcoholism, drives much of the novels' action. In *Voyage in the Dark* money seems to have a will of its own. The novel illustrates how women of Anna's social position have a highly unstable relationship to money, which shapes and determines their lives. Anna knows she cannot control money and is fully aware of the dangers that come with her economic precarity. She nonetheless gives her money unselfishly away to help her friend Maudie, only soberly reflecting "It's always like that with money. You never know where it goes to. You change a fiver and then it's gone."[30] Like Rhys's other heroines, Anna has no source of a sustainable income. Her situation becomes even more dire when her lover Walter convinces her to quit her job as a chorus girl, to be more freely at his disposal. Tellingly, upon their first meeting they discuss her salary as a chorus girl and Walter casually notes that it barely suffices to make a living. While this might not solely function to ensure that Anna is financially destitute, and therefore more likely to accept his advances supplemented by money and gifts, this focus sets up a social inequality between them where gender and capital or class intersect. When Walter fails in his first attempt at seducing Anna, he sends her money and the text clarifies how money is the truly seductive of the two: "I was accustomed to it already. It was as if I had always had it. Money ought to be everybody's. It ought to be like water. You can tell that because you get accustomed to it so quickly."[31]

---

30 Rhys 1934, p. 137.
31 Rhys, Jean: *Voyage in the Dark*. (1934). Penguin Books: London 2000, p. 24.

Anna's work as a chorus girl, a job that relies on the sexualisation of her body, along with her insufficient pay, paves the way for her path into prostitution. Schößler observes that even though sex work was a marginal phenomenon in labour sociological terms, the literary imaginary was drawn to it. The extent to which working women were subject to this sexualising gaze in the literature and the film of the age was noticeably class-specific; while upper- and middle-class working women were not often sexualised in conjunction with their labour, working-class women were often presented in explicit proximity to prostitution or sexualised labour.[32] Rhys's novels, however, do not indulge in the scintillating narratives about prostitutes. On the contrary, her focalizers are the mistresses, and their perspectives do not allow for sentimentality and romance, or scandalous entertainment. Rhys's women are trapped in pervasive structural inequality.

Anna's materialism throughout the novel shows the imbalance of her role as consumer and as a waged worker. This imbalance triggers her failure as a capitalist subject. Even though she is deeply embedded in a consumerist culture, she rejects its promises of social progression. Neither materialism, nor work, nor love can reward her and grant her stability in life. She realises that all three roles combined are the cause for her precarity. This becomes obvious when she reflects:

> The clothes of most of the women who passed were like caricatures of the clothes in the shop-windows, but when they stopped to look you saw that their eyes were fixed on the future. 'If I could by this, then of course I'd be quite different.' Keep hope alive and you can do anything, and that's the way the world goes round, that's the way they keep the world rolling. So much hope for each person. And damned cleverly done too. But what happens if you don't hope anymore, if your back's broken?[33]

Anna's insight into exploitation via the constructed desire for clothes reveals how the desire for an escape from disenfranchisement is channelled and contained by capitalist materialism, so that women's desire can only be fulfilled by, literally, buying into the system that disadvantages them. However, the text tentatively suggests how to throw a spanner in the works by means of failure. In other words, failure can be liberating for Anna, by

32 Schößler, p. 31.
33 Rhys 1934, pp. 111–2.

being fashioned into tools that help her see through this system and refuse it: "'I can't stand here staring at these dresses for ever,' I thought. I turned around."[34] The novel teases out the conflation of clothes and the commodification of not only femininity, but also women in general. Maudie tells Anna about one of her lovers who complains "a girl's clothes cost more than the girl inside them. [...] you can even get a very nice girl for nothing if you know how to go about it. But you can't get a very nice costume for her for five pounds."[35] While clothes are firmly established at a market value, women are doubly vulnerable with their undefined status as a commodity and the notion that men deserve free access to their bodies.

Commenting on the repetitive experience of exploitation, Anne Cunningham finds that the trope of circularity in *Voyage in the Dark* undermines notions of linear progress.[36] The tension between progression and circularity plays into the novel's critique of capitalism.[37] The text calls into question all notions of 'fresh starts' or 'getting on', and illuminates the precariousness experienced by many who have no privileged access to resources, like Anna. The idea of self-fashioning success through willpower runs through the novel like a red thread. Virtually all characters advise Anna to 'get on.' Frustrated with these forms of advice, Anna starts questioning their validity:

> Everybody says, 'Get on.' Of course, some people get on. Yes, but how many? What about what's-her-name? She got on, didn't she? 'Chorus-Girl Marries Peer's Son.' Well, *what* about her? Get on or get out, they say. Get on or get out.[38]

She rejects the logic of 'getting on' and identifies the ideological pitfalls behind it. By choosing a chorus girl, like herself, to illustrate her point, she shows the unrealistic career paths available to women, as it stands to reason that not everyone can marry a peer. Moreover, she exposes that the only way to escape precarious living conditions is through marriage. Finally, she deconstructs the notion of success by narrating the example

---

34 Rhys 1934, p. 112.
35 Rhys 1934, p. 40.
36 Cunningham, p. 375.
37 I have discussed this theme further in Behrendt, Aileen: *Gender Politics and British Women Writers of the 1930s*. Königshausen & Neumann: Würzburg 2020.
38 Rhys 1934, p. 64 (emphasis in the original)

of the chorus girl like a newspaper headline, which reduces the woman recently risen to an upper social position back to her position as chorus girl, suggesting that society will always see her as such and her upward mobility, though financially sound, is illusory. The italicised 'what' adds a note of rebellion which initiates Anna's deconstruction of the chorus girl example. To Anne Cunningham, who has analysed this trope in her essay, this means that the text proposes that Rhys's heroines' female subjectivities based on failure and negation is preferable to the prescribed choices available to women.[39] The context of the 1930s significantly shape female experience of ambivalent independence. Anna's rejection of 'getting on' also exemplifies the historical moment when women could be socially independent but had few options to realise financial independence.[40] Anna's rejection therefore exposes two hypocrisies, one that complicates the interwar gender conventions about women and work and one at the heart of a capitalist ideology.

The Failed Flâneuse

Rhys's last interwar protagonist, Sasha Jansen, has held a variety of precarious occupations, from model, to shop assistant, to tourist guide, and even to ghost writer. However, her previous employment only lowered her self-esteem and made her feel powerless. For instance, while she was writing up "fairy stories for a very rich woman,"[41] her commissioners criticised her writing style, annoyed that she used words of one syllable, consequently implying that she lacks erudition. As a city guide, she tries to accommodate vague wishes of tourists who insist on going to an exhibition whose name or place they do not recall.[42] Moreover, her job as a tourist guide made her nervous so that she lost her sense of direction, indicating not only the power her employers have over her mental capacities but also the hierarchy that differentiates between her urban experiences as a vagabond and those of literal tourists. This momentary lapse is not a

39 Cunningham, p. 376.
40 Cunningham, p. 387.
41 Rhys, Jean: *Good Morning, Midnight.* (1939). Penguin Books: London 2000, p. 139.
42 Rhys 1939, p. 27.

lack of competence because, as the reader learns, Sasha is well acquainted with the streets of Paris. It is testament to the pressure on women whose professional success depends on how well they cater to others' needs. This pressure does not subside even when the parties involved are all female, because it sits at the intersection between gender and economy. The privileged and socially acceptable women who do not have to work can command the women who do. I want to read Rhys's *Good Morning, Midnight* to show how female employees face certain gendered expectations that effect their psyche and add to their precarity. Sasha serves as a prime example of how women's work depends on the recognition and often benevolence of their employers, who have very little incentive to give either. Sasha has no network of security she can mobilise in her defence and is therefore subjected to her boss's will.

Sasha's psyche greatly suffers from the lack of respect she experiences in her professional life. While she was working as a shop assistant she was constantly humiliated. In a pivotal scene of the novel, her English boss gives her instructions to deliver a note, but his poor French misdirects her. Instead of recognising this mistake, he patronisingly blames her and questions her intellect. Retrospectively, she challenges his presumptions and privileges:

> Well, let's argue this out, Mr Blank. You, who represent Society, have the right to pay me four hundred francs a month. That's my market value, for I am an inefficient member of Society, slow in the uptake, uncertain, slightly damaged in the fray, there's no denying it. So you have the right to pay me four hundred francs a month, to lodge me in a small, dark room, to clothe me shabbily, to harass me with worry and monotony and unsatisfied longing till you get me to the point when I blush at a look, cry at a word. We can't all be happy, we can't all be rich, we can't all be lucky – and it would be so much less fun if we were. Isn't it so, Mr Blank? […] Let's say that you have this mystical right to cut my legs off. But the right to ridicule me afterwards because I am a cripple – no, that I think you haven't got. And that's the right you hold most dearly, isn't it? You must be able to despise the people you exploit. […] Did I say all this? Of course I didn't. I didn't even think it.[43]

Sasha identifies a sadistic streak that plays into the imbalance between the two groups. She deconstructs the legitimacy of those in power with her

43 Rhys 1939, pp. 25–6.

example of the severed legs by comparing the exploitation of the work force to mutilation. This outlines the psychological effects resulting from the precarious living conditions, choosing a metaphor to highlight the crippling effect of the vagabond life.

At the same time, the above passage shows the far-reaching indoctrination of a capitalist ideology as Sasha has fully accepted her 'market value,' convinced that she is 'inefficient.' She does not challenge a capitalist prioritizing of efficiency. Still, she recognises the arbitrary and unjust measuring of efficiency that puts her at a disadvantage from the start. She also understands how her objection is effectively silenced as the system ensures her lack of confidence to voice it. From within this logic, she can only carve out a small space of resistance that sets boundaries on the exploiter's privileges.

When Sasha inherits enough money to get by without a job, she still does not become the female equivalent of Mackenzie. She cannot be a woman of leisure who can freely roam the streets of the city. Instead Sasha moves through Paris looking in on the bohemian lives of others. Her experience of mobility is marked by loss and uncertainty, rather than freedom and choice. As an unmarried woman, she is socially suspicious, and landladies and hotel owners are reluctant to grant her lodging. Jeremy Hawthorne shows how despite the sense of bohemianism, Rhys' early heroines are trapped by their lack of money, emotional deprivations and cultural restrictions that make it hard for single women to move at ease in public spaces.[44] But Sasha proves that even having a small amount of money does not change that as long as she remains an independent woman, separated from her husband. Rhys's novel offers elaborate descriptions of how Sasha interacts with the public urban spaces she inhabits. Nagihan Haliloğlu proposes that *Good Morning, Midnight* captures Sasha's failed flâneur life-style in Paris.[45] The text sets the city with the streets and bars Sasha frequents in opposition to the hotel rooms in which Sasha hides:

44 Hawthorn, Jeremy: "Travel as Incarceration: Jean Rhys's 'After Leaving Mr. Mackenzie'" In: Lange, Attie de (ed.): *Literary Landscapes: From Modernism to Postcolonialism*. Palgrave Macmillan: Basingstoke et al. 2008, pp. 58–74, p. 64.

45 Haliloğlu, Nagihan: *Narrating from the Margins: Self-Representation of Female and Colonial Subjectivities in Jean Rhys's Novels*. Rodopi: Amsterdam 2011, p. 87.

> My life, which seems so simple and monotonous, is really a complicated affair of cafés where they like me and cafés where they don't, streets that are friendly, streets that aren't, rooms where I might be happy, rooms where I never shall be…[46]

The way Sasha arranges spaces implies her position between being a tourist or a vagabond. She has enough means to lead a moderately comfortable life, but her entry into the bohemian lifestyle is fraught with difficulty. Not only does her allowance not suffice, she cannot claim spaces with the same self-assurance of a Mackenzie. As a wanderer, her position is too close to a prostitute, but she is even more dangerous to the social order because she cannot be contained by male desire. Moreover, the spaces can reject her, which prevents her from assuming the role of the flâneuse. The spatial arrangement is notably absent of people, despite the division's reliance on words indicating human affection. It not only humanises these spaces, in Sasha's perception, they even have direct power over her. As a result, Sasha's relationship to these urban spaces is unmediated. It increases, on the one hand, Sasha's isolation from human interaction, and on the other, it highlights her intimate connection to the spaces she inhabits but can never fully claim.

In that sense, she is a literal vagabond, but she also personifies a critique of the structural inequality at the heart of modern life. Rhys's text shows that outside marriage and inherited wealth, there are no paths that lead women out of precarity towards economic and social stability. Female vagabonds are the flipside of the international interwar bohemia. In the end, Sasha has to pay the price for her threatening ambivalence as a vagabond. When she rejects the advances of a male prostitute due to her sexual insecurity, she is not only robbed of her money, but also raped by a neighbouring hotel guest, who had preyed on her throughout the novel.

The Capitalist Narrative of Success and Failure

Rhys's novels portray the economically and socially precarious lives of women in the interwar years. They struggle with the capitalist narrative of success and failure in a society that regards women who work as suspicious. Thus they fail to fulfil the economic imperative of progress, and

46 Rhys 1939, p. 40.

instead spiral downwards into prostitution, untethered and abandoned. As women who entered the economic market, they were immediately sexualised, while their work and selves were devalued by their employers, to increase their own profit, or by men who wanted to be their lovers without facing social responsibilities. Rhys's unattached women therefore have to constantly cater to male desires. Their status as independent women and as women who work displaced them from any social networks, but Rhys shows how little security these would have offered them in the first place. Their labour only ensures their continued exploitation and none of the occupations they can take up can be considered rewarding. The various middle and lower class jobs featured in Rhys's work all lead to a vagabond life. Rhys's women are forever on the move, shut away in cheap hotel rooms, because the world proves inhospitable for them. When they finally force their way into visibility, they do so at their own social and economic risk.

References

Balducci, Temma: *Gender, Space, and the Gaze in Post-Haussmann Visual Culture: Beyond the Flâneur*. New York et al.: Routledge 2017.

Bauman, Zygmunt: *Postmodernity and its Discontents*. Polity Press: Cambridge 1997.

Bauman, Zygmunt: *Liquid Modernity*. Polity Press: Cambridge 2000.

Behrendt, Aileen: *Gender Politics and British Women Writers of the 1930s*. Königshausen & Neumann: Würzburg 2020.

Beilharz, Peter: "Zygmunt Bauman." In: Jon Simmons (ed.): *From Agamben to Zizek*. Edinburgh University Press: Edinburgh 2011, pp. 45–59.

Colesworthy, Rebecca: "Jean Rhys and the Fiction of Failed Reciprocity." *Journal of Modern Literature* 37(2), 2014, pp. 92–108, retrieved 20.09.2018, from DOI: 10.2979/jmodelite.37.2.92.

Cunningham, Anne: " 'Get on or Get Out': Failure and Negative Femininity in Jean Rhys's 'Voyage in the Dark'." *Modern Fiction Studies* 59(2), 2013, pp. 373–94. Retrieved 20 Sept. 2018. DOI:10.1353/mfs.2013.0022.

Davidson, Arnold E: "The Art and Economics of Destitution in Jean Rhys's 'After Leaving Mr. Mackenzie'" *Studies in the Novel* 16(2), 1984, pp. 215–27, retrieved 20.09.2018, from https://www.jstor.org/stable/29532275.

Dreyer, Elfriede / McDowall, Estelle: "Imagining the flâneur as a woman." *Communicatio: South African Journal for Communication Theory and Research* 38(1), 2012, pp. 30–44, retrieved 8. 12.2020 from DOI: 10.1080/02500167.2011.634425.

D'Souza, Aruna / McDonough, Tom: *The Invisible Flâneuse?: Gender, Public Space, and Visual Culture in Nineteenth-Century Paris.* Manchester University Press: Manchester 2006.

Elkin, Lauren: *Flaneuse: Women Walk the City in Paris, New York, Tokyo, Venice and London.* London: Penguin Random House 2016.

Grandy, Christine: "Paying for Love: Women's Work and Love in Popular Film in Interwar Britain." *Journal of the History of Sexuality* 19(3), 2010, pp. 483–507, retrieved 19.11.2019, from https://www.jstor.org/stable/40986336.

Haliloğlu, Nagihan: *Narrating from the Margins: Self-Representation of Female and Colonial Subjectivities in Jean Rhys's Novels.* Rodopi: Amsterdam 2011.

Hawthorn, Jeremy. "Travel as Incarceration: Jean Rhys's 'After Leaving Mr. Mackenzie'" In: Lange, Attie de (ed.): *Literary Landscapes: From Modernism to Postcolonialism.* Palgrave Macmillan: Basingstoke et al. 2008, pp. 58–74.

Kalleberg, Arne L. / Vallas, Steven P.: "Probing Precarious Work: Theory, Research, and Politics." In: Kalleberg, Arne L. / Vallas, Steven P. (eds.): *Precarious Work.* Emerald Publishing Limited: Bingley, UK 2018, pp. 1–30.

Neckel, Sighard: "The refeudalization of modern capitalism." *Journal for Sociology* 56(3), 2020, pp. 472–486, retrieved 8.12.2020, from DOI: 10.1177/1440783319857904.

Parsons, Deborah L.: *Streetwalking the Metropolis: Women, the City, and Modernity.* Oxford University Press: Oxford 2000.

Rhys, Jean: *After Leaving Mr Mackenzie.* (1930). Penguin Books: London 2000.

Rhys, Jean: *Good Morning, Midnight.* (1939). Penguin Books: London 2000.

Rhys, Jean: *Voyage in the Dark.* (1934). Penguin Books: London 2000.

Schößler, Franziska: *Femina Oeconomica: Arbeit, Konsum und Geschlecht in der Literatur – Von Goethe bis Händler.* Peter Lang: Frankfurt am Main et al. 2017.

Weeks, Kathi: "Down with Love: Feminist Critique and the New Ideologies of Work." *WSQ: Women's Studies Quarterly. The Feminist Press* 45(3&4), 2017, pp. 37–58, retrieved 8.12.2020, from DOI: 10.1353/wsq.2017.0043.

Katrin Frisch

Violence as a Currency in the Neoliberal Order – Challenging the Literary Commodification of Lower-Class Masculinities in an Economy of Privilege

Abstract: *This chapter brings two seemingly very disparate books into conversation to discuss different forms of violence and their interdependency with class. In Alan Hollinghurst's novel* The Swimming-Pool Library *the affluent gay protagonist Will pursues a lifestyle of leisure and casual sex. In a pivotal moment of the book, Will becomes the victim of a skinhead attack. This scene is mirrored in a passage from DJ Stalingrad's* Exodus, *a skinhead-autobiografiction, where the narrator-protagonist beats up his unsuspecting victim. Despite the similarity, the shift in perspective complicates the seemingly apparent victim/attacker dichotomy. The skinheads in Hollinghurst and DJ Stalingrad disrupt a neoliberal system that disadvantages lower-class subjects and continues to displace (literary) lower class identities. In both cases they do so, unapologetically, with violence. This chapter argues for a critical reading that makes the multiple forms of violence within these texts visible and illustrates how they intersect with the logics of neoliberalism.*

Keywords: violence, masculinity, lower classes, commodification

> For a long time I didn't want to write, now I do. I need it. I am relaxed and simply write down images, one after another, as they pop up in my memories. They have lived in me for all this time, held me hostage and tortured me, I couldn't think of anything else. Now I am writing them down, and with every page, one of the demons, who had been stuck in my head, can leave and transforms into something new on the page. The longer I write the lighter I feel; to the ever-patient pages I banish my sorrows.[1]

---

1 DJ Stalingrad: *Exodus*, Matthes & Seitz: Berlin 2013, 5–6. *Exodus* is not officially available in English. All translations in the text are mine. I would like to thank Christopher Widdison for his help. Page references refer to the German translation of the book. The Russian original, published by the literary journal *Znamya* in 2010, can still be accessed online: http://magazines.russ.ru/znamia/2010/9/d9.html.

Those are the words the young skinhead narrator-protagonist of DJ Stalingrad's book *Exodus* uses to describe the process of writing, more specifically, his urge to write. Writing becomes an act of liberation from the internal demons, yet the final product also serves another purpose, namely that of the subjectification of the skinhead as artistic creator. Skinheads, one of the dominant British working-class subcultures that developed in the late 1960s,[2] have become symbolic stand-ins for a brutish unregenerate masculinity – notwithstanding the fact that women are part of the scene – whose primary language is violence. The skinhead as symbol is so monofacetted that it does not seem to need any further explanation, whether it is used in political debate or in literary representation. Alan Hollinghurst's novel *The Swimming-Pool Library* is an example of the latter, where the skinheads who beat up the protagonist Will in one of the pivotal moments of the book become the model antagonists within the Thatcherite society. There is, however, a different reading the novel offers; one that can only be fully coaxed out when Hollinghurst's book is read in conjunction with DJ Stalingrad's skinhead-autobiografiction.[3] This reading complicates the trope of violence by making the different overlapping and interacting discourses of violence visible. Narrated by a lower-class skinhead, who unapologetically employs different forms of violence, *Exodus* destabilizes

2 Cf. Farin, Klaus / Seidel-Pielen, Eberhard: *Skinheads*. C.H. Beck: München 1993, pp. 23–58.

3 The term autobiografiction was first coined by Stephen Reynolds in 1906. The most comprehensive study on the subject is Max Saunders's *Self-Impression: Life-Writing, Autobiografiction, and the forms of Modern Literature*. Oxford University Press: Oxford 2010. I use the term here in a simplified form to draw attention to the intersection of autobiography and fiction in *Exodus*. In the few accounts on the book it is usually presented as a document from Russia's dark underbelly that is worth reading precisely because it chronicles the life stories that seldom reach an audience. Especially in the postscript of the German translation it becomes obvious to the reader that the narrated exploits of the unnamed protagonist are modelled on the experiences of the author during his years as a skinhead. Moreover, the fact that author and narrator share identities is crucial for my reading. However, the book also writes itself into certain literary traditions, such as the *Künstlerroman*, which it imitates and at the same time undermines. Thus *Exodus* needs to be read as both autobiographical and fictional.

easy attacker/victim binaries. In both books, the skinheads disrupt a capitalist system that discriminates against the lower classes by challenging the neoliberal mantra that hard work pays off in the end. They not only attack the middle classes, figuratively and literally, but also refuse to toil to become middle class themselves. Moreover, the skinheads' violence also disturbs the hegemonic middle class discourses that continually displace non-middle-class identities. By turning the skinhead, the anti-thesis of bourgeois culture, into a writer, *Exodus* challenges the objectification of skinheads in particular and economically marginalised people in general, as well as notions of cultural production.

The act of writing as lower class subjects may be different than brute acts of violence, but it is still considered an attack on middle class hegemony as it challenges established discourses, which a comparative reading of Hollinghurst's *The Swimming-Pool Library* and DJ Stalingrad's *Exodus* will tease out. Lower class literature is often criticised for its vulgar language, while the same characteristic is seen as daring and praised for its unconventionality in middle class literature.[4] Hollinghurst's protagonist Will is not shy in using strong language, especially when referring to sexual acts and desires. For a gay man in conservative Britain this is seen as daring and empowering. Yet Hollinghurst's novel, without overlooking its merits, leaves large parts of the hegemonic discourse intact. It is an uncomfortable read for the bigots, but also for many marginalised people. The first seem to be the intended aim, the second collateral damage. *Exodus* proves to be an uncomfortable read to almost all of its readers: to those privileged and in power by showing them the structural violence they impose, to the oblivious, who would love to close their eyes to these things, but also to those it considers its own kind, for destroying any illusion of improvement. Like the skinheads' physical violence, it primarily destroys, but it also helps its antagonistic readers to see "the world in a new light".[5]

4 The practice of cultural appropriation in terms of race and class was also especially widespread with Modernist writers, who exploited forms of language they deemed experimental and conventional, while they at the same time denigrated the true originators of these linguistic practices; see, for example, North, Michael: *The Dialect of Modernism: Race, Language, and Twentieth-Century Literature*. Oxford University Press: Oxford 1994.

5 DJ Stalingrad, p. 118.

As the language of violence disturbs middle class audiences, it exposes the inherent violence of the dominant discourses and the systems which they uphold. The skinheads' violence does not constitute an outlier in an otherwise non-violent system. On the contrary, the skinheads in Hollinghurst and DJ Stalingrad receive their agency via the use of violence. Despite their differences in setting *Exodus* reads like a counter-narrative to *The Swimming-Pool Library*, mirroring the circularity of its plot, the aimlessness of the protagonist and the skinhead violence, yet with a fundamental shift in perspective. The scene in Hollinghurst's novel where the skinheads beat up Will can be paired with a similar scene in *Exodus*, this time seen through the eyes of the skinhead attacker. The graphic depiction of violence (in *Exodus* more so than in *The Swimming-Pool Library*) at first glance obscures the forms of oppression the victim represents. Will might not strike readers as an agent of violence, but he exploits the power hierarchies of a system that privileges him. As Júlia Braga Neves has observed, *The Swimming-Pool Library* presents "features that point to the effects of the protagonist's complicity with his conservative and neoliberal environment".[6] While Hollinghurst's novel needs to be read in respect to its lower class characters as hegemonic, *Exodus* offers a subversive reading of class-based violence that is at once more complicated and more disturbing, as it confronts readers with graphic displays of nihilistic violence, while making the compelling claim for sympathy with the attackers. The following analysis is not meant to glorify or condone the physical violence employed by the skinheads in both books, nor is it an attempt to rank different forms of violence in their severity. Instead I will analyse the machinations of violence and show how contingent they are with a given power dynamic, in this example hegemonic discourses on class in a capitalist system. Especially *Exodus* reveals the structural violence that often remains invisible as those who fall victim to it are silenced.

6 Neves, Júlia Braga: *London, Queer Spaces and Historiography in the Works of Sarah Waters and Alan Hollinghurst*. dissertation 2018, p. 214.

Writing Between Precarity and Privilege

The production of literature is a unique type of labour that frequently pretends to exist outside the realm of the marketplace but is intensely intertwined with the mechanics of power within and beyond the logics of capitalism.[7] Who gets to write literature is determined by more than just class affiliation. However, class remains one of the most salient determinants of who gets to be considered an author. Writing commands money and time, elements the economically disadvantaged often lack along with their supposed lack of education. Yet, when members of the lower classes attain education (and money), they are often considered to have moved up the social ladder. In his essay "You Are Not Working-Class", Nathan Connolly meditates on class membership:

> I work in publishing. [...] Does that make me middle class now? If it does, then it ignores all of the social, cultural and economic limitations that initially held me back? Does that all vanish now? [...] There is a vision of the working class that we like to cling to: a romanticised, fetishized idea that is still rooted somewhere around the publication of *The Road to Wigan Pier* in 1937, an account of working class life written by a man educated at Eton.[8]

I concur with Connolly that class identity goes beyond the level of education, type of employment or taste. Individual class trajectory, representation, and participation in discourse formation seem just as relevant to determine class membership as Pierre Bourdieu's different forms of capital. Writing while lower class means finding a voice in a system that is built on its objectification.

Writing on class brings with it the difficulty of what designations to use. Theories on class and competing terms are plentiful. As this essay deals primarily with literature I will use the more colloquial (and therefore less exact terms) lower class and middle class, even if that means

---

7 The urge to create is not necessarily subject to the logics of the marketplace, even though the finished product is meant to be sold and consumed. This becomes especially apparent when art is praised precisely for its commercial non-success. Although a facetious mantra, the idea that a product of art is valuable precisely because it has no mass appeal (and thus is a capitalist failure) is surprisingly resilient.

8 Connolly, Nathan: *Know Your Place*. Dead Ink: Liverpool 2017, p. 238.

sacrificing some of the sociological complexities. Due to my focus on literature, class membership will be based, apart from socio-economic factors, on representation and participation in discourses and their formation, which translates to different forms of power. Unless working class is the more appropriate term, I will use the term lower class in this essay to refer to the broad group of people in a given society whose lived reality and identity is shaped by their lack of different forms of capital and their subsequent marginalisation by the system in power and the hegemonic discourses it produces, which simultaneously help to uphold it. The lower classes wield little to no power, whether politically, economically, or symbolically, an observation especially relevant when the phenomenon of violence is discussed.

The Multiple Dimensions of Violence

To know what constitutes violence seems to come intuitively to many. The skinhead's boot "slamming towards [Will's] face",[9] as well as the protagonist in *Exodus* who smashes some stranger's head with an iron pipe, are obvious examples of violent acts, and do not seem to need to be defined as such. Yet, these acts are more complicated when they are analysed beyond the boot-slamming and head-smashing. In both cases the set-up seems to suggest that the attackers are acting for individual gain, or for violence's sake, out of a position of physical power. In Hollinghurst's novel, the attackers are in a position of power by dint of physical superiority and strength in numbers; in *Exodus*, their power derives from the mere fact of being armed. However, in both scenes the victim of the attack (i.e. the victim of physical power) actually holds the position of political power, being a representative of the privileged classes. It is illuminating to approach these scenes with the theory of Johan Galtung on the multiple dimensions of violence in mind. Especially important for my endeavour is his distinction between personal and structural violence:

> We shall refer to the type of violence where there is an actor that commits the violence as personal or direct, and to violence where there is no such actor as

9 Hollinghurst, Alan: *The Swimming-Pool Library*. Penguin: London 1988, p. 174.

> structural or indirect. In both cases individuals may be killed or mutilated, hit or hurt in both senses of these words, and manipulated by means of stick or carrot strategies. But whereas in the first case these consequences can be traced back to concrete persons as actors, in the second case this is no longer meaningful. There may not be any person who directly harms another person in the structure. The violence is built into the structure and shows up as unequal power and consequently as unequal life chances.[10]

Galtung later added the category of "cultural violence", which he defines as "those aspects of culture [...] that can be used to justify or legitimize direct or structural violence".[11] Cultural violence, he posits, "makes direct and structural violence look, even feel, right - or at least not wrong".[12]

Both of the texts analysed in this chapter negotiate different dimensions of violence in a complex manner. Personal as well as structural violence is present as part of the narrated story, with two important differences: the aspects of structural violence that are actively addressed differ, as does the locus of the narrating character within the general power dynamic. This fundamentally influences how both protagonists view themselves. The unnamed protagonist in *Exodus* is an agent of personal violence but less so of structural violence, hence he is violent but feels powerless. Will, on the other hand, is a beneficiary of structural violence and less of personal violence (although in his fantasies he sometimes reveals a more violent version of himself), thus he feels powerful but does not consider himself violent. The cultural aspects that legitimise violence that both novels share are the capitalist system and homophobia. Moreover, in *Exodus* religion plays a fundamental role as a cultural aspect to make violence look and feel right. More importantly, *The Swimming-Pool Library* and *Exodus* can also be read as examples of cultural violence. This seems especially obvious for the latter text, but Hollinghurst's novel is selective in what kinds of oppression it problematizes. It would be too easy to consider only the character of Will as the locus of cultural violence, from which

---

10 Galtung, Johan: Galtung, Johan: "Violence, Peace, and Peace Research". *Journal of Peace Research*, 6(3) 1969, retrieved 2.1.2021, from https://www.jstor.org/stable/422690, pp. 170–1.

11 Galtung, Johan: "Cultural Violence". *Journal of Peace Research*, 27(3) 1990, retrieved 2.1.2021, from https://www.jstor.org/stable/423472, p. 291.

12 ibid.

the rest of the narrative could conveniently distance itself. However, the perspective of the novel and of its central character are more intertwined than some of the more critical passages indicate. While readers might want to pause and reflect on Will's behaviour, the novel's autodiegetic narration effectively reproduces the power dynamics of the Thatcherite society that give centre stage to the wealthy individual but silences large groups of the marginalised. The latter, so one could argue based on these two novels, have only two options left: to withdraw themselves or to disrupt the dynamic via the use of violence.[13] Both options are not depicted as on par with Will's eloquent musings and autonomous decision-making. Even if the novel could be read as implicitly criticising Will's behaviour, this critique comes from a decidedly middle-class stance that is only too happy to reproduce class-based prejudices to score a point against the hypocrisy of the wealthy. The fact that the book can be read as a narrative of sexual liberation bears further testimony to the neoliberal idea that the freedom of the individual may be bought at the expense of other people's liberation.[14] This is the path Will successfully pursues and the book offers little space or consideration to those who pay the prize for Will's antics. The

---

13 Surely there are other ways of challenging the status quo, like non-violent protests, petitions, or establishing a counter culture, yet I would argue that they fall into a different category. First these alternative forms rely on privilege such as different forms of capital and (spare) time. Secondly, and no less importantly, they are often only effective when they can elicit the support or cooperation of the middle classes. For example an academic essay on middle-class hegemony will only be printed by a traditional publishing house if it gets the approval of middle-class gatekeepers. Thus in general these alternative forms leave the overall power matrix intact. While incrementalism is an important method to achieve societal change, especially *Exodus* points to the failure of these alternatives.

14 The novel's paratexts, in particular the blurbs found on the cover and inside, celebrate the book for the defiant stance of its gay protagonist, calling it 'the ultimate example of gay literature' and 'the first major novel in Britain to put gay life in its modern place and context'. Of course, these texts are meant to advertise the book, but they do so by creating a pedestal for its 'homosexual and reckless' protagonist and cast those who dislike the book as its moral enemies: 'This is a brave book. It doesn't polemicize and it doesn't apologize. It can only shock those who care or need to be shocked' (blurbs in Hollinghurst, front matter).

question is not whether readers find Will likeable, but that he is part of a set of complex characters, all hailing from the moneyed classes, in contrast to the one-dimensional, clichéd, and hackneyed representation of the marginalised. This is no exclusive feat of Hollinghurst's *The Swimming-Pool Library*, literature abounds in the one-dimensional and clichéd depiction of individuals from marginalised groups. It should be obvious that this is problematic, even in the cases when those individuals are portrayed as positive. Denying characters agency and complexity upholds ideas of dominance and thus is a form of cultural violence. The skinheads in Hollinghurst's novel might be violent within the story, but they are made the victims of the narrative perspective. In short, they hurt Will, but the book does them harm.[15]

In addition to the personal, structural, and cultural dimension of violence, I also want to give some thought to violence as a political force. Preceding the description of the assault, readers in *Exodus* are confronted with the words "Tell me why? Why? Secretly I know why", challenging the idea that what readers are about to witness is not an act of senseless violence, but is instead imbued with meaning.[16] The imbalance in political power indicates that both skinhead attacks could be classified as political violence, with both parties involved being at once victim and assailant. In his study *Democracy and Political Violence*, John Schwarzmantel defines political violence as

> the infliction of physical harm on individuals, or the threat to do this, in the pursuit of some political goal. A political goal can be distinguished from a private one in that the aim to be pursued through the use of violence is some change in the overall nature and structure of society, whether that involves a change in position of some group within it, or the nature of the laws, values and norms, which govern that society.[17]

---

15 This distinction is based on William C. Gay's essays 'The Role of Language in Justifying and Eliminating Cultural Violence' In: Fuat Gursozlu (ed.). *Peace, Culture, and Violence*; Brill Rodopi: Leiden, Boston 2018, in which he further develops Stephanie Ross' theory of offensive versus oppressive language.

16 DJ Stalingrad, p. 14.

17 Schwarzmantel, John: *Democracy and Political Violence*. Edinburgh University Press: Edinburgh 2011, p.14.

Will seems completely oblivious to the fact that he could be an agent of political violence, despite the fact that he knowingly exploits power imbalances to gratify his sexual desires.[18] When Will encounters the skinheads in the council estate, he does not only represent the upper-class interloper but also the male gaze, doubly objectifying the skinheads as 'white trash' and sex objects. As I am going to argue in more detail below, the skinhead's attack can thus be read not only as a defence of 'their' space, but as a resistance to their commodification. He also benefits from a political system – the politics of austerity, which marginalises groups deemed 'the other' based on race and class as well as its intersections – that, despite his homosexuality, revolves around his needs, safety, and well-being. His dark fantasies, in which he sexually assaults those (marginalised) individuals who do not submit to his sexual advances, do not merely bear witness to Will's amoral character, but to the mechanics of a society that has taught him from early on that those beneath him exist to obey and serve him, and deserve punishment should they refuse to do so. Thus when Will is denied by a young lower class boy whom he fancies, he channels his feelings of powerlessness into fantasies of sexual domination: "I saw myself pissing over him, jamming my cock down his throat, forcing my fingers up his ass – disturbing images with which to enter a Boys' Club. I resented his ability to resist me, and that I had no power over someone so young".[19] What should be noted is that the boy did not outright refuse Will, but resisted his *gratis* commodification and offers Will a transaction – money for sex – an act that makes the commodification within this sexual encounter visible, something which Will refuses (although Will would have been able to pay the boy any price he demanded, something Will readily admits). However, more than sex it is sex plus subordination he wants from lower-class boys. Will meeting with or lusting after young men from the lower classes can be read essentially as a commodification of lower-class bodies to satiate upper-class carnal appetites. His power is often visible as privilege but seldom as violence. Yet the violence becomes

18 In fact, Will's conquests frequently rely on the intersection of race and class, as his lovers are often young Black boys from working class backgrounds.

19 Hollinghurst, p. 134. It is ambiguous whether Will considers these ideas disturbing in general, or only disturbing in the context of going to a Boys' Club.

apparent when Will's position is challenged. His daydream reveals how structural violence has the potential to turn into personal direct violence. What Will lacks in self-awareness here is made up by the narrative perspective, at least implicitly. However, at other times the novel's representation of the lower class fuel the structural violence on which Will acts.

With its graphic depictions of violence, and its revelling in fighting and endurance, *Exodus* offers its readers a narrator who is fully aware of the violence he inflicts, at times gleefully so. At the same time, he uses the same drastic language to describe the violence that is done to him and his kind, "the crippled, the ill, the children of the proletariat, the stupid, the infantile, the failures, who make up a fucking huge percentage of this society."[20] He thereby deconstructs the capitalist myth of personal responsibility, for in a system based on exploitation and inequality, progress is only open to the privileged few (and, as readers are going to learn, to the 'class traitors' as well). The circularity of the plot emphasises this central argument. Compared to *The Swimming-Pool Library*, where the circularity of the plot is based on Will's volition, the vicious cycle in which DJ Stalingrad's protagonist and his friends are trapped is one of structural violence.[21] This does not legitimise the skinheads' direct violence against (privileged) individuals as representatives and agents of this structural violence, but it disrupts the hegemonic view that their violence is the disturbance of an otherwise harmonious social order. As *Exodus* makes so painfully clear, in a violent system, all individuals become agents of violence, differing only in their amount of political power and the form of violence.

---

20 DJ Stalingrad, pp. 14–15.

21 Read from a critical class perspective one can read the two circular plots in a way to tease out the way choice intersects with class. In Hollinghurst's novel, Will is confronted with the homophobia of the skinheads as well as of the heteronormative system, which both can result in violence. Yet even when Will learns that the wealth that sustains his lifestyle is built on the persecution of homosexuals, his response is neither political nor does it challenge the system in place. Uncovering his grandfather's political actions dismays him, but it does not endanger his privileges as indicated by the fact that Will prioritises his pleasure and a retreat into the private realm over political change. In contrast, in Exodus the only escape from the circularity of the plot is death or flight.

There is one form of violence that needs to be addressed before I will take a closer look at the literature: Epistemological violence. Based on Gayatri Spivak's text "Can the Subaltern Speak?",[22] epistemological violence can be understood as the knowledge production by those in power on the so-called 'other' that overrides the actual experiences of those marginalised and which thus creates and sustains systems of oppression and exploitation. In my reading, this pertains to the fact that knowledge on the lower classes and their lived experiences is rarely produced by those with a lower-class background. In the anthology *Know Your Place. Essays on the Working Class by the Working Class*, Andrew McMillan writes that:

> It's worth noting how many essays from 'The Academy' on the working class approach the subject almost as a zoological species to be observed and studied; they are already othered by the academic who strides in and tells them what their lives 'mean' or how they might be 'interpreted'.[23]

This asymmetric knowledge-production also affects how, for example, urban topography is read, labelling lower-class spaces as bleak, ugly, and problematic, and therefore spaces to avoid or to flee from. The same asymmetry is rampant among cultural products, like literature, music, and film. As a corollary, many lower-class characters and settings who are part of a cultural consciousness have not only sprung from the pen of someone decidedly unlike them, but more importantly steeped in hegemonic discourses of the (white, often male, often Christian) middle classes, as Connolly's example above shows. In the two books I analyse in this essay this difference in representation becomes especially salient.

22 Spivak, Gayatri: "Can the Subaltern Speak?". In: Cary Nelson & Lawrence Grossberg (eds.): *Marxism and the Interpretation of Culture*, University of Illinois Press: Chicago 1988.

23 McMillan, Andrew: "One of Us: Some Thoughts on Sexuality". In: Connolly, Nathan: *Know Your Place: Essays on the Working Class by the Working Class*; Dead Ink: Liverpool 2017, p. 93.

Violence to Resist Commodification in *The Swimming-Pool Library*

When the different strata of society mingle in Hollinghurst's novel, they mostly follow conventional power dynamics. This is best illustrated by Will's entirely lust-driven affair with Arthur Hope, a young Black lower-class boy. While I will not go into the details of their problematic relationship, it is Will's urge to see Arthur that brings him to the London council estate where he will eventually meet a group of skinheads. It is interesting to note how much Will identifies the council estate as "foreign territory", a place where he does not belong. Noting his bleak surroundings – the concrete, the stench of urine, racist graffiti – Will moves through the council estate as the unwelcome guest he truly is. Will's description of the council estates taps into the dominant cultural consciousness. Even to middle-class readers more critical of Will's antics, the council estates in *The Swimming-Pool Library* might seem like an apt copy of London's real urban lower-class landscape, since the novel essentially reproduces the popular fiction of council estates as abject places infested with crime, drugs, and poverty. While the history of the council estate can be read as the failure of a social utopia, the mono-dimensional characterisation of them as hellish both for their inhabitants and society at large must be considered a construct, which was specially furthered in the Thatcherite era.[24] Compare Lynsey Hanley's *Estates: An Intimate History*, which describes, council estates as "isolating, fear-filled, and abject"[25] with Gena-mour Barrett's "Living on an Estate Gave me a Community I Never Knew I Needed", which offers a very different picture.[26] It would be wrong to suggest that one

---

24 Cf. Duff, Kim: *Contemporary British Literature and Urban Space: After Thatcher*. Palgrave Macmillan: Basingstoke 2014, p. 57.

25 Duff, p. 61.

26 Consider the following passage: "Still, despite the idea that your only aspiration living on an estate should be to leave, I continue to question just how much better life actually becomes once we move. The truth is, I felt safer living on our rundown estate among people I trusted than in a house, isolated and alone, among people I didn't." (Barrett, Gena-mour: "Living on an Estate Gave me a Community I Never Knew I Needed". In: Connolly, Nathan (ed.): *Know Your Place*, p. 163). Comparing this passage to the representation of council estates in *The Swimming-Pool Library*, it becomes evident that their depiction as unsafe

representation is more correct than the other, instead we should accord lower-class spaces the plurality we normally accord middle and upper-class places. Moreover, in the novel the council estates become projections of entrapment. Will imagines Arthur's family almost as prisoners, and – after his unsuccessful attempt to meet Arthur – he himself is eager to leave, thinking that it would be best if they would meet "on common ground – a bar or club or out in the open air."[27] Will does not understand that the places he has in mind are not common ground, but spaces that mirror society's power dynamics, where Will feels at home, but which are structurally hostile to people like Arthur. Bars and clubs are also places of commerce that rely on consumption and are thus by design safe spaces for people with money. Will seems unaware of the economic logic that pervades the different spaces he inhabits. Moreover, Will, due to being part of the wealthy, is used to being welcomed into any kind of place, as most spatial exclusions are based on capital. The uncomfortable feeling of being unwanted in a certain space is therefore negotiated by othering the unwelcoming space, i.e. the council estate, and its inhabitants. Here the perspective of the narrative seems to align closely with Will's perspective by making the council estate seem particularly threatening, with the skinheads as the ultimate threat, preventing him from leaving. While Will quite palpably feels his being out-of-place, he seems only able to articulate this feeling by projecting it onto Arthur's family: "I thought with yearning of the Hopes [Arthur's family], whom I did not know, forced to contain their anger, contempt, and hurt in such a world."[28] Ironically the austerity politics that benefit people like Will have produced the setting he now so facetiously abhors.

For, as Will's meeting with the skinheads and preceding erotic fantasies revolving around one of them will make clear, his sexual attraction is inextricably linked to class dynamics:

---

and unwelcome spaces is a middle-class construction. In her chapter, Barrett argues not so much that council estates are ideal living environments but that for lower-class Black people white middle-class spaces can prove to be a lot more hostile, a perspective that is seldom covered in the debate surrounding council estates.

27 Hollinghurst, p. 171.

28 Hollinghurst, p. 171.

> They were a challenge, skinheads, and made me feel shifty as they stood about the streets and shopping precincts, magnetising the attention they aimed to repel. Cretinously simplified to booted feet, bum and bullet head, they had some, if not all, of the things one was looking for.[29]

Skinheads are idealised sex objects for Will primarily because they (seemingly) fulfil lower-class clichés of stupidity, bruteness, and corporality as opposed to the cultured, refined, and sophisticated members of the upper echelons of society. Subjected to the middle class male gay gaze, the skinheads are fragmented into pieces ready for (carnal) consumption. When Will sees the group of skinheads for the first time he muses:

> One of them, slobbish, with moronic sideburns, and braces hoisting his jeans up around a fat ass and a fat dick, was very good. I looked at him for only a second; a phrase from the Firbank I had just been reading came back to me: 'Très gutter, ma'am'.[30]

Looking at the skinheads, Will's description of them is informed by his sexual desires as much as it is by his prejudices. Yet his explicitly stated superiority is in the end challenged by the skinheads' seeming reversal of power and resort to violence, a turn that seems to confirm Will's image of them in the first place. Through the eyes of Firbank, the skinheads become objects in the council house tableau, appealing if they can be consumed like a commodity, but problematic when they gain agency to refuse consumption. Standing among the estate's trashcans and sporting badly tattooed swastikas, the skinheads become the embodiment of 'white trash', delineating not only their place in society, but also in the chain of consumption. It is no coincidence that before beating up Will, the skinheads also destroy his copy of Firbank, incidentally the book that was used to label them as inferior a few pages before:

> I saw two things: my beautiful new copy of [Firbank's novel] had been jerked from my pocket in the scuffle. [...] A boot slammed down on it, buckling the binding, and then again and again, grinding the pages into the warm-smelling spilt rubbish...[31]

---

29 Hollinghurst, p. 172.
30 Hollinghurst, p. 170.
31 Hollinghurst, p. 174.

The book becomes one with the rubbish that litters the pavement: A crime not so much because of its connotations of theft, but because the novel is downgraded from an object of cultural significance to a disposable commodity. Thus their act of violence evokes a double symbolic significance: they are a threat to liberal society and destroyers of culture. Their set-up as 'moronic' and fascist[32] makes this reading jarringly obvious as much as it is troubling, for it attempts to hide Will's predatory power. He invades the space, the council estate, that has been set up by the politics in power to marginalise poor people, an act that would constitute trespassing if it were done the other way around. Housing politics, the privatisation of public space and increased surveillance are concrete topographic manifestations of the power hierarchies that determine who is allowed to use which space. While there is no excuse for the skinhead's right-wing attitude and homophobia, Will is far away from being a proponent of a liberal, tolerant, and just society. In fact, Will is only willing to stand up for and defend his own liberties (emphasised by his remark "It was actually happening. It was actually happening to me" that precede his recounting of the attack);[33] something that is not that different, when his hyper-privileged position as a white upper-class man is taken into account, from the crude nationalism of the skinheads.[34] While the skinheads' adherence to right-wing ideology is obvious enough, Will embraces a system in which individual freedom, well-being, and self-fulfilment relies on whiteness, wealth, and masculinity. It is thus a form of bourgeois nationalism that does not primarily commit physical violence against "the other" (as the skinheads do) but keeps "the other" contained by consuming them.

---

32 One of the characters is described as having a crude swastika tattoo, linking the skinheads to the numerous National Front graffiti Will spots around the estate.

33 Hollinghurst, p. 174.

34 Compare this to Neves: "In displaying a protagonist whose freedom is granted by his class, whiteness and education, Hollinghurst shows that this image of 'sexual freedom' is not available to all people, but only to those who can afford to be part of a selected community of gay men. [...] If neoliberal politics prospered under the promise of individual freedom, Hollinghurst certainly makes the point that this freedom is only achievable to a very small percentage of the population, who enjoys the privileges of whiteness, wealth and masculinity", p. 203.

The construction of the skinheads as not only model clichés but also by the evocation of strength through violence distracts from the fact that Will is, after all, the more problematic character. Read in this way, the novel exposes a common double standard in the evaluation of members of different classes. Initially set up as the antithesis to the upper-class Will, readers might come to the conclusion that the skinheads do not differ radically from Hollinghurst's protagonist: both idle away their time, find joy in simple and physical activities and exploit given power dynamics in their favour. From his privileged position, Will has the possibility to go about in a more cultured and supposedly sophisticated manner. Yet, his underlying racist exoticism that feeds into his relationship with Arthur is not morally superior to the skinheads' outright white supremacy; his sexual adventures in bars and clubs are not inherently more meaningful than the skinheads' mock fights. There is little ground to find Will a more sympathetic and valuable member of society were it not for class dynamics that benefit people like him (and the fact that the novel is narrated by him increases the bias). The novel echoes the dominant discourse that only members of the privileged classes are in a position where their safety, needs, and individuality matter. This double standard might predispose readers to be revolted at the violence aimed at Will, but not at the violence Will employs (or fantasises about), although it is magnified by the system that in matters of gender, race, and class acts in his favour. Making the skinhead scene one of the book's pivotal moments suggests that the novel primarily draws attention to Will as victim, while it downplays his agency in systems of structural violence, especially so since the skinheads as stock British characters are constructed to be personifications of the troubled aspects of British society.

Being beaten up by the skinheads in a homophobic attack seems to make the skinheads agents of society's homophobic policies, as Will and his friends understand it. Read in this way the novel mirrors the words of the famous gay German filmmaker Rosa von Praunheim whose best-known documentary is titled: *Nicht der Homosexuelle ist pervers, sondern die Situation, in der er lebt* [Not the homosexual is a pervert, but the situation, in which he exists]. Decades later, one can read DJ Stalingrad's *Exodus* as a possible reply: maybe it is not the skinhead who is violent, but the society in which he lives, something that might be true for Hollinghurst's novel as well.

Literary Writing as Violence in *Exodus*

In *Exodus* readers find a scene similar to the one described in Hollinghurst's novel, yet here the narrative roles are reversed. The skinhead becomes the narrating subject, approaching his victim unaware from behind. In a short scene preceding the attack, he constructs a comparison between the two men, himself and his victim, which could not be starker:

> The guy is nicely dressed, humble, stylish. Proper haircut, sharp-featured, athletic, into sports, hopeful gaze from brown eyes.
>
> He is not one of those dressed-up faggots, he is a serious, good guy – a strong, courageous, okay kind of guy. [...] One night this guy stands in front of a shop and I approach him from behind. Dressed in a shabby sweater, dirty trainers, badly-shaven head, bumfluff, face full of pimples, rotten teeth.[35]

Couched in homophobic language, the narrator paints an admiring picture of his victim; he seemingly has everything the narrator lacks. This does not save him from the violence he is about to fall victim to. In fact, it makes it worse:

> Within one second this great guy is transformed into a pile of shit. An iron pipe turns his head into bloody mincemeat. Teeth, shreds of skin, and blood fly in all directions. I am a failure at school, detested by my classmates, I drink and wank. Sunken chest, rickets, asthma prone, and a weak heart, never had a normal job, never had a father, never had a girlfriend. Now within one second that wanker is paying for all these years, my whole life, for all these idiots like me, the crippled, the ill, the children of the proletariat, the stupid, the infantile, the failures, who make up a fucking huge percentage of this society. I will smash his head in with this iron pipe for all of us, and there will be something sacred to it; everything sacred has something of this.[36]

Underneath the graphic display of violent language lies a meditation on the different layers of power. The power suggested by the force of the violent blows that sends "teeth, shreds of skin, and blood fly[ing] in all directions" is instantly contradicted by a self-description that focuses on

35 DJ Stalingrad, p. 14.
36 DJ Stalingrad, pp. 14–15.

the very powerlessness of the narrator. It adds to a scene that is almost cliché (a skinhead beating up his unsuspecting victim) a depth that allows readers maybe not exactly to sympathise with the narrator, but to grasp this act of violence as part of a structural dynamic, in which different forms of violence have been inflicted upon the narrator. As the narrator declares his individual act of violence as a revenge for the many, he creates a case of divine justice. The description of himself works as a *pars pro toto* and so does his action. By comparing himself to his outwardly flawless victim, the narrator, at first, conveys notions of individual responsibility. However, the narrator's continued description of himself, while inflicting violence, shows his traits to be products of systemic oppression. Poverty, ill health exacerbated by poverty and environmental discrimination – rickets is primarily caused by malnutrition and vitamin deficiency, the combination with asthma points to pollution – and the lack of social ties determine the narrator's existence. Not living up to societal expectations and standards – failing at school, hailing from a dysfunctional family, lack of a girlfriend – can be seen as individual predicaments, yet they are interdependent with a system of epistemological violence that assigns values to things like the nuclear family, romantic relationships, and success in a standardised testing environment. His identification with a diverse set of the disadvantaged suggest that the failures that are perceived as products of individual (ir)responsibility, are in fact, products of systemic oppression.

The predatory capitalism that developed in Russia after the break-up of the Soviet Union and its accompanying political system brought extreme economic inequality and destitution to many.[37] The narrator's answer to

37 The 1990s were a time of great economic and political turmoil and upheaval. *Exodus* devotes several passages to this time of transition in Russia and the many people it left behind; see, for example, pp. 50–51, 73, and pp. 124–5. In her book *The Future is History,* in which Masha Gessen looks at the nineties and aughts through the lens of personal biographies, she brings up the following: "There was a specific Russian expression: *budushchego net*, 'There is no future.' As though it could indeed by canceled. People said it when a particular vision of the future collapsed. For many people […] the future ended when the Soviet Union collapsed and the narrow hallways disappeared. Many struggled on, but the anxiety caused by uncertainty rendered them incapable of meaningful action", Gessen, Masha: *The Future is History. How Totalitarianism Reclaimed Russia.* Granta: London 2017, p. 309. This is the backdrop against which *Exodus* needs

this system of inequality is levelling it down. Not by following the dominant discourse of upwards class mobility through hard work, education, and grit, but by forcing those privileged by the use of brute force to become 'a pile of shit', or in other words: just as worthless as the narrator and his kind. The reversal of violence inflicted happens on multiple levels as well. It is not only the skinhead narrator who takes physical revenge on a random man he identifies as a representative of the systemic violence, which has made his life, and the life of others, miserable, where nothing that constitutes a so-called normal life was ever attainable. The narrator also reverses the epistemological power imbalance, by turning the middle-class man into an interchangeable nameless individual, while he gives voice to those who normally remain invisible. His violent act becomes a symbolic act "for all of us", a group that deliberately excludes those individuals privileged and in power. The victim becomes a prop in a narrative that centres those usually marginalised and marginalises those who are usually centred in narratives. What should be noted, however, is that by making himself the defender of all the disadvantaged, the narrator erases his own involvement in society's power dynamics. In his simple binary, pitching those with power against those without, he conveniently brushes over any inner-group hierarchies. By presenting himself and his friends as existing at the bottom of society, the narrator withholds that some groups range even lower on the societal ladder. This holds especially true with regards to women. While the book's main targets are the middle classes and middle class (capitalist) discourses, women become the collateral damage in this attack, not by having physical violence but epistemological violence inflicted upon them. This is especially important since *Exodus* is not so much an unbridled revelling in physical violence, but an attempt of writing back against epistemological violence.

At the heart of *Exodus,* so I would argue, lies thus not the physical brutality of the skinheads, but a critique of the ubiquity of middle-class narratives that are used to hold existing power structures in place by

---

to be read. Interestingly the Russian *budushchego net* mirrors the British subculture slogan "no future", popularised by the Sex Pistols as an attack against the establishment, but by many during that time also used to express pessimism in the face of a possible nuclear war.

creating hopes which cannot be fulfilled. These narratives work in conjunction with an oppressive system that keeps the lower classes in destitution and despair while they are being fed the neoliberal myth of personal responsibility to lift yourself out of your present (socio-economic) position.

> They have swindled us, the clever and the rich bastards. They have told us, the masses of the crippled, the poor and stupid, that we are worthy of many things. That we could create something great or at least something good. [...]. They have divided us and taken possession of us. Now they use us for their aims, those great and clever people [...] I don't need your fairy tales and fantasies, made up out of nothing. Everything was invented by those clever fucks, with their business plans and iPhones, talents and scholarships, they sneer at you and watch as you struggle while you're trying to console each other. The paradise doesn't exist and will never exist, forget that shit.[38]

The narrator dissects the role of hegemonic narratives to keep systems of oppression in place. One can identify elements of religion (the idea of paradise to come), political strategy (*divide et impera*) as well as commodity fetishism. As he makes clear the violence of oppression depends on discursive myths to 'sell' the virtue of a system to those victimised by it. Promises of future bliss (or at least well-being) are coupled with tactics to undermine intra-group solidarity ensuring that the system itself escapes critique, because the (unwilling) cooperation of the marginalised is needed to keep the system functioning. As becomes apparent in a later scene, even the violence of the skinheads can become an element to uphold the system of power if they are willing to cooperate with the state. The same type of violence by the same set of people can thus be subversive or hegemonic depending on the way it is discursively framed. The quote above ends with a reference to paradise, denouncing it a myth. While this at first glance may seem like a dejected finish, I would argue that it could be read as empowering the marginalised. The myth of paradise is a prominent element of religious discourses,[39] and is an especially insidious one by dint

38 DJ Stalingrad, pp. 22–23.

39 As the title of the book indicates, religion plays an important, albeit ambivalent, role in *Exodus*. The frequent use of religious imagery suggests that violence is or can be sacred and that religion also thrives on violence. Religion also offers an alternative to violence, yet its entanglement with the system in power leave it tainted.

of its ability to legitimate suffering by promising a just reward in the form of eternal happiness. As a narrative it functions similarly to capitalist discourses, which encourage toil with the potential of wealth. Both narratives are hegemonic as they keep existing power structures in place and serve as explanations for the existence of oppression and suffering. From within they leave little room to imagine (or affect) change, as they punish dissenters with absolute misery (either hell or severe deprivation) and exclusion from the community. Read in this way, the myth of paradise becomes a soothing narrative to relieve the suffering lower classes of some of their worries by pretending that everything will be well in the end. More importantly it becomes a smokescreen for violence inflicted upon those it sets out to comfort. When the narrator appeals to his imagined audience of the downtrodden to "forget that shit", he does not ask them to refrain from imagining a better future, but to stop acquiescing to a narrative that sells them their present suffering as meaningful.

But in the contemporary Russia of DJ Stalingrad, a better future for the downtrodden is hardly achievable. Life for the lower classes is one of toil and pain and of little reward:

> Imagine you are a piece of living meat in the cattle shed, not clever, not talented, not rich, not healthy. […] Now your main task for the rest of your life is to navigate the revolting pain and madness, which your generous fate has so abundantly planted in your life. This is your only purpose, and not the creation of a better world, the development of talents, individual fulfilment in the sciences or art, the accumulation of riches and prosperity. You don't have and never had the mental or financial resources for all of this; that is nonsense. No matter how much you work, the only success you may dream of is buying a Zhiguli. Artistic achievement? The only thing you can achieve is idiocy just like you are an idiot. The only thing you should strive for in life is to not become homeless, severely disabled or obviously mad and then a swift and painless death.[40]

A good life for the downtrodden, so the passage indicates, is primarily one of escape: avoiding homelessness, madness, and pain is the best you can hope for. The metaphor of the piece of meat in the cattle shed frames the

---

40 DJ Stalingrad, p. 24. A Zhiguli (Russian: Жигули) was a type of car aimed at the middle-class market produced by the Russian company AwtoWAS. In Western Europe (including the former GDR) it is more commonly known as Lada, a name that was later also used for the Russian market.

existence of the lower classes as part of a logic of exploitation, in which the lower classes exist solely to be used; to be the objects of somebody else's individual fulfilment, but never the subjects of their own. What is noteworthy about the quote is that it is addressed at an imagined middle-class audience, one for which the life described is not lived reality. It also contradicts itself. For the narrator-protagonist who speaks to us does so via a product of artistic achievement. This does not invalidate his argument here. Rather, it points to the fact that the dominance of middle-class discourses is causally linked to the lack of life-opportunities the lower classes have. As they cannot participate in discourse formation, they become further victimised by hegemonic discourses that legitimise their oppression. The skinheads' violence is thus a 'talking back', using one form of violence against another. While this strategy seems to be successful for DJ Stalingrad, after all with the help of *Exodus* he inserts himself into the discourse, the skinheads' violence also perpetuates ideas of the lower classes as brutish and uncultured. In the examples discussed, using physical violence reshuffles power imbalances on the streets, but largely leaves the systemic power dynamics intact. Only when DJ Stalingrad employs a form of violence that those in power usually rely on, in this case epistemological violence, can he effectively disturb the system. In his short introductory text, Sergey Chuprinin, editor-in-chief of *Znamya*, the literary magazine that published *Exodus*, writes that "without these voices, without these lives, our idea of the country and the people will also be wilfully incomplete" as a defense against potential critics, who might be outraged by the subject matter and language of the text.[41]

The only possibility for the lower classes to actively participate in society is through consumption. Buying a Zhiguli suggests that success, namely upwards class mobility, is a matter of economic transaction and not self-fulfilment. Consumption, the great pacifier, keeps people locked in a system of labour while giving them the illusion of choice. True choice, however, is a privilege of the middle class, as *Exodus* suggests again and again. Yet the narrator and his friends disrupt the logic of consumption: not merely

---

41 Chuprinin, Sergey ["Потому что без этих голосов, без этих жизней наше представление о стране и народе будет тоже заведомо неполным."] foreword to DJ Stalingrad; Исход. In: Журнальный зал: Знамя, 2010 №9.

by reverting to theft whenever possible, but by substituting the materialist status symbols of a capitalist society with the destructive force of violence:

> [Fedja] told us once, how he met an old school friend, who works in an office, cheap jacket, just grinning and telling him for an hour how he just bought a new home exercise machine, how great it is, lauding himself. Fedja is tired, hung over, and just returned from work and that guy asked him: So what did you achieve? Fedja is fucking annoyed and brutally direct: 'Don't have a home exercise machine, don't have any money either, but yesterday I beat up a guy on Ryazansky Prospekt with a bucket. He even had to be taken away by an ambulance…'[42]

Fedja's old school friend has (quite literally) bought into hegemonic discourses of success that equate achievement with consumption. Fedja, on the other hand, lacks the money to do so despite being employed. More importantly, he refuses to participate in capitalist cycles of labour and consumption. Instead, he elevates the violence he inflicts on other people to a status symbol, measured by absurdity ("with a bucket") and severity ("even had to be taken away by an ambulance"). Passing of his violent but ridiculous act as an achievement, he caricatures society's (and his old friend's) notion of success. Moreover, violence becomes a form of self-fulfilment, an identity building method on par with consumption, with the added benefit that it doubly antagonises the system. It is destructive but more importantly it is a refusal of cooperation with the system in power. This can be read as a reply to the passage quoted earlier, which identified consumption as the only possible success for the lower classes, whereas individual fulfilment was a privilege of the wealthy. Violence thus becomes an integral part of an identity construct; just as the objects people purchase often reflect their identity more than fulfilling any real need. While Fedja's glorification of violence appears problematic, the narrator-protagonist offers a more complex take on the role of violence in and for a given society.

The skinheads' violence seems problematic because it is destructive and meaningless. However, it is not only the brute force of violence that truly makes it problematic, but the fact that it undermines social conventions, rules, and laws. On the contrary, there are agents who commit similar

42 DJ Stalingrad, p. 9.

violence as the skinheads and who remain accepted members of society not despite, but precisely because of their use of violence: the police. The police can commit violence in the name of the system in power, thereby operating as the personification of the rules and norms imposed. Their behaviour receives legitimacy by existing laws but also by those discourses that frame violations of the norm as crimes. Thus joining the police would be a form of cooperation with the system. Success, i.e. the chance to leave poverty, comes at a price of becoming a traitor to your own class, upholding systemic force against the marginalised. Violence can become an acceptable means of work when it is employed by the state and for the state to uphold the hegemonic system. Thus men, who have "the valuable characteristic of inflicting and enduring pain"[43] become useful assets when recruited by the police, but problematic when they act upon their own volition. The difference lies not in the means or forms of violence, but in the way it is framed by discourses.[44] The narrator- protagonist makes this clear when he muses on war as a "socially beneficial bloodbath":

> In human societies there was always a process of natural selection that weeded out the useless part of the male species. From birth they are unable to productively participate in society, they would be bad husbands, fathers, workers, CEOs. This is genetic, these people have a destructive disposition from the very start. [...] When they are ready, they are sent on their predestined path: into the socially beneficial bloodbath. Usually that means war. [...] If this does not happen [...] the male blood, that has not been drained, starts to ferment and poison everything.

43 Cf. DJ Stalingrad, p. 49.

44 Of course, theoretically, police violence is curtailed by the means they are allowed to employ as well as concerning the range. In practice the police has the right to maim and kill to restore order or to ward off an attack and is frequently exempt from legal prosecution. There is a whole media industry that fuels the narrative of the police as a force to protect and solve crimes. It is mostly in counter-cultural discourses where the police as a brutal and at times deadly force is emphasised. Thus while #BlackLivesMatter has gained currency, it is often challenged by the colour-blind #AllLivesMatter and the pro-police #BlueLivesMatter. It is noteworthy that every time legitimate criticism of police violence is voiced, it is immediately countered by narrative defence mechanisms that stress the central and exceptional role of the police. This does not mean that all cops are bastards, but that the police as a force is couched in a narrative that legitimises their violent deeds, even when the very same acts committed by non-police individuals would be considered (hate) crimes.

> [...] Now war is shifted into the midst of society, one part of these useless men are called *police*, the rest *criminals*.[45]

The useless violent male population is seemingly arbitrarily divided into those who uphold state power and those who undermine it. It is not by chance that the police are among the most hated by the narrator-protagonist and his friends. Not only because they are their direct antagonists, but because they have become the henchmen of a system which now helps to facilitate their suffering. In *Exodus* central narratives on violence are turned upside down. Subversive, disruptive violence is lauded, whereas state violence that puts discourses of oppression into practice is condemned. Yet what the book does not – maybe cannot – present is a way out of this. The anti-development plot entirely ridicules the notion of progress, the narrative of upward mobility the lower classes are meant to strive for. Instead it describes an existence in gridlock, in which the circular plot mirrors the lack of choices the lower classes have in contemporary Russia, in which they are forced to gyrate "in this morass, trying to escape, but no one ever does."[46]

The narrator's ideas of genetic determinism stand in stark contrast to capitalist notions of choice, where everyone can – with the right amount of talent and labour – become anything. Despite its nihilistic subtext, the narrator in the above quote still relies on a logic of exploitation. These so-called useless men do, in fact, have a use by being the material for wars. Despite their supposed uselessness, these men fulfil a certain (dialectic) function, which grants them a group identity. Yet the narrator's explanation is noticeably gendered, completely disregarding women. This leaves open whether women are not considered genetically useless or if they range even lower in the hierarchy of uselessness by not even serving any function whatsoever and thus becoming invisible; an invisibility the text reinforces.

---

45 DJ Stalingrad, pp. 48–49. An idea that is reminiscent of the Futurist manifesto's exhortation of war as the sole hygiene of the world. This is not to suggest that the narrator-protagonist shares the same political outlook as the Futurists, namely fascism, but that the idea of war as a cleansing force and humanity as in need of such cleansing has remained popular. With the Futurists it was a claim dealt from above, in *Exodus* it is a claim from below, where the narrator-protagonist imagines himself to die in such a war.

46 DJ Stalingrad, p. 117.

In general, women are continually side-lined in *Exodus*, primarily relegated to their accessory function as mothers, wives, and lovers. It is not surprising but warrants mentioning that despite the book's harsh condemnation of existing power imbalances concerning class, *Exodus* leaves the patriarchy very much intact and uncontested.[47] Violence as a means and as an identity seems only available to men. The few instances in the book when women are shown to be violent, for example the protagonist's mother hitting her son, they become objects of pity and derision. Female violence, which often happens in a domestic context, is presented as the antithesis of care. Thus while violence bestows agency upon men and acts as a subversive means against the system in power, female violence signifies a lack of agency and makes women enablers of systemic oppression. This becomes especially problematic when set against *Exodus*' presentation of violence as the only thing that will set you free:

> But then I suddenly got it, as if someone had whispered it to me. You just need to beat up everyone. Simply beat up everyone. Don't listen to stories, disregard epaulettes and hierarchies – just beat them up. That was the language everyone was lacking. And there you have it: it worked. Every little fucker, bandit, nazi, policeman or bully, who simply got one in the face with no explanation, suddenly became sensible, as if some fucking vicious cycle in his head had been broken for a moment. For a few seconds he saw the world in a new light – and we helped them do it.[48]

Engaging in violence becomes a form of communication. As the skinheads are denied any form of cooperation unless they fully collaborate with the state, violence becomes the only tool to pry the closed-off discourse open for them. Subversive violence becomes a language that facilitates understanding, because it acts as a response within the dominant logic but also directly antagonistic to it. What is interesting about this passage is that violence is not only portrayed as cathartic, but as a positive force. Again this seems to endorse theories from the beginning of the twentieth century, more specifically in this case Georges Sorel's *Reflections on Violence*, in which he argued that violence is always also constructive in its destructiveness

47 In this respect *Exodus* also reproduces certain dimensions of structural violence.
48 DJ Stalingrad, p. 118.

by producing those qualities a bourgeois degenerate society is lacking.[49] Even more important than Sorel are two Russian figures, Mikhail Bakunin and Boris Savinkov, to contextualise the idea of violence as language here. Bakunin, the founder of collectivist anarchism, championed the idea of the violent rebellion by the peasants and even the *lumpenproletariat* against "all vestiges of the existing order".[50] Unsurprisingly, Bakunin's ideas also drew heavy criticism from within revolutionary circles, who saw "the economic and political struggle of the workers for their emancipation [] replaced by universal pan-destructive acts of heroes of the underworld".[51] *Exodus*'s embrace of violence situates itself squarely on Bakunin's side, although it seems to have less faith in the revolutionary power of violence. Instead personal violence is used to disrupt the structural violence in society, yet with no overarching utopia or political plan in tow. In this respect, *Exodus* calls to mind Savinkov writing, first and foremost his book *The Pale Horse*, which is equally suffused with violence as well as religious allusions and could also be read as an autobiografiction. Narrated from the perspective of a terrorist and written by a terrorist, the novel devotes itself to a negotiation of violence as an act that seemingly transcends mere politics. When *Exodus* inscribes itself into this literary tradition it seems to imbue the idea of 'violence as language' with an additional layer of meaning, but it also suggests a circular entrapment that foreshadows that this kind of violence brings no progress, neither to society nor to the violent individual. Boris Savinkov's career ended on the pavement outside the Lubyanka prison. In *Exodus* the ever-escalating violence will eventually force the narrator-protagonist to leave the country, and to move full circle, to write. It is, after all, writing that will truly set him free: The language of violence that informed his life now informs his writing, producing graphic images and a literary whirlpool of hate and self-hate. Just as the

49 Cf. Sorel, Georges: *Reflections on Violence*. Dover Publications: Mineola, New York, 2004, pp. 274–276. It may not surprise that Sorel's ideas on violence influenced the genesis of fascist ideology; One of Sorel's most notable readers was the *duce* Benito Mussolini himself.

50 Goodwin, J. Frank: "Violence and the Legacy of 'Bakuninism'". In: Levitt, Marcus C. / Novikov, Tatyana. *Times of Trouble: Violence in Russian Literature and Culture*. University of Wisconsin Press: Madison 2007, p. 104.

51 Quoted in Goodwin, p. 104.

narrator-protagonist identified physical violence as a kind of language, writing can become a type of violence.

This is not meant to glorify violence, or to promote subversive violence in particular. Yet violence has to be understood as a pervasive phenomenon that shapes societies and the lived realities of individuals in many ways beyond the sphere of physical violence. These other dimensions of violence, may they be structural or epistemological, often remain hidden. Laying them bare, as *Exodus* does, threatens to disturb established power dynamics, an act that by is often perceived by those in power as an attack. For the narrator-protagonist and his friends, violence is the only way to interact with their society on their own terms. It offers them agency and it is the only language that enables them to make themselves heard.

Conclusion

Skinhead violence is not in itself particularly interesting. The narrator-protagonist's claim that there is something sacred to it is equally void. These were not the claims I was making in this chapter when I argued that violence for the literary subjects was a viable option to counteract the systemic violence that entraps them daily. In Hollinghurst's *The Swimming-Pool Library* the privileged protagonist lives relatively unencumbered from structural violence. The ostensible brutality in his encounter with the skinheads forcefully brings physical violence into Will's life. Yet by turning Will into a victim, the novel helps to hide his own agency in systems of power and oppression. On the other hand, the narrator-protagonist from *Exodus* and his friends revel in physical violence, while they are simultaneously acutely aware of their lack of power. The many levels of structural violence weigh heavily on those who have to bear the brunt of them. Moreover, structural violence and individual subversive violence can come in similar forms. The police (or on another level, soldiers) attacking individuals or groups would appear quite similar to subversive physical violence, were it not discursively framed differently. Yet the former helps to uphold the current power system as well as dominant discourses, which at the same time constructs institutionalised forms of violence as legitimate and oftentimes necessary. The protagonist-narrator in *Exodus* understands this; Will from *The Swimming-Pool Library* arguably does not. Yet Will's well-being is not dependent on grasping the societal dynamics of violence, on the other hand DJ Stalingrad's narrator-protagonist gains no benefit from this realisation. While the use of subversive violence offers him and his skinhead friends a short-lived and thus perilous position of power the only long-term options available are his exodus, prison or death.

References

Chuprinin, Sergey: foreword to DJ Stalingrad. *Исход*. In: *Знамя*, 2010 №9.

Connolly, Nathan: *Know Your Place: Essays on the Working Class by the Working Class*; Dead Ink: Liverpool 2017.

DJ Stalingrad: *Exodus*. Matthes & Seitz: Berlin 2013.

Duff, Kim. *Contemporary British Literature and Urban Space: After Thatcher*: Palgrave Macmillan: Basingstoke 2014.

Farin, Klaus / Seidel-Pielen, Eberhard: *Skinheads*. C.H. Beck: München 1993.Galtung, Johan: "Violence, Peace, and Peace Research". *Journal of Peace Research*, 6(3) 1969, pp. 167–191, retrieved 2.1.2021, from https://www.jstor.org/stable/422690.

Galtung, Johan: "Cultural Violence". *Journal of Peace Research*, 27(3) 1990, pp. 291–305, retrieved 2.1.2021, from https://www.jstor.org/stable/423472.

Gay, William C: "The Role of Language in Justifying and Eliminating Cultural Violence". In: Fuat Gursozlu (ed.). *Peace, Culture, and Violence*; Brill Rodopi: Leiden, Boston 2018.

Gessen, Masha: *The Future is History. How Totalitarianism Reclaimed Russia*. Granta: London 2017.

Goodwin, J. Frank: "Violence and the Legacy of 'Bakuninism' ". In: Levitt, Marcus C. / Novikov, Tatyana: *Times of Trouble: Violence in Russian Literature and Culture*. University of Wisconsin Press: Madison 2007.

Hollinghurst, Alan: *The Swimming-Pool Library*. Penguin: London 1988.

Neves, Júlia Braga: *London, Queer Spaces and Historiography in the Works of Sarah Waters and Alan Hollinghurst*. dissertation; 2018.

North, Michael: *The Dialect of Modernism: Race, Language, and Twentieth-Century Literature*. Oxford University Press: Oxford 1994

Saunders, Max: *Self-Impression: Life-Writing, Autobiografiction, and the forms of Modern Literature*. Oxford University Press: Oxford 2010.

Schwarzmantel, John: *Democracy and Political Violence*. Edinburgh University Press: Edinburgh 2011.

Sorel, Georges: *Reflections on Violence*. Dover Publications: Mineola, New York 2004.

Spivak, Gayatri: "Can the Subaltern Speak?". In: Cary Nelson & Lawrence Grossberg (eds.): *Marxism and the Interpretation of Culture*, University of Illinois Press: Chicago 1988.

Dorothea Trotter

Right to Work: The Humanitarian Migrant as Economic Subject in Contemporary German Literature

Abstract: *Global migration flows in the 21st century have cast old debates about the complicated relationship between work, integration, and the nation-state into new light. Literary texts in particular provide a medium for the critique of state policies and social discourses, often by articulating a criticism of the treatment of asylum seekers in relation to the central values which those societies allege to follow. Considering Elfriede Jelinek's 2013* Die Schutzbefohlenen, *Jenny Erpenbeck's 2015* Gehen, ging, gegangen, *and Abbas Khider's 2016* Ohrfeige, *this paper provides some insight into the intricate relationship between work and refugee status. Specifically, it looks at how lack of access to the labour market affects feelings of space, time, integration, and belonging for migrants, and how these representations can critique the system of which the character is made a subject.*

Keywords: transnational, asylum, refugees, integration, labour market, nation-state

Introduction

Our lives and livelihoods are often defined by our work: how hard we work, how much money it makes us, and how much time we spend working and not working. Given the centrality of work to so many aspects of our lives, it is not surprising that those who do not work are excluded from social discourse in significant ways. A proportion of the population has restricted access to jobs because of age, lack of training, or mental or physical disability. However, most nation-states also exclude a small percentage of trained adults not living with a disability from the labour market, not because they do not want to work or are physically or mentally unable to do so, but because they are not citizens. While nearly three-fourths of the world's international migrants are of working age,[1] the numbers of

1 74 % of the world's working migrants are ages 20–64; International Organization for Migration (IOM): *World Migration Report 2020*. International Organization for Migration: Geneva 2019, p. 3.

unemployed asylum seekers and refugees are responsible for a relatively high average international foreign-born unemployment rate of around ten percent.[2]

In the UK, Germany, and especially the US,[3] where immigration rates are among the highest in the world, laws governing access to the labour market are strict. In Germany, for example, most refugees are allowed to work after four years of taking up residence if they can provide the appropriate professional qualifications and language skills.[4] While a select few are permitted to work after three months, even ninety days can be a long time to spend without a routine, feelings of accomplishment, social interactions, and at least minimum wage—and this is assuming the person can find work after three months.[5] State regulations result in visible and invisible groups of people on the border of survival, forced to seek work illegally (often thereby inadvertently threatening their asylum applications) or else be accused of 'loitering about,' causing social disturbance or depleting state resources provided by the taxpayers.

At the same time, access to good jobs is an important driver of social cohesion.[6] In the conversations about regulations for migrants entering the labour market, policy makers reason that work provides both practical self-sufficiency and enhanced integration.[7] With this, one refers to the

---

2 OECD (2020), "Foreign-born unemployment (indicator)", 2020, retrieved 24.4.2020. doi: 10.1787/ba5d2ce0-en.

3 Coincidentally (or perhaps not) also the three countries represented at the 2018 Trilateral Conference.

4 The right to work in Germany is determined by the status of asylum granted and the amount of time already in Germany. "Beschäftigung oder Erwerbstätigkeit gestattet" needs to stand in the papers in order to be permitted to work. After four years of being in the country, this right is usually given.

5 Asylum seekers are given financial support in the time it takes for their applications to be reviewed and/or before finding work. However, these sums, varying based on whether the migrant lives in federal accommodation or private are all less than the average social welfare check in Europe. This information can be found on the *The Asylum Information Database* (AIDA).

6 Wietzke, Frank-Borge: "Policy Research Working Paper 6804: Pathways from jobs to social cohesion". *The World Bank Research Observer,* 2014.

7 Trines, Stephen: "The State of Refugee Integration in Germany in 2019". *WENR World Education News and Reviews* 8.8.2019., retrieved 28.2.2020, from https://wenr.wes.org/2019/08/the-state-of-refugee-integration-in-germany-in-2019

social interactions and the language skills that can be gained by working together with members of the workforce, in this case assumed to be mostly citizens. However, what is implied is that the migrant will be more quickly exposed to the social values and norms of their new community, which would lead to a quicker assimilation and initiate the process of becoming full citizens. While assimilation is the simple way of removing tensions in heterogenous communities, many view it as less preferable to integration, which involves the two-way adaptation efforts of both the migrants and receiving community.[8] The resulting incorporation into social, economic, cultural and political life ultimately leads, as sociologist Jane Jenson puts it, to a "socially cohesive society" where all members have a sense of "belonging, participation, recognition and legitimacy".[9] I take social cohesion and its potential contribution to national community feeling, especially in how it can lead to a feeling of civic culture, social solidarity, and territorial belonging and identity,[10] as my premise for linking integration into the workforce to integration into the nation, taking into account that a myriad of factors will affect a migrant's feeling of belonging to a nation.[11]

Work, despite being an unruly concept, may be that which creates the most stable relationship to the likewise unstable concept of the nation, especially in case of European countries where the rise of industrialization, capitalism, and the nation are intimately connected. As early as Adam Smith's 1776 *An Inquiry into the Nature and Causes of the Wealth of Nations*, the anglophone sphere has conceived of the relationship between economics and politics as vital to the understanding of the nation-state,

---

8 International Organization for Migration (IOM): *N 34 International Migration Law Glossary*. International Organization for Migration: Geneva 2019, p. 106.

9 Spoonley, Paul: "Social Cohesion: A Policy and Indicator Framework for Assessing Immigrant and Host Outcomes." *Social Policy Journal of New Zealand = Te Puna Whakaaro* 24(1), 2005, pp. 85–110.

10 Spoonly 2005, p. 85

11 Furthermore, while I will assume that the nation-state corresponds to the nation it exercises control over as a sovereign governmental body, I am aware that the bureaucratic systems of the state are rarely, if ever exercising control over a homogenous, unchanging community. In fact, we will see later in the paper how this conception is played with in literature. However, for the purpose of the paper, it is important to note the link between the bureaucracy and its supposed role in the nation-state.

noting how each part ensured the success of the others.[12] In Prussia around the same time, G. W. F. Hegel conceived of civil society as a work-oriented society,[13] while Max Weber argued nearly 100 years later that the capitalist promise of work as a prerequisite to happiness and salvation was already closely entangled into the conceptual myths of such protestant nation-states as England, Prussia, and later Germany.[14] With this history of economic thought, one could argue that the existential necessity of payment for work is closely bound with the conception of the nation-state, not least since the state that determines citizenship and residence status also determines who is legally permitted to accept payment for work. With the emergence of the welfare state in the latter half of the 20th century, the state's role in society and work intensified with its policies to uphold the economic and social well-being of those within its borders. This same obligation results in special consideration of migration, which, unrestricted and/or unskilled, is often feared to disturb the financial soundness of the state.[15]

These relationships, difficult enough to argue in political and sociological contexts, are clearly picked up by the contemporary literatures of today, as I intend to show with a select look at three German-language texts: Elfriede Jelinek's 2013 *Die Schutzbefohlenen*,[16] Jenny Erpenbeck's 2015 *Gehen, ging, gegangen*,[17] and Abbas Khider's 2016 *Ohrfeige*.[18] All three texts were written in the context of the contemporary global trend of migration flow from the Global South to the Global North that resulted in growing public interest in migration politics and asylum regulations

---

12 See Smith, Adam: *An Inquiry into the Nature and Causes of the Wealth of Nations*. Ed. by Cannan, Edwin. Modern Library: New York, 2000.

13 See Hegel, GWF: *Grundlinien der Philosophie des Rechts*. Suhrkamp: Frankfurt a.M. 1986.

14 See Weber, Max / Parsons, Talcott (transl.): *The Protestant Ethic and the Spirit of Capitalism*. Routledge: New York, 2001.

15 Razin, Assaf et al: *Migration and the Welfare State: Political-Economy Policy Formation*. The MIT Press: Cambridge, MA, 2011, p. 2. It should be noted that Razin et al also note that this fear is mostly unsubstantiated.

16 Jelinek, Elfriede: *Die Schutzbefohlenen,* retrieved 5.7.2018, from elfriedejelinek.com/fschutzbefohlene.htm.

17 Erpenbeck, Jenny: *Gehen, ging, gegangen*. Penguin: Munich 2017.

18 Khider, Abbas: *Ohrfeige*. Hanser Verlag: Munich 2016.

and began even before the European Migration Crisis of 2015,[19] but has dramatically increased since then. However, each author refers to different migration drives and specific national contexts.

In narratives of migration, work is often what literally keeps the characters—and the text—going. Amidst descriptions of observations of difference in culture or the protagonists' experiences of racism, the work of the author's plot moves the narrative forward through the characters' searches for work, the struggles of keeping work, failing to perform the duties that come with it, or more rarely, finding a job matching one's training and talents and with good conditions. Often these novels seem to be moved forward by negative affects related to work: desperation that leads to feelings of shame and degradation as the character takes on work no one else is willing to do, even exchanging their bodies, or parts thereof, for renumeration if it can be made commodifiable on the market. This paradigm supports the stereotype of a desperate migrant who is willing to do anything in order to survive or to send money home to their families.

While literary representations can perpetuate this stereotype, contemporary literature works with the representation of the intimate results of strict labour market laws on humanitarian migrants:[20] depression, anxiety, deportation, and sometimes even death. One can see individual effects of work, and lack thereof, for a person, as well as be reminded that economic activity is just one of the aspects of human life over which the modern-day nation-state can be considered to have some claim and control. It also enforces an economic order that governs the emergence of migrant subjectivities as well.

---

19 Although I do not see migrants coming to various European countries since 2015, largely as a result of the civil war in Syria as a crisis, I do understand the term "migration crisis" as the acute and longer-term migration management challenges that result out of the "complex and often large-scale migration flows and mobility patterns caused by a crisis which typically involve significant vulnerabilities for individuals and affected communities" (IOM *Glossary* 137)

20 According to the *IOM* these are persons in need of protection, including but not limited to refugees, persons with urgent protection needs, migrants in vulnerable situations, extended family members, or persons in need of medical assistance and care (IOM, "humanitarian admission" 2019a, p. 96)

Considering *Die Schutzbefohlenen, Gehen, ging, gegangen*, and *Ohrfeige*, this paper will provide some insight into the intricate relationship between work and refugee status, and how these representations can critique the system of which the character is made a subject. I am interested in the way that the state determines the right of non-citizens to enter the labour market and how lack of access affects feelings of space, time, integration, and belonging for migrants. I believe literature can provide a medium for the critique of state policies and agencies, and also of wider discourses and processes within the societies that take up (or reject) those migrants, often by articulating a criticism of the treatment of refugees in relation to the central values which those societies allege to follow.

Working Values in *Die Schutzbefohlenen*

In highlighting hypocritical practices of societies in regards to their values, Elfriede Jelinek's 2013 play *Die Schutzbefohlenen* provides a strong example.[21] Written in response to protests about asylum seekers' rights and asylum application processes in Vienna in November 2012 and all over Europe, Jelinek writes in assumed voices, most of which seem recognizable as refugee voices. Near the beginning of the text, the refugees respond to a "Willkommen" pamphlet designed by the Austrian ministries for integration and international affairs.[22]

> Die Kenntnis Ihrer Werte haben Sie uns vermittelt, vielen Dank, wir können sie nachlesen und steigen jetzt auf dieses *Fundament der gemeinsamen Werte*, wir wollen die Grundlage dieser Gesellschaft kennenlernen, bitte sagen Sie uns, wie wir zu dieser *Grundlage* kommen können, damit wir dann von dort aus auf das *Fundament der Werte* steigen können, bevor die noch auf uns draufsteigen. Die wollen ja vielleicht auch höher hinauf. Die erste Klippe müssen wir schaffen, die müssen wir nehmen. Sonst wäre der Schritt für uns Unkenntliche, Unwissende zu groß, die Stufe von uns zu Ihnen zu hoch; wir wollen ein Teil davon sein, *wir*

21 Referred to in German as a *Sprachkunstwerk*, written in 2013 but first performed in Hamburg in 2014.

22 Previously called Federal Ministry for External Affairs (Bundesministerium für auswärtige Angelegenheiten, BMaA) and the "Federal Ministry for European and International Affairs," it is as of 1 March 2014 called the "Federal Ministry for Europe, Integration and Foreign Affairs" (Bundesministerium für Europa, Integration und Äußeres).

wollen ein Teil dieser Gesellschaft sein, ja, genau!, wir wollen herzlich eingeladen werden und das keinesfalls als Anstoß verstehen, vom Fundament Ihrer Werte wieder runtergeworfen zu werden wie eine Klippe, äh, wie von einer Klippe, danke, das wäre nicht nötig gewesen, [...] wir wollen *Ihre Werte unbedingt, in Beruf, Schule, Berufsschule und Familie*, die ich nicht mehr habe, sie sind alle tot [...] wir wollen das alles, wir wollen es wirklich, wir wollen Arbeit, Schule, Freizeit mit Leben erfüllen, wenn auch nicht mit unserem, denn davon haben wir zuwenig und schon zuviel hergegeben, damit könnten wir nicht mal ein Windrad antreiben, kein einziges, und viele sind sowieso weg.

[You have given us knowledge of your values, thank you very much, we can read about them and now climb onto this *foundation of common values*, we want to get to know the basis of this society, please tell us how we can get to this foundation so that we can then climb from there *onto the foundation of values before they climb on top of us*. They might want to climb higher, too. We have to get over the first cliff, we have to take it. Otherwise the step would be too big for us unknowable, unknowing people, the step from us to you would be too high; we want to be a part of it, *we want to be a part of this society*, yes, exactly! we want to be cordially invited and in no way understand this as an impulse to be thrown off the foundation of your values again like a rock, uh, like off a rock, thank you, that would not have been necessary, [...] we want your values absolutely, *in vocation, school, vocational school and family*, which I no longer have, they are all dead [...] we want it all, we really want it, we want work, school, to fill leisure time with life, even if not with ours, because we have too little of it and have already given away too much, we couldn't even power a windmill with it, not a single one, and many are gone anyway].[23]

The irony in the refugees' response is immediately noticeable. A short paraphrase of the first sentence could read: 'Thank you for sharing these values with us, which you call the foundational values of your society, but please, tell us how we can learn them, because the values are the same ones that are used to exclude us', or "we would like to have your values, certainly, like family values, but how, when we have lost our families". The adroit use of anadiplosis reminds one of the rhetoric of ancient Greek tragedies, including Aeschylus' *The Suppliants*, which serves as Jelinek's primary intertextual reference for her text. Furthermore, the long sentences, flowing into one another with words repeated in different senses, give one the feeling of trying to keep up to make it to the next idea. While being forced to imagine the "Fundament der gemeinsamen Werte" as they are turned into a literal block onto which one can climb, one is reading/

23 Jelinek 2013. My emphasis; all translations in this paper are my own.

hearing how these values become personified and can climb on top of the migrants, since the values "wollen ja vielleicht auch höher hinauf," like on the proverbial career ladder. At the same time, the speakers only have enough life left in them to live, but "damit könnten wir nicht mal ein Windrad antreiben."

With "[d]ie erste Klippe müssen wir schaffen," and then the movement, like the language, "von Klippe zu Klippe," one gains a sense of instability and impossibility for rest. Jelinek's writing of the refugees' recognition and aspiration of the Austrian/European values reproduces the quick-paced adaptations expected from workers in a capitalist society. Her arrangement "Beruf,[24] Schule, Berufschule, Familie" evokes the *Arbeitsgesellschaft* debate from 1982 around Hannah Arendt's claims in *The Human Condition* (1958),[25] that of the three human activities—labouring, working, and acting (demonstrating agency), modern European societies focused on work as their most important activity.[26] "Whatever we do, we are supposed to do for the sake of 'making a living'; such is the verdict of society".[27] However, just as the refugees describe, Arendt noted "permanence, stability, and durability, have been sacrificed to abundance, the ideal of the animal labourans".[28]

Not only are the fundamental values grounded by the values of diligence and industry, but in their presentation Jelinek questions the logic

---

24 According to Max Weber in *The Protestant Ethic and the Spirit of Capitalism*, *Beruf* automatically implies a connection to heaven, since as Martin Luther coined, it is an occupation in response to a calling (*Ruf*) by God. One serves God in one's calling during life, and then attains salvation in the afterlife (Weber 2001, p. 39).

25 Arendt, Hannah: *The Human Condition*. University of Chicago Press: Chicago, 1998, p. 73.

26 I refer here to debate that started at the 21st Deutsche Soziologentag 1982 in Bamberg, *Krise der Arbeitsgesellschaft?* where Ralf Dahrendorf and Claus Offe consider the new constellations of the prospects for a working society that has run out of work in light of the current economic situation, suggesting that work no longer plays the same role since the 1980s that they did in Arendt's conceptions of the 17th century through the 1950s. In light of neo-liberal tendencies in many countries, I am not sure if that is true.

27 Arendt, pp. 126–127

28 Arendt, p. 126

of the relationship between work, dignity, and belonging. Recalling the Hegelian assumption that "not only the individual's subsistence but also her worth and dignity are mediated by work",[29] Rahel Jaeggi has recently argued that contemporary economic relationships, affected by globalism, have also shifted the historical understanding of the meaning of work to one necessitating social cooperation, in particular in regards to work-oriented societies where work plays a preeminent role.[30] This particular aspect deserves further attention, but if we recognize that the economic interests of political and social actors are already predetermined by the logic of the economic mechanisms that constitute contemporary capitalism, then Jelinek's piece, structured to replicate this mechanism, may simultaneously be a piece about integration and disintegration.

That is to say, the refugee, based on their personal story and situation, could perhaps ascribe to diligence and industry easily, since often in their situation as a precarious migrant there is a lack of stability, durability, and permanence. At the same time, Jelinek points out how these feelings cannot necessarily be granted through involvement in a capitalist economic system, the logic of which defies stability and permanence. The speakers feel the unstable ground beneath their feet and the sheer impossibility of reaching these values, because they are based on things the refugees lost or had to leave behind, or on the support of a society that threatens to cast them off any moment.

This "Fundament der gemeinsamen Werte" is built up only to be broken down again by one word: "tot". The death of the speakers' families points out the relative insignificance of the other three foci of work and study, and contributes to the understanding that there is something that the authors of the pamphlet are not considering. In conveying the values meant to help the migrants assimilate, they reinforce the fact that they can contribute and share in the economic and educational aspects, but not in family and life, and so their statements lead the audience back to the situation at the beginning of the passage, where the gaps are too wide to be overcome, and the migrant speaker is excluded, waiting to be invited again.

---

29 Jaeggi, Rahel: "Pathologies of Work". *WSQ: Women's Studies Quarterly* 45(3&4), 2017, pp. 59–71, p.61.

30 Jaeggi, p. 61

Time and Frames in *Gehen, Ging, Gegangen*

Jelinek's text clearly engages with Max Weber's *The Protestant Ethic and the Spirit of Capitalism*, where he argues that modern capitalist societies benefited from a certain protestant ethic, which entailed a profane redirection of the desire to secure salvation through the work done on earth away from spiritual and towards economic activity. This ethic and its historical baggage stand in the centre of another recent German-language piece of literature focusing on the treatment of refugees within Europe, namely Jenny Erpenbeck's 2015 novel *Gehen, Ging, Gegangen*, also written in response to a protest camp of asylum seekers. Erpenbeck concentrates attention on the inherent violence in immigration and asylum laws that do not seem to enforce justice for the refugees,[31] often working against them, which includes laws about access to the labour market. Early on, the novel's focalized narrator, Richard, asks "[w]arum eigentlich wird den Männern in einem Land, in dem selbst der Anspruch auf einen Himmel im Jenseits von der Arbeit abhängt, das Recht, arbeiten zu gehen, verweigert? [Why, actually, are the men denied the right to work in a country where even the right to heaven in the afterlife depends on work?]".[32] The succinct manner of Richard's criticism of the German state's exclusion of migrants from the labour market relies on the understanding of the so-called protestant work ethic and its relationship to the nation, but it is only through engagement with and investment in the migrants that Richard comes to this understanding.

The novel itself opens with Richard's first day of retirement from teaching Classics at the Humboldt University, and concerns itself for a considerable section of the opening with his difficulties adjusting to his new lifestyle. Used to a lifetime of work, Richard finds an affinity with other individuals "die aus [der Zeit] hinausgefallen sind [who have fallen out of time]".[33] Except in this case, as Richard later recognizes, it is because the asylum

31 Speaking of the police clearing of a protest, Richard notes that „[d]ie Gewalt, mit der dabei vorgegangen wird, hat ihre Wurzeln in der Inzucht, die die Gesetze mit ihrer Auslegung treiben, denkt Richard, im Grunde genommen nichts anderem als ein bisschen Tinte auf ein bisschen Papier" (Erpenbeck 301).

32 Erpenbeck, p. 84

33 Erpenbeck, p. 51

seekers are not allowed to work,[34] which makes their relationship to work and time different as a result. The socio-legal scholar Sarah Turnball describes the temporal experience of such individuals as consisting of a form of "stretched time," a period of waiting and uncertainty without a sense of personal agency.[35] While detained and going through the bureaucratic processes needed to gain asylum, residency status, and the right to work, irregular migrants or asylum seekers see themselves as wasting time, compounded by the suspension of an uncertain future. As a result, they seek out activities with which that time can be filled. Richard observes this in the migrants he meets: Rashid from Nigeria, Karon Anubo from Ghana, Osarobo from Niger, and many others, some of whose names Richard knows, many that he does not. They are even willing to participate in unpaid activities, which Rashid organises for them: "Unentgeltlich harken sie Laub in den Parkumlagen Berlins, putzen in Kindergärten und Schulen, waschen Teller in einem Wohngebietclub. Wir sind froh, wenn wir etwas zu tun haben, sagt Raschid. [They rake leaves in Berlin's park surrounds, clean kindergartens and schools, and wash dishes at a neighbourhood club for free. We are happy to have something to do, says Rashid]".[36] "Froh" or "happy" is expressed as the key affect, but gratefulness is implied, and this presentation clearly speaks back to a negative discourse about migrants.

Unlike Jelinek, Erpenbeck frames work as an overwhelmingly positive experience, constructed from the opening pages as a panacea,[37] important to people's personality,[38] and a primary concern for all the men.[39] In contrast to Richard, the other characters are constantly presented as without rhythm, not working while wanting to work. Though one might consider

---

34 Erpenbeck, p. 119

35 Turnball, Sarah: "Stuck in the Middle: Waiting and Uncertainty in Immigration Detention". *Time & Society* 25(1), 2016, pp. 61–79. Nicholas Courtman calls this an extended present, which I find a useful way of thinking about it. See Courtman, Nicholas: "Seeing the Human in the (Queer) Migrant in Jenny Erpenbeck's *Gehen, Ging, Gegangen* and Terézia Mora's *Alle Tage*". In: Dawson, Leanne (Ed.): *Queering German Culture*. Camden House: Rochester, NY 2018, pp. 153–76.

36 Erpenbeck, p. 205

37 Erpenbeck, p. 10

38 Erpenbeck, p. 241

39 Erpenbeck, p. 172

this to be counter-intuitive, I believe this is part of Erpenbeck's positive framing of the migrants for a non-migrant reader,[40] as well as her implied critique. Consider the repeated use of the word "wollen": "Und was wollen die Männer? Arbeit wollen sie. Und von der Arbeit leben. In Deutschland bleiben wollen sie".[41] In the third person narration, Erpenbeck simultaneously defines what the migrants want, while emphatically depicting the humanity of her characters with a desire that her German readers could understand. To prevent negative assumptions about the migrants, she emphasises their desire to work, but she, as a pre-emptive strike, also blurs the line between economic migrants and refugees.[42] Economic opportunity was not the main driving force of their migration, but these men do not want to rely on the economic support of the state either, as asylum seekers must do while their applications are reviewed.

At the same time, Erpenbeck implicitly differentiates between Arendt's delineation in *The Human Condition* of the three core human activities. Richard's activities, meticulously noted on nearly every page, are comprised of labour, production, and action: tasks of the domestic sort or privileged pursuits of human sensibility and intellectual stimulation, and

40 This positive framing, as Nicholas Courtman also puts it, or didacticism, as Sophie Salvo most recently puts it in her recent article "The Ambivalent Didacticism of Jenny Erpenbeck's *Gehen, Ging, Gegangen*". *The Germanic Review*, 94(4), 2019, pp. 345–62, seems to be a direct response to the negative attitudes of many of the readers, often non-migrant, white Germans, whom Erpenbeck seems to want to educate. This is not to say, however, that the book will reach the most negative attitudes of anti-migration or racist mindsets.

41 Erpenbeck, p. 18

42 Often distinguished from one another in a hierarchy of which kind of migrant is more justified in seeking residence in Germany, "economic migrant" and "refugee" are tricky labels to apply, and both labels could be acceptable since there are complex, often overlapping, drivers of migration. In the case of the migrants in *Gehen, ging, gegangen,* humanitarian migrant seems more appropriate. Humanitarian admission is a "process offering a pathway for admission into a country on a temporary or permanent basis to persons or groups of persons with protection needs. Humanitarian admission is often an expedited process used for persons in need of protection, including but not limited to refugees, persons with urgent protection needs, migrants in vulnerable situations, extended family members, or persons in need of medical assistance and care" (IOM *Glossary*, pp. 96)

human activity that are rarely acknowledged in the consideration of labour markets.[43] Despite his retired status, Richard settles into what economic philosopher Sonya Marie Scott calls "the assertion of a certain inherent economic temporality, often in the form of smooth and quantifiable rhythms, or predictable and knowable cycles" that comes with the desire to "posit coherent laws of the economy".[44] Even after Richard becomes interested in the stories of the refugees at Alexanderplatz and begins to engage in visits, interviews, conversations and invitations, he follows this rhythm.

On the other hand, the migrants are excluded from any economic activity. They are occasionally able to complete *Handeln,* despite some significant barriers,[45] but they are excluded from labour and production. "Was machen die Männer eigentlich hier den ganzen Tag, wenn sie nicht arbeiten dürfen? Nichts sagt die knochige Frau. Und im Abwenden sagt sie noch: Wenn das Nichtstun zu schlimm wird, organisieren wir eine Demo. [What do the men actually do here all day if they are not allowed to work? The bony woman says nothing. And as she turns away, she says: 'If doing nothing gets too bad, we organize a protest.']".[46] Protests are public means of exercising the political right of being seen and heard, however, the first protest in the novel is the one Richard fails to see, and through these depictions Erpenbeck points sharply toward the irony of contributing to the political community while being excluded from the other two activities. In this, one must ask about the citizenship-granting body's open-handedness with non-material rights while restricting access to the labour and productive ones, and whether this upholds Arendt's argument that in modern *Arbeitsgeselleschaften,* action is the least important activity, which is why it would be the first one to which the asylum seekers would have access.

43 Whyte, David: "Naked Labour: Putting Agamben to Work". *Australian Feminist Law Journal,* 31(1), 2009, pp. 57–76, p. 74.

44 Scott, Sonya Marie: *Architectures of Economic Subjectivity: The Philosophical Foundations of the Subject in the History of Economic Thought.* Routledge: New York, 2012, p. 5.

45 Consider here the description of the second demonstration (Erpenbeck, pp. 265–268).

46 Erpenbeck, p. 48

At the same time, foregrounding the men's partiality to labour and production, which is a response to the prevalence of paranoid and negative language about migrants in the media and on the political stage–a negative framing–, also upholds conceptions of citizenship status that are repeated in Richard's visible framework. A few of the men Richard refers to were invisible to him the first time he walked by their protest on Alexanderplatz, Berlin, and his first time seeing them is mediated through a television report.[47] Richard's limited perspective comes from being framed, as Judith Butler calls it, by an active "strategy of containment, selectively producing and enforcing what will count as reality".[48] His reality is in part structured by having all the rights of a citizen, which includes being able to carry out all the activities necessary to human fulfilment. The migrants, on the other hand, are strategically contained and conveniently excluded by this framework.

As a result, *Gehen, ging, gegangen* works on two levels: first, by mimetically representing the gaze of the outsider when they finally look into the world of the migrant and how they can see the reality of the migrant's position in Germany, and, second, by communicating the stories of the migrants' lives in the countries of origin and the story of the journey they took to get to Germany. It must be noted, however, that the novel clearly underlines that the migrants' authentic perspective is not given to us, since their stories are relayed mostly through Richard's third person focalized narration.[49] Instead, the migrants and their depicted relationship to work are used as blank slates, allowing for the European's projection of their own imagining of what refugees go through onto what they call "the Other",[50] threatening to open up gaps that overlook the negative

---

47 Erpenbeck, p. 27

48 Butler, Judith. *Frames of War: When is Life Grievable*. Verso: London and New York 2009, p. xiii.

49 One notable exception is Awad, whom Richard initially calls Tristan, because Awad is how he imagines Tristan.

50 In his introduction to *Orientalism* in 1978, Edward Said describes that Orientalism is, among other things, a projection of the European onto what it labels the "Orient": a world that emerged, first according to general ideas about who or what was an Oriental, then according to a "detailed logic governed not simply by empirical reality but by a battery of desires, regressions, investments, and projections". Said, Edward: *Orientalism*. Vintage: New York, 1979, p. 8.

experiences caused by the paradoxes inherent in the relationship between nation-states, work regulations, and migrants. It is to these paradoxes that I will turn in the analysis of Abbas Khider's fourth novel, *Ohrfeige*..

Integration: Being a Good Burger in *Ohrfeige*

Ohrfeige was published in 2016, just a few months after the start of the refugee crisis of 2015. Following on the heels of a number of commercially successful novels such as Erpenbeck's *Gehen, ging, gegangen,* though noticeably claiming some authenticity of experience which Erpenbeck and Jelinek cannot,[51] the novel's protagonist is Karim, a young Iraqi asylum seeker. In the novel's framing narrative, Karim takes his asylum case worker, Frau Schulz, hostage and forces her to listen to his experiences of marginalization and precarity as a refugee in Germany. *Ohrfeige* earned Khider praise from various critics for, among other things, "forcing German readers to listen to those seeking and who are granted temporary asylum".[52] In a sense, the reader takes the position of Frau Schulz, rendered a captive audience whose mouth is taped shut so all she can do is listen without interrupting. Through her embodiment of the bureaucracy of the state, Khider criticizes the dual nature of the state, described as both "eine Göttin. Eine Naturgewalt, die Macht über andere Menschen hat [a goddess, a force of nature with a power over other people]",[53] and a cold, inhumane being. Karim concludes that „[f]ür Sie war ich wohl Asylant 3873 oder so. Nicht mehr wert als die Nummern […] [to you I was probably Asylum Seeker 3873 or so. Not worth more than the numbers]".[54] Such an entity could impossibly design fair standards for residency and citizenship, but she chooses to focus on quantifiable values, and Khider does not let this go unexamined.

Next to the violent, eponymous slap that Karim gives to Frau Schulz, Karim attempts to take back some of the power that she had exercised in

51 Khider came to Germany at age 23 seeking asylum after fleeing Iraq for political reasons and after two years of imprisonment.

52 Kämmerlings, Richard: „Man sollte uns zwingen, den Flüchtlingen zuzuhören". *Die Welt* 8.8.2016.

53 Khider, p. 11

54 Khider, p. 12

rejecting his legal right to stay in the country, first by removing a social barrier in suggesting to call her by her first name, then by speaking in Arabic, which Frau Schulz does not understand.[55] Karim wants to tell Frau Schulz his story, so that she understands what he has been through and what having his asylum revoked means to him, but he tells it in a language she cannot understand. While Karim admits that this seems unproductive,[56] he also asserts language is not the problem, anyway. Just as Richard in *Gehen, ging, gegangen* could not see things outside his framework, Frau Schulz would not hear things outside of hers. While her situation is another problematic devoicing of people in precarious situations by those in power, the situation parallels some of the paradoxes inherent in the regulatory practices of the state in regards to refugees, for example, that they are expected to contribute to social cohesion, yet are placed in housing in city suburbs or small towns. While telling her (and the reader) Karim's story of flight and settling, further paradoxes in the regulatory policies of the states become clear.

Karim describes his experiences after he was approved to leave the asylum seeker accommodation centre. After being sent from office to office, and advised to first find work before seeking private accommodation, Karim finds his designated caseworker at the job centre.

> Herr Sepp vom Arbeitsamt riet mir dann, ich solle irgendwo jobben. Rafid war extra mit mir mitgekommen und übersetzte alles.
>
> »Ich will gern vorher die Sprache erlernen und brauche dafür Unterstützung.«
>
> »Das ist kein Problem. Das freut uns, dass Sie die Sprache lernen wollen«, sagte Herr Sepp. »Sie müssen aber erst ein Jahr lang arbeiten und Steuern zahlen. Danach können wir Ihnen einen Sprachkurs finanzieren«
>
> »Aber wie soll ich ein Jahr lang ohne Sprachkenntnisse arbeiten oder überhaupt einen Job zu finden?«
>
> »Wie alle Ihre fleißigen Landsmänner auch. Ich könnte Ihnen eine Stelle bei Burger King vermitteln. Es ist nur eine Teilzeitarbeit, aber für den Anfang ist das genau das Richtige für Sie. Sie sind krankenversichert, verdienen etwas Geld und können langsam ein guter Bürger werden. «
>
> »Entschuldigen Sie«, sagte Rafid. »Wie meinen Sie das, ein Burger werden? «

---

55 It may be interesting to consider here Gayatri Chakravorty Spivak's idea of epistemic violence and how it occurs in multiple ways here by both Karim and Frau Schulz and the bureaucratic system.

56 Khider, p. 10

»Nein«, sagte Herr Sepp. »Nicht Burger. Bürger! Bürger. Bewohner des Landes. Bürger. Mit Umlaut. Also Staatsbürger. Deutscher. Bei Burger King. Arbeit. Dann. Bürger.«

» Oh, ich verstehe. Entschuldigung.«

[Mr. Sepp from the employment agency then advised me to take a job somewhere. Rafid had come along with me and translated everything.

"I would like to learn the language beforehand and need support for that."

"That's not a problem. We're glad you want to learn the language," Mr. Sepp said. "But first you have to work and pay taxes for a year. After that, we can finance a language course for you."

"But how can I work for a year, or even find a job, without knowing the language?"

"Just like all your hardworking compatriots. I could get you a job at Burger King. It's only part-time work, but it's just right for you to start. You'll have health insurance, make some money, and you can slowly become a good *Bürger*."

"Excuse me," Rafid said. "What do you mean, become a burger?"

"No," said Mr. Sepp. "Not burger. *Bürger*. Citizen. Inhabitant of the land. Citizen. With an umlaut. Staatsbürger. German. At Burger King. Work. Then. Citizen."

"Oh, I see. Sorry."][57]

After several patronizing remarks about approving of Karim's desire to learn the language and the industriousness of his compatriots, the encounter between Karim and Herr Sepp ends with the strange clarification of the difference between a burger, the food, and a Bürger, the German word for citizen. They are nearly homophones and heterographs marked by a single typographical and articulated difference between an umlaut. There is only a slight etymological relationship between the two words Burger and Bürger, but it comes from the fact that hamburger, from which the word burger derives, is a demonym of Hamburg, the German city. Herr Sepp does not consider that the two words could be confused,[58] but Rafid is not sure if Karim is supposed to become a good citizen or a good burger in this burger-joint, even if it would be absurd to ask someone to become a meat patty sandwiched by bread. His confusion implies that

57 Khider, p. 157

58 It is also a question of whether Herr Sepp is speaking in a southern Bavarian dialect that would make the vowels even more similar, making them bona fide homophones. However, the point would remain that Herr Seep overlooked the potential confusion.

Herr Sepp's prioritization of finding a part-time job and being insured to become a good citizen, rather than taking a language course to attain the qualifications for attending university, for example, is just as absurd.

However, Herr Sepp (perhaps optimistically) also suggests that fulfilling this work requirement will make Karim a "Staatsbürger" and a "Deutscher," a citizen of the state and a German. In implying that they are coterminous, Herr Sepp equates being a working, tax paying member to being accepted as a member of the nation, complicating the idea of German citizenship, often still conceived as a "community of descent".[59] Still, in the same promise of Germany nationality, Herr Sepp demands the implied step of working first, as though work is the most important requirement for being a member of the German national community. In their exchange, Herr Sepp prioritizes the activities that the migrants in *Gehen, ging, gegangen* were excluded from. He reinforces the primacy in nation-states of economic activity in constituting political belonging, and disregards the spheres of language and communication, which is where the real political belonging is created, according to Arendt. "In acting and speaking, men show who they are, reveal actively their unique personal identities and thus make their appearance in the human world".[60] Speaking and acting, according to Arendt, is how people become visible. Instead, Herr Sepp renders Karim an economic subject, though an invisible one.

One could say this is partly due to the difficulty of constructing such an "imagined community" as the nation, a difficulty compounded by large-scale migration and the development of diasporas.[61] For most people, work

59 Brubaker, Rogers. *Citizenship and Nationhood in France and Germany*. Harvard University Press: Cambridge, Mass., 1992, p. x. Herr Sepp's use of these terms, which are part of ongoing public debates, can also be explored further by considering Gosewinkel, Dieter: "Staatsbürgerschaft und Staatsangehörigkeit". *Geschichte und Gesellschaft* 21(4), 1995, pp. 533–56, in which he illuminates the differences between citizenship and nationality and complicates the legacy of *ius sanguinis*.

60 Arendt, p. 179

61 For more on Benedict Anderson's ground-breaking explanations of nationalism, see Anderson, Benedict: *Imagined Communities: Reflections on Origin and Spread of Nationalism*. Verso: London, 2016.

is not the most obvious requirement on entering into what Homi Bhabha calls an "impossible unity," composed of myriad actors and forces such as language and common heritage. However, since "the quest to secure this impossible unity drives states to various forms of coercion aimed at both inclusion [...] and exclusion",[62] states have found one way by imposing strict regulations on whether migrants can work. According to sociologist Lucy Mayblin, whose research focuses on the politics of asylum, "differential access to the labour market is one of the ways in which the state maintains a distinction between [...] citizens and non-citizens".[63] In fact, Mayblin argues, the governments of most liberal nation states enforce policies that will exclude asylum seekers "as far as possible territorially, socially and economically" since "[a]sylum seeking is linked to welfare support and therefore seen as an unfair economic burden".[64] As we have seen, this is exactly Karim's experience.

However, Khider's novel makes a valuable contribution to this discourse by providing an important reminder that citizenship extends beyond having work. Practically, it makes sense that Karim would work and pay taxes so that he can take the language courses, and thus state inclusion happens before cultural inclusion, but only after going through the regulatory path of the state. In principle, migrants to any country are allowed to work in the professions they have learned. However, in reality, there are often obstacles -- such as informal working relations, failing to recognize foreign educational and professions qualifications, or discrimination -- to practicing the profession learned, or practicing any profession at all. The ability to work under one's own name and/or practice one's chosen profession, often the one for which one was educated or trained, is an important standard for upholding the dignity of a human being. One's value as a human is tied to one's skills and talents, and these are aspects of human dignity the state is legally obligated to uphold. Working for the state precedes the necessary measures needed to actually begin to belong

62 Bhabha, p. 83

63 Mayblin, Lucy: "Troubling the Exclusive Privileges of Citizenship: Mobile Solidarities, Asylum Seekers, and the Right to Work." Citizenship Studies 20(2), 2016, p. 192

64 Mayblin, p. 194

to the nation, such as language learning and exposure to the customs and values.

However, without knowing the language, Karim is automatically deskilled, employed in a lower skill level that requires no language skills, and he is isolated, because he cannot communicate with his colleagues. Recognizing the low wages, and the impossibility of earning enough in such a job to save for an important surgery to treat his gynecomastia, which was the reason for his flight from Iraq,[65] Karim rejects the Burger-joint job only to find himself working in factories as an undocumented construction worker. The situation reflects what Judith Butler and Gayatri Chakravorty Spivak discuss in *Who Sings the Nation State,* where Judith Butler argues, "there are a set of powers that produce and maintain this situation of destitution".[66] As the construction work does not give him the participatory status in society that he was hoping for, Karim is pushed towards believing that he needs to switch jobs, in order to become that which he makes. "Ich war sogar so weit, ein guter Burger oder Bürger im Burger King zu werden [I'd come to the point that I would even have become a good burger or Bürger at Burger King]".[67] Not only does the case worker make obvious that a language course would be much more useful for helping Karim integrate—that is, move through German spaces and interact with other German speakers and eventually become a citizen, but that it is difficult to disentangle the concept of the nation from the concept of the state, and the migrant's relation to both will often be recognized from their positioning as a working subject.

Conclusion

Khider's *Ohrfeige* as well as Jelinek's *Die Schutzbefohlenen* and Erpenbeck's *Gehen, ging, gegangen*, and other narratives featuring migration show some of the underlying expectations of communities for their newcomers,

---

65 Although it is perhaps not of essential importance within the frame of this paper, it is interesting to point out that with this, Khider undermines the most common reasons for migrating from Iraq: political persecution or economic opportunity.

66 Butler, Judith/ Spivak, Gayatri Chakravorty: Who Sings the Nation-State? Language, Politics, Belonging. Seagull Books London: London, 2007, p. 10

67 Khider, p. 162

but they also reveal a hypocrisy in attaining these values, because the expectations often ignore the positions or experiences of the migrants. Some of this difficulty results from the paradox of creating national belonging and political community, which is that it relies on exclusion. This is made evident by the policies in place to secure borders, workforces and the rights guaranteed to citizens. Often upon arrival, asylum seekers are rendered invisible by measures taken to neither completely include, nor exclude them. However, recent literature that focuses on those who are excluded from the labour market manages to bring them back into visibility as well as provide some voices of commentary about the nation-states that try to exclude them. Voices from the margins are able to remind the majority that their experiences of work and life in Europe are not the only ones, but that their situation deserves a second glance as well. Not only do these narratives reveal the centrality of work in German society and in the societies of nation-states that are similarly formed, but they also point out the policies of state and citizenship participation that could be improved for everyone.

Although these narratives are praised for giving visibility to people who are otherwise marginalized in European societies, in many ways these texts shed more light on the societies than on the migrants. It may seem ethnocentric that these texts mostly tell the European citizens about themselves, but given the European situatedness of these authors, I think they are turning society's gaze towards the centre by casting from the periphery. By looking at people who are excluded from the workforce, these texts reveal a preoccupation with work, its regulation of lifestyle and time, and how people belong to and can engage in communities in which are lived and worked. In summary, they seem to prompt the reader to question the responsibilities and foci that come with German or Austrian citizenship and consider changes that may benefit both citizens and newcomers.

References

Anderson, Benedict: *Imagined Communities: On the Origin and Spread of Nationalism*. Verso: London, 2016.

Arendt, Hannah: *The Human Condition*. 2nd ed. Univ. of Chicago Press: Chicago, 1998.

Brubaker, Rogers. *Citizenship and Nationhood in France and Germany*. Harvard University Press: Cambridge, MA, 1992.

Butler, Judith/ Spivak, Gayatri Chakravorty: *Who Sings the Nation-State? Language, Politics, Belonging*. Seagull Books London: London, 2007.

Butler, Judith. *Frames of War: When is Life Grievable*. Verso: London and New York, 2009.

Courtman, Nicholas: "Seeing the Human in the (Queer) Migrant in Jenny Erpenbeck's *Gehen, ging, gegangen* and Terézia Mora's *Alle Tage*." In: Dawson, Leanne (ed): *Queering German Culture*. (German Yearbook 10). Camden House: Rochester, New York 2018, pp. 153–176.

Erpenbeck, Jenny. *Gehen, ging, gegangen*. Penguin: Munich, 2017.

Gosewinkel, Dieter: "Staatsbürgerschaft und Staatsangehörigkeit". *Geschichte und Gesellschaft* 21(4), 1995, pp. 533–56.

Hegel, GWF: *Grundlinien der Philosophie des Rechts*. Suhrkamp: Frankfurt a.M. 1986.

International Organization for Migration (IOM): *N 34 International Migration Law Glossary*. International Organization for Migration: Geneva, 2019a.

International Organization for Migration (IOM): *World Migration Report 2020*. International Organization for Migration: Geneva, 2019b.

Jaeggi, Rahel: "Pathologies of Work". *WSQ: Women's Studies Quarterly* 45(3&4), 2017, pp.59–76.

Jelinek, Elfriede: *Die Schutzbefohlenen*, retrieved 5.7.2018, from elfriedejelinek.com/fschutzbefohlene.htm.

Kämmerlings, Richard: „Man sollte uns zwingen, den Flüchtlingen zuzuhören". *Die Welt* 8.8.2016.

Khider, Abbas: *Ohrfeige*. Paperback, Hanser Verlag: Munich, 2016.

Mayblin, Lucy: "Troubling the Exclusive Privileges of Citizenship: Mobile Solidarities, Asylum Seekers, and the Right to Work." *Citizenship Studies* 20(2), 2016, pp. 192–207.

OECD (2020), "Foreign-born unemployment (indicator)", 2020, retrieved 24.4.2020. doi: 10.1787/ba5d2ce0-en

Razin, Assaf, Efraim Sadka, and Benjarong Suwankiri. *Migration and the Welfare State: Political-Economy Policy Formation.* The MIT Press: Cambridge, MA, 2011.

Said, Edward. *Orientalism.* Vintage: New York, 1979.

Scott, Sonya Marie: *Architectures of Economic Subjectivity: The Philosophical Foundations of the Subject in the History of Economic Thought.* Routledge: New York, 2012, p. 1–10.

Smith, Adam: *An Inquiry into the Nature and Causes of the Wealth of Nations.* Ed. by Edwin Cannan. Modern Library: New York, 2000.

Spoonley, Paul: "Social Cohesion: A Policy and Indicator Framework for Assessing Immigrant and Host Outcomes." *Social Policy Journal of New Zealand = Te Puna Whakaaro* 24(1), 2005, pp. 85–110.

Trines, Stephen: "The State of Refugee Integration in Germany in 2019". *WENR World Education News and Reviews* 8.8.2019., retrieved 28.2.2020, from https://wenr.wes.org/2019/08/the-state-of-refugee-integration-in-germany-in-2019

Turnball, Sarah: "Stuck in the Middle: Waiting and Uncertainty in Immigration Detention". *Time & Society* 25(1), 2016, pp. 61–79.

Weber, Max, trans. Talcott Parsons: *The Protestant Ethic and the Spirit of Capitalism.* Routledge: New York 2001.

Whyte, David: "Naked Labour: Putting Agamben to Work". *Australian Feminist Law Journal,* 31(1), 2009, pp 57–76.

Wietzke, Frank-Borge. "Policy Research Working Paper 6804: Pathways from jobs to social cohesion". *The World Bank research observer,* 2014.

About the Authors

Aileen Behrendt works as a lecturer at the University of Potsdam, from which she also received her PhD in 2019. Her research and teaching interests include modernist and interwar literature, gender studies, British comedy and fandom cultures. In 2017 and 2018, she was a Visiting Scholar at the University of Washington, Seattle. Recent publications include a book on *Gender Politics and British Women Writers of the 1930s* (Königshausen & Neumann 2020) and an essay on Winifred Watson's *Miss Pettigrew Lives for a Day*, published in *Comedy and Intermodernism in Fiction by British Women Authors, 1930–1960*, (Cambridge Scholars Publishing 2020).

Nicholas Courtman completed his PhD at the University of Cambridge on literary engagements with sex work, forced labour, and state socialist labour ideologies in contemporary German-language literature in 2021, and is currently working as a researcher at the Expert Council on Migration and Integration in Berlin. His next research project will examine the history of citizenship law and naturalisation practice in West Germany after 1949.

Katrin Frisch, PhD has studied English and Gender Studies at Humboldt-Universität zu Berlin and King's College London. In 2019 she completed her PhD in English Literature, which was jointly awarded by both universities. In her doctoral thesis she explored the interdependencies of right-wing ideology and Anglophone Modernist writing, raising fundamental questions about the relationship between aesthetics and politics. It was published in 2019 under the title *The F-Word: Pound, Eliot, Lewis, and the Far Right* (Logos 2019). Other research interests include human/animal studies, the contemporary Far Right as well as class matters in literature and society. She is currently working in the field of research integrity.

Simon Godart is post-doctoral researcher at the EXC 2020 "Temporal Communities" at the Free University Berlin in research area 3 "Future Perfect" where he is working on the theory of complex literary temporalities. He studied philosophy and literary studies in Berlin. In 2019, he received his PhD in philosophy with a study on the theory of quotation in Montaigne's Essais and Bayle's Dictionnaire historique et critique.

His monograph has been published under the title „Passagen. Zitat und skeptische Poetik bei Michel de Montaigne und Pierre Bayle" (Fink 2021). Since 2020, he is one of the editors of the online journal „Bildbruch. Beobachtungen an Metaphern" (Berlin/Basel).

Anat Messing Marcus received her PhD from the University of Cambridge. She holds an MA from the Cohn Institute for the History and Philosophy of Science and Ideas, Tel-Aviv University. Her research focuses on critical theory, philosophy, psychoanalysis, feminist theory and aesthetic theory. Her doctoral thesis explores the work of the senses, philosophy of language and political aesthetics in Benjamin's work, taking as its touchstone the substantially poetics of architecture and the sensorial experience of "tactility" across his writings. Among her publications is the article " 'Im Taktischen': Figures of Touch in the Work of Walter Benjamin", *The Germanic Review: Literature, Culture, Theory* (2018). Her current project explores the relationship between language, emotion, affect and gender.

Elena Stingl has been a doctoral candidate at the Friedrich Schlegel Graduate School for Literary Studies at the Free University Berlin since 2017. Her dissertation examines twentieth century literary and philosophical texts that engage with the crushing of workers' movements by fascism and the failure of proletarian revolutions on the Eurasian continent. The authors at the centre of the dissertation are Georges Bataille, Simone Weil, and Alfred Sohn-Rethel, among others. She completed her earlier studies at the Institute of Comparative Literature at the Ludwig-Maximilians-Universität in Munich, where she was employed as a research assistant in 2015/16. Her research interests lie at the intersections of literary studies, sociology, and political theory.

Dorothea Trotter holds a B.A. in Literature from New College of Florida, an M.A. in Comparative Literature from Florida Atlantic University. She completed her PhD as a fellow of the Friedrich Schlegel Graduate School for Literary Studies at the Freie Universität of Berlin, in which she examined the relationship between television references and identity expression in transnational German and English millennial literature. She specializes in narratives of migration in German, British, and US contexts, and she is interested in the intersection of postcolonial and intermedial studies.

Focalizing on questions of representation and identity, her current project looks at representations of facial difference in television, film, and literature.

Nora Weinelt is a research fellow at the Chair of Comparative Literature at the University of Augsburg. She received her PhD in Comparative Literature for a thesis on *Versagen. Geschichte, Theorie und Poetik einer modernen Denkfigur* from the Humboldt University of Berlin in 2020. Recent publications include a paper on Bruce Nauman's *Contrapposto Studies* (forthcoming with Kadmos Berlin), a paper entitled „'Do you recognize me?' Bemerkungen zur Zeitlichkeit der Oberfläche in *TwinPeaks*" (Wiesbaden: Springer VS 2020), and *Minimale Männlichkeit. Figurationen und Refigurationen des Anzugs* (Berlin: Neofelis 2016), a book on masculinity and the suit.

Literatur – Kultur – Ökonomie
Literature – Culture – Economy

Herausgegeben von / Edited by
Christine Künzel, Axel Haunschild, Birger P. Priddat,
Thomas Rommel, Franziska Schößler und / and Yvette Sánchez

Vol. 1 Franziska Schößler: Femina Oeconomica: Arbeit, Konsum und Geschlecht in der Literatur. Von Goethe bis Händler. 2017.

Vol. 2 Yvette Sánchez (Hrsg.): Business-Fiktionen und Management-Inszenierungen. 2018.

Vol. 3 Manuel Pombo: Trueques discursivos entre Literatura y *Management*. 2019.

Vol. 4 Franziska Jekel / Anna-Katharina Krüger / Myriam-Naomi Walburg (eds.): Writing (for) the Market. Narratives of the Global Economy. 2020.

Vol. 5 Ulrich Fritsche / Roman Köster / Laetitia Lenel : Futures Past. Economic Forecasting in the 20th and 21st Century. 2020.

Vol. 6 Lucas Alt: Genuss und Arbeit im Angestelltenroman. Von Irmgard Keun bis Elfriede Jelinek. 2021.

Vol. 7 Silke Schmidt: Narrative Change Management in American Studies. A Pragmatic Reading. 2021.

Vol. 8 Kurt Hahn / Marita Liebermann (Hrsg.): Finanznarrative als Krisennarrative. Literarische und filmische Modellierungen *kapitaler* Erschütterungen in der Romania. 2021.

Vol. 9 Aileen Behrendt / Nicholas Courtman (eds.): Writing the Economic Subject in Modern Western Europe. Representation, Contestation, Critique. 2021.

www.peterlang.com

www.ingramcontent.com/pod-product-compliance
Ingram Content Group UK Ltd.
Pitfield, Milton Keynes, MK11 3LW, UK
UKHW041828100926
8556IPUK00002B/69